SENTENCE COMBINING AND PARAGRAPH BUILDING

SENTENCE COMBINING AND PARAGRAPH BUILDING

WILLIAM STRONG
Utah State University

RANDOM HOUSE ♦ NEW YORK

First Edition
987654
Copyright © 1981 by Random House, Inc.

Library of Congress Cataloging in Publication Data
Strong, William, 1940–
   Sentence combining and paragraph building.

   1. English language—Rhetoric. I. Title.
PE1408.S7714   808'.042   80–27438
ISBN 0-394-31264-3
ISBN 0-394-32772-1 (Teacher's Edition)

Cover and text design by Dana Kasarsky Design
Cover and text illustrations by Lonni Sue Johnson

Manufactured in the United States of America

ESPECIALLY
FOR
KRISTIN AND ERIC STRONG

Combine these sentences:

Your smiles echo.
They fill my heart.

A man who teaches about writing should certainly, I think, write two or three books in his life to show that he has at least tried to practice the craft he discourses upon.

—Bonamy Dobrée

PREFACE

This book is written in the form of a story. Its core consists of ten sequential episodes that are set in a classroom. The story, told from the point-of-view of one of its characters—a writing teacher, deals with both the theory and technique of sentence combining. While this teacher *persona* is based in part on my own classroom experience, it mainly grows out of my observations of excellent writing teachers in action. (If I were as good as the "I" telling the story, I probably would not have needed to write it.)

In other words, both the narrator and the class inhabit a *dream reality*. These characters exist only in print and only, therefore, in our imaginations. Let me emphasize, just for the record, that no actual teacher and class work as smoothly as those in the story. Reality, more often, is false starts and unanswered questions. Like any idealized narrative, the book's story leaves out much of the nitty-gritty, banal richness of real life. It shows life better—and duller—than it really is.

I chose to put the lessons in narrative form so that I could *show* how writing can be taught and learned in new ways. Moreover, I wanted to respond to the tough questions about sentence combining that people often ask once the technique begins to work both on and for them. My hope is that *real* students and teachers will have their questions answered by watching fictional characters master the "how" and "why" of combining.

I also hope that instructors using this text will regard the narrator as a colleague worthy of a team-teaching effort and that students will see the fictional class as an extension of their day-to-day writing program. Certainly the book's story and exercises are intended as a *catalyst* for productive classwork, not as a substitute for it.

Sentence Combining and Paragraph Building is designed for use in one-term or one-semester writing courses. Because its explanations and exercises cover a range of basics, the book is especially appropriate for students

who are improving their skills in constructing sentences and paragraphs.

In addition to combining practice immediately after each narrative unit, the text contains two large sections of exercises—one focused on single-paragraph combining, the other on multiple-paragraph work. These exercises have been arranged in order of increasing difficulty. Both "open" (uncued) and "signaled" (cued) exercises are included, the former to teach stylistic decision-making, the latter to teach specific "target" sentences.

A second purpose of these exercises is to provide insight into paragraph building. Rereading instructions, which focus on paragraph organization or intersentence cohesion, accompany each exercise. I have included these instructions to show *how* sentences connect and link together to build paragraphs. (Advance organizers for the Part Two exercises, which focus on links between paragraphs, not sentences, show *how* paragraphs connect and link together to create stories and essays.)

I have attached *Paragraph-Building Options* to each exercise in order to accomplish the third goal—connecting personal writing to exercise paragraphs and constructing paragraphs that parallel those in an exercise. Such writing not only involves applying the skills acquired in combining and the insights gleaned from rereading but also involves making decisions about ideas—how to select, organize, and express them. Because it demands invention and planning, paragraph building puts sentence combining in perspective as a *means* to an end, not as an end in itself.

ACKNOWLEDGMENTS

In 1958, on a warm spring afternoon, the late Lloyd ("Shorty") Johnson talked to a squirmy high school class about the difficulty of getting words down on paper. Eying his captives over horn-rimmed glasses, he described writing as a process of personal discovery and intellectual invention, not as a simple-minded mechanical routine. Writing is hard work, he stressed, but the results are well worth the effort.

After four years of work on *Sentence Combining and Paragraph Building*, I've begun to understand what that skilled and witty teacher was getting at. To get this book into print, it was necessary to write my way through two other manuscripts.

Both of those efforts—including the original collaboration with my good friend, Lawrence McKinney—will now be published separately. Larry helped with some practice exercises in this book and contributed much to earlier versions of the narrative. In addition, his readings of the manuscript were done with a skilled, sensitive eye. His teaching voice, like Shorty Johnson's, echoes in the pages that follow.

Development of this text has been guided by the intelligence and balanced criticism of Richard L. Larson and Elizabeth McPherson. Both have a sane and humane perspective on writing instruction. Their thoughtful responses to various drafts have made this a far better book than it otherwise would have been.

Many reviewers have also contributed reactions and suggestions for improvement: John Brereton (Wayne State University), Sharon Crowley (Northern Arizona University), Jerry Howard (Northeastern Illinois University), Erika Lindemann (University of North Carolina, Chapel Hill), Michael Miller (Longview Community College), Carol Rossi (University of Santa Clara), and Joseph Trimmer (Ball State University). Helpful "unofficial" reviews were provided by Freeman Anderson (Portland State University), Patsy Candal (Coastal Carolina College), William E. Smith (Utah

State University), and members of a writing response group at the Bay Area Writing Project (University of California, Berkeley) in 1978. For sharing their perspectives on sentence combining, I also wish to acknowledge in particular Warren Combs, Charles Cooper, Donald Daiker, Charles Duke, Dave Holden, Bill Horst, Kellogg Hunt, Andy Kerek, Rebecca Johnson, John Mellon, Max Morenberg, Will Pitkin, Herm Schmeling, Charles Suhor, and Vince and Patty Wixon.

For their support during the book's development, special thanks go to Carol Strong; to Richard Garretson, my editor at Random House, as well as to Christine Pellicano and Dorchen Leidholdt; to typists Kae Lynn Beecher, Carlene Claflin, Kristin Strong, and Kathrynn Whitney; to Donn Beck, whose friendship and correspondence helped me through darker times; and to my colleagues in the Departments of Secondary Education and English at Utah State University.

Kudos, finally, to my students and to the many teachers, workshop participants, and student teachers who have generously field-tested exercises in the text. Their advice, encouragement, and common sense have been essential to the evolution of *Sentence Combining and Paragraph Building* as well as to my spiritual health.

William Strong
Logan, Utah
November 1980

TO THE TEACHER

Exercises in sentence combining and paragraph building do not in and of themselves teach writing. What they do, quite simply, is facilitate the learning of writing.

The key assumptions of the book are described below:

1. *Sentence combining works.* Many research studies since the late 1960s have documented the effectiveness of this approach. Recent research with nearly 300 freshman college students at Miami University concluded that combining practice produces dramatic, demonstrable gains in syntactic maturity and overall writing quality. (Details of this study and others are presented in the *Teacher's Edition.*)

2. *In learning to write, playing it safe is playing it stupid.* The experience of many writers and teachers suggests that linguistic growth is accelerated as a person takes risks with language; plays with it; explores its structure, diction, and intersentence cohesion; and solicits feedback from others. More than anything, *focused practice* is essential for acquiring and improving skills.

3. *Long, complex sentences are not necessarily the most effective ones.* When approached in the right way, combining practice improves sentence variety by heightening awareness of stylistic options. But the central point of sentence-combining practice is being *able* to make longer, more complex sentences, not being *obliged* to do so. Brevity, at times, has its virtues. Communication—not obfuscation—is the goal of skill-building.

4. *Sentence combining promotes the development of a range of language skills.* Learning punctuation, mastering basic mechanics, varying the emphasis of sentences, evoking different nuances of tone, handling

coordination and subordination, forging cohesion links—each is a possible focus for combining. Exercises can be studied and restudied from different angles. Language learning involves a network of skills.

5. *"Open" and "signaled" sentence combining serve different purposes.* Educational research has documented the effectiveness of both "open" and "signaled" sentence combining. "Open" exercises—those that call for a *variety* of solutions—help teach decision making and sentence emphasis. "Signaled" exercises—those that have a right answer specified in transformational "cues"—help teach specific structures. Because they have complementary goals, both kinds of exercises are included in this book.

6. *Links between sentences and paragraphs can be better understood through sentence combining.* Disconnected sentences—even when technically correct and syntactically mature—are in no sense "good writing." To be effective, sentences must be *connected* to one another, both in content and in structure and semantics. Because intersentence and interparagraph links are so important to coherent prose, they are the focus of rereading instructions and *Paragraph Building Options.* The theory base for rereading derives from the seminal work of M. A. K. Halliday and Ruqaiya Hasan, *Cohesion in English* (1976).

The underlying premise of all six assumptions is that *sentence combining is a means to an end.* Such exercises can add variety to the length and patterning of sentences, improve skills of usage and punctuation, and heighten understanding of unity and cohesion in paragraphs. But, clearly, it's the transfer of sentence combining skills and knowledge to the student's own writing that really counts. That application is the aim of this book.

CONTENTS

1

ONE   SENTENCE BASICS

SINGLE-PARAGRAPH EXERCISES 99

TWO   SENTENCE STYLISTICS 131

MULTIPLE-PARAGRAPH EXERCISES   227

TO THE STUDENT

Sentence combining works best when the exercises are whispered aloud at first, then done silently. Developing an "inner voice"—one that tries first one sentence, then another, until the best possible candidate is selected—takes time and patience. But it pays off.

On the one hand, every neurologically-normal person has vast language powers already built into his/her brain. (Our ability to spin jillions of spoken sentences without thinking about *how* they are structured is self-evident proof of this fact.) On the other hand, however, many of us experience painful silence when faced with a blank sheet of paper. Suddenly, we don't know how to talk or what to say. Self-consciousness overwhelms us.

Sentence combining helps switch on our built-in powers of composition. It gives us access to our own sentence-spinning, idea-connecting genius. This transfer of power from speech to written expression is facilitated by friendly groupwork and by paragraph-building practice.

Here, then, are some sentence combining hints:

1. Explore various ways to say the same thing; experiment for emphasis; get others' opinions of the most effective transformations.

2. Imitate particularly interesting or effective sentences. (Copies don't need to duplicate every detail of the original—just its main structural features.)

3. Do all of your practice combining in a writing notebook. Keep all sentence imitations, rewrites, usage items, spelling problems, and so on. Reserve a section for "writing starters" such as quotes, interesting ideas, questions, and fragments of class conversation.

4. Try combining two or more clusters of short sentences to make one "super sentence"; try leaving an occasional cluster uncombined for dramatic emphasis. Remember: long sentences are not necessarily good ones. Sometimes shorter is better.

5. Insert your own sentences between the sentences in the combining exercises. Your original sentences will help develop the *content* of an exercise by adding details, clarifying points, providing examples, making generalizations, and so forth.

6. Use sentence combining as a *catalyst* for writing. Argue with an exercise. Rewrite it from another *point-of-view* (from the point-of-view of a particular character or from the perspective of a narrator who "knows all"); in a different *mode* (in story-telling form or as an impersonal news report) or in an altered *tone* (from serious to humorous).

There are two special learning aids at the back of the book. The first, a glossary, provides short definitions of technical terms. Refer to this section when questions arise about terminology or when a quick review is needed. The second aid, an answer key, provides possible answers to exercises within as well as after the narrative units. Refer to this section only *after* you have completed assigned exercises to get feedback on your skill development.

A SENTENCE COMBINING PRE-TEST

Directions. Make a *single* sentence out of each cluster of short sentences. You may delete words, change the forms of words, or add connecting words. After checking with the *Answer Key*, p. 275, give yourself 5 points for each correct writeout. *More than one correct writeout is possible for each cluster.* (50 points possible)

MODELS

The funeral director has doubts.
The doubts are grave.
The doubts are about Mortimer.

Writeout: The funeral director has grave doubts about Mortimer.

Robert is my brother.
This is speaking relatively.
He is an orphan.
The orphan was adopted.

Writeout: Robert, an adopted orphan, is my brother, relatively speaking.

1. The photographer took the picture.
   The photographer shuddered.

2. The students have a club.
   The club is called "The Bored of Education."

3. The baker kneaded dough.
   The baker was hard-working.
   The baker wanted to avoid bankruptcy.

4. The writer spent his nights at a table.
   The table was round.
   He called himself "King Author."

5. The farmer was out standing in her field.
   This was after four years of training.
   The training was arduous.
   The training was in college.

6. The Corporal administered punishment to the Private.
   The punishment was corporal.
   The administering was sometimes public.
   The administering was sometimes private.

7. The car roared out of the parking lot.
   It was low-slung.

It was fishtailing.
It left an autograph.
The autograph was black.

8. The hermit lived in an outhouse.
The living was for seven years.
The outhouse was abandoned.
He established a legal claim.
The claim was by "Squatter's Rights."

9. The dentist testified in a suit.
The dentist was nicely-dressed.

The suit was for malpractice.
She swore to tell the whole tooth.
She swore to tell nothing but the tooth.

10. The rancher's daughter spied a rustler.
The rancher was dottering.
The rustler was a bull-shooter.
The rustler was hiding in the bullrushes.
The bullrushes were rustling.
The rustler was listening to bluegrass.
The rustler was smoking.

PART ONE

SENTENCE BASICS

UNIT ONE
HOW SENTENCE COMBINING WORKS

I'm sitting on the front edge of the desk, checking the crease in my slacks. It's the beginning of a new term, and there's tension in the room.

"This is a writing class," I say. "You already know how to do much of what we'll be practicing. Right now I'm just going to summarize some basics about language and writing. Then I'll give you a few sentence-combining exercises so that you can check your skills. If anything isn't clear, please ask questions. I'll try to answer them."

My edginess is beginning to fade. "You all know how to talk," I continue. "Therefore you know a lot about writing."

No-kidding expressions drift across a few students' faces.

"What I'm trying to say is that all of you hear, speak, and understand by using the same basic rules. You know how to put words in order and connect pieces of language. You know how to invent new ways of saying the same thing."

At the back of the room one of the students is doodling on his name card. His name is Eric, and he looks a little sleepy.

"We all learn talking first and writing later," I add. "In other words, we all learn *automatic* ways of putting words together. Of course, sometimes it's hard to find just the

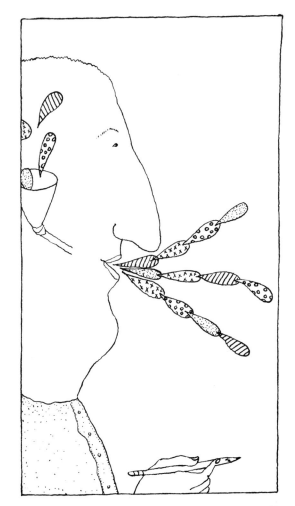

right word or to communicate new thoughts clearly. But we're all like computers that are organized the same basic way. Our data are words. And we already know how to put these words together."

Eric rubs the tough, dark stubble on his chin and raises his hand. "If we all know the same way to talk and write," he asks, "why is writing so hard?"

I'm glad that this question is coming up early. "Well, first," I begin, "you get daily practice in talking. Usually, you don't have to think about *how* to do it. You practice talking all the time until it's a natural happening—like breathing. And another thing about talk: Someone's out there *listening*. If you don't make yourself understood, someone will yawn or look puzzled or ask questions or say, 'Hey, I don't follow you.' "

Eric is frowning slightly. "But when you write, isn't somebody *listening* to what you say? I mean, just like talking?"

"Good question. And the answer is *yes*—sort of. You see, the listening happens all at once when someone *reads* what you've written. In a conversation, though, the talking and listening are usually a back-and-forth thing."

"So?"

"So in a conversation—like this one, say—there's flexibility. You can question me, and I can repeat or fill in the gaps. Your feedback helps me get the message across. But when I'm writing, things are different. You're not there to question or challenge me, so I have to *imagine* you as a reader and *imagine* where you may not be getting my message. It's like a guessing game. I put the words down and *hope* you're able to understand what I'm saying. That makes writing harder than the back-and-forth process we're in right now."

Eric shrugs. "Yeah, maybe so."

"In writing," I add, "you string your words out on paper, but there's no way of knowing whether your audience will *get* what you're saying. There's no immediate response."

"Until those words start getting *corrected*," Anne murmurs with a hint of challenge.

"Right," I say to her. "In writing the feedback from your reader-listener, sometimes a teacher, comes afterward. And that's often a painful experience, as many of us here know all too well. It's too late then to add to an explanation, clear up a misunderstanding, or fix a problem in usage."

"Or spelling," Rob adds, testing me with a grin.

"That too. All of which points to one conclusion: In practicing writing, you also have to practice *listening*—being an audience for your own talk."

Several students are looking confused. "I don't know if I understand," Carlos says. "You mean writing is like talking to yourself?"

"That's *exactly* what I mean. When you're writing, you're talking to yourself and trying to imagine that you're a reader."

"Crazy business," he mumbles.

"Right again. But it's a nice kind of craziness when it works. To get good

at writing, you have to listen to your words as you imagine your audience will."

Carlos glances doubtfully at a friend. Then Jill raises her hand. "Yes, but how?"

"That's what this class will be about. You see, being able to talk to yourself with no holes in the conversation—and then getting it down so that people can make sense of what you're saying—doesn't happen overnight. Writing takes *time* to learn. And like many other skills, it's something you can get better at with study, practice, and feedback from others."

Glancing at Eric, I click back to his original question—why writing is so hard when talking is relatively easy. "One other thing about talking and writing: Writing is harder because it's such a *deliberate* act. You have to sit down and face a blank sheet of paper. You have to think not only of *what* you're saying but *how* to say it. You have to imagine yourself as a reader. You have to check over what you've written for errors in usage and spelling. You have to rewrite to make it better. Talking, on the other hand, is usually more spontaneous, unrehearsed."

Something in this interests Christopher; he catches my attention. "I've heard that people don't really write like they talk. I mean, the sentences are *different*, you know?"

"Good point. Conversational sentences are usually looser, more rambling, with lots of starts and stops, and interruptions. An exception, of course, is a prepared formal speech, which is really writing that's read aloud. Written sentences tend to be longer and more sophisticated in their structure. They use more subordination and more obvious transitions."

Christopher nods, but some of the others look lost.

"Back to this thing about *feedback*," Anne says, stroking the hollow of her throat. "Like, it's natural when you're talking. People ask questions and you explain or whatever. But feedback when you're writing? I don't get it."

"Feedback is one reason we'll use an approach called *sentence combining* in this class," I reply. "It's designed to give you feedback about your writing—from yourself, from your classmates, and sometimes from me. I think you'll find that it doesn't hurt like the feedback you may have gotten in the past. The whole approach is different."

"How's that?"

"Well, sentence combining teaches you how to *listen* to various ways of saying the same thing. It gives you practice making choices among similar sentences. But it also teaches you ways of making sentences that may be different from what you're used to. During the process of combining, you'll be continually making *judgments* about sentences. So that's what I mean by feedback: making better and more informed choices, step by step. Sometimes you'll do this in a group, sometimes by yourself."

"What kind of judgments?" Tony asks.

"Sometimes you'll combine sentences and ask yourself whether the result sounds grammatical—like 'good English,' in other words. This is the most basic level of judgment about sentences. Sometimes you'll be comparing

sentences on the basis of phrasing or sentence rhythm, asking yourself which one 'sounds better' or 'reads more smoothly.' This is a higher-level judgment about sentences. And sometimes you'll be considering differences in sentence emphasis and logic so that you can express meanings clearly and precisely. This is probably the highest-level judgment of all. Making these various judgments over and over helps you improve the writing you do on your own."

"Sounds weird," Carlos says.

I can feel myself liking Carlos. "Well, maybe not so weird," I say to him. "Look at it this way: All of us use the same basic language rules; the fact that we can understand each other right now tells us that. The rules apply to both talking and writing; that's obvious to anyone who learns how to read. The task we're facing, you see, is to take those built-in rules that we *already* use in talking and practice them in writing."

"Which means practicing talking to yourself." He pokes his tongue around the inside of his cheek, and two of his buddies chuckle soundlessly.

I can't keep from laughing as I scribble the words *feedback* and *practice* on the chalkboard. I'm sensing that this class will keep me on my toes throughout the term.

"Practice," I continue. "That's the second reason we'll use the *sentence-combining* approach. My belief is that *any* skill takes lots of practice to acquire. It doesn't matter whether we're talking about welding, macramé, banjo strumming, bartending, jewelry making, cooking, nail pounding, or writing. To learn something, you have to *do* it. It's that simple. And to maintain the skills you've gotten, you have to *practice* them."

Eric looks hopeful and a little less sleepy. "So, we're going to *do* writing —not just talk about it?"

"Right. Sentence combining is a way to get both feedback and practice. Its purpose is to help you transfer your natural talking power into the not-so-natural situation called writing. Why? So that you'll know more about your skills—and so that you'll apply them more often."

"I'm not quite clear on that," Nate says.

"Let me put it this way," I continue. "When you combine sentences, you'll do what you've been doing in speech for years—only now you'll do it on paper, where the results can be talked about by you, me, and others in class. The *practice* in combining—and the *practice* in making various kinds of judgments about the resulting sentences—will teach you a lot about the basics of writing."

"So, knowing more about what you're doing helps you do it better."

"Exactly. Nicely put."

Theresa raises her hand impatiently. "Will we be using a lot of grammar terms?"

"We won't spend time learning parts of speech, doing diagrams, or memorizing definitions and rules. If you already know some grammar terms, that's fine. But terminology isn't really necessary to do combining. You'll encounter a few terms now and then in my explanations, but I'll

keep those to a minimum. Don't worry about them. You'll find they're pretty easy once you're comfortable with the combining work."

"How come no grammar?"

"We're not going to spend time naming sentence parts because we'll be too busy learning how to write. You've probably played the naming game before. And you're therefore aware that it doesn't give you much feedback or practice in *writing*."

A small silence joins us together.

"So how does sentence combining work?" Anne asks.

I pick up a piece of chalk, flip it end over end, and write the following sentences on the board.

Sentence combining builds skills.
The skills are for writing.
The building is systematic.

"Now, make *one* sentence out of those three," I say to the class. "Use the first sentence as your *base* and add words from the other sentences to it. We'll call the result a *writeout*."

"Base?" Andrea asks.

"The base sentence is the one the others hook onto. You can put other sentences *into* the base; this is called *embedding*. Or you can join other sentences *to* the base with connecting words." I pause, then ask for volunteers to give their writeouts.

"*Sentence combining builds writing skills systematically.*"

"*Skills for writing are systematically built through sentence combining.*"

"Good. Any others?"

Some students seem uncertain.

Chico gives his version in the form of a question: "*Sentence combining systematically builds skills that are for writing?*"

"Right. You're getting it."

Kristin leans forward in her desk. "Do you *have* to use the first sentence as the base?"

"No, you can use others as well. What's your writeout?"

"*Skill building is systematic with sentence combining.*"

"Nice. You used the third sentence as the base."

"Can you *add* words?"

"Right. You can put in connecting words, change the form of words, or delete words. The only requirement is to keep the basic meaning of what's given to you."

"*What sentence combining does is systematically build writing skills.*"

"Well done again. Any others?"

Tony clears his throat. "Uhm . . . *The writing skills that sentence combining builds* . . ." He hesitates, biting his lip. "That's not right, is it?"

"It's not complete. It's part of a sentence—a sentence fragment. You've got a good start. Keep it going."

Tony gives it another try: *"The writing skills that sentence combining builds . . . uhm . . . are systematic."* He squints at me, listening to the inner echo of his writeout. "That's changed something."

"You've got a complete sentence now, but its meaning is different from the others. It's the *building* of skills that's systematic."

"First day out and I blow it, huh?"

"Not at all. It's okay to make mistakes. You see, I *want* you to experiment with sentences and try out different ways to say the same thing. Making mistakes is *part* of learning and nothing to be afraid of."

"Sort of strange for an English class," he says.

I put another cluster on the board.

> The clusters are short.
> The clusters are simple.
> The clusters are easy to combine.
> This happens at first.

"Same rules," I say. "See if you can get all four into one. If that's a problem—or if you like the sound of a two-sentence combination better—then put four into two."

Carlos raises his hand. *"At first the clusters are short, simple, and easy to combine."*

"Short, simple clusters are easy to combine at first," Rob volunteers.

Janet's voice comes next. *"The clusters are short and simple, and at first they are easy to combine."*

"Very good. Those are all stylistically unique. Now how about some others?" A long pause follows.

Anne finally reads her sentence. *"Because the clusters are short and simple, they are easy to combine at first."*

"Nice. You've made a causal connection."

"The clusters—short and simple—are at first easily combined," Maria offers.

"It's easy at first to combine short, simple clusters," Tim adds from the corner.

"You're doing fine. Let's try another cluster. Again, it's four into one if you can manage—or four into two if you prefer."

> Then the clusters get longer.
> The clusters get more complicated.
> This stretches your skills.
> The skills are mental.

STOP. PUT THE ABOVE CLUSTER INTO THE FORM OF A WRITEOUT. THEN RESUME YOUR READING.

Nate leads off. *"Then the clusters get longer and more complicated. This stretches your mental skills."*

"Your mental skills are stretched as the clusters then get longer and more complicated," Chico says in a half-whisper.

Laura raises her hand. *"Then because the clusters get longer and more complicated, your mental skills are stretched."*

I can feel the class begin to relax. "All are excellent writeouts. Any more possibilities?"

"Longer, more complicated clusters stretch your mental skills," Eric volunteers.

"Ah, a short, vigorous writeout."

"Clusters that are longer and more complicated are then used for stretching your mental skills," Kim offers.

"And another good one. You see, there's nothing to it. You're using your built-in speech power and transferring it to writing. So let's try another cluster."

Five more sentences go up on the board.

> This approach transfers power.
> The transfer is from speech.
> The transfer is to writing.
> This approach increases options.
> The options are related to style.

I hand out pieces of chalk at random. "Take a moment and put these five sentences into one—or five into two if that's your preference. Go to the board and do your writeout. Then give your piece of chalk to someone else. If your answer is the same as someone else's, don't put it up twice."

Walking to the side of the room, I begin reading the writeouts as they appear on the board:

A. This approach transfers power from speech to writing and increases stylistic options.

B. Transferring power from speech to writing, this approach increases options in style.

C. a speech-to-writing power transfer happens with this approach, it thus increases style-related options.

D. With this approach, theres a transfer of power from speech to writing; which increases the options of style.

E. Stylistic options are increased as this approach transfers power from speech to writing.

F. This approach, which transfers power from speech to writing. It increases style options.

G. Because this approach transfers power from speech to writing, it increases options related to style.

H. Power is transferred from speech to writing with this approach, and style options are increased.

"Now this was a fairly tough cluster," I tell the class. "There *are* some proofreading problems that we'll deal with later—things like spelling and punctuation. And there's even a sentence fragment, which many readers consider more serious. But *all* these matters are no cause for gnashing of teeth. They're fairly easy to learn once you get the speech-to-writing transfer happening smoothly. Besides, you'll find many errors clearing up automatically as you start listening to your sentences and puzzling your way through combining exercises. The idea now is to team up and help each other with usage skills. This is the most basic level of feedback about writing."

Chuck is squinting at the board. "Uhm, maybe I made a mistake in the one I did. I left off a capital letter."

The class focuses on Chuck's writeout as I capitalize the first word.

C.   A speech-to-writing power transfer happens with this approach, it thus increases style-related options.

"That takes care of one usage problem," I say to him. "But there's another that needs to be fixed. Try whispering the sentence aloud. Think about the punctuation."

Hands start going up as Chuck murmurs the words. "Something to do with the comma?"

"That's right. Who's got a solution to the problem?"

"You need a stronger punctuation mark to separate the two sentences," Maria volunteers. "Either a semicolon or a period should replace the comma."

"And a capital letter follows the period," Chuck says with a grin.

I make this correction. "That's right. A simple proofreading change makes a run-on sentence into two independent sentences."

C.   A speech-to-writing power transfer happens with this approach. It thus increases style-related options.

"Of course not all of our talk about sentences will be at this basic level," I continue. "We'll also make judgments about sentences that are technically correct but somehow awkward. And we'll be getting feedback on the emphasis and logic in comparable sentences so that writeouts really say what we want them to."

Carlos has a skeptical look on his face. "This combining seems too good to be true. How do we know it works?"

"It works if you do."

"No, I'm serious."

"So am I. Sentence combining isn't any kind of magic answer for learning how to write. But it *does* give you feedback on your sentences and lots of practice making them. It helps you do new things with sentences so that you begin seeing and hearing the options available to you. And it even teaches

you how sentences link together—as we'll learn later." I pause to look the class over. "But you have to get *into* the exercises. This means listening to what you're saying and paying attention to your writeouts."

"You mean the punctuation and stuff?"

"For starters, yes. Proofreading your work. Making sure that it not only makes sense but also *appears* literate."

I scribble another cluster on the board.

> Sentence combining provides practice.
> It provides feedback.
> It leads to awareness.
> The awareness is of skills.
> The skills are in writing.

Students begin whispering their writeouts to one another—a sign that they're catching on.

"Volunteers for writeouts?" I ask.

"Why don't you try the other students who are reading this book?" Kristin replies. "They can do combining as well as we can."

She's right, of course.

Your writeout goes here:

_____

_____

_____

_____

"How about homework?" Eric asks.

"You'll find some exercises in comparing writeouts, proofreading, and discussing your inner voice—the voice you hear when you're thinking to yourself. There's also an oral dialogue in the form of a script. This is fun because you get to trade friendly insults with a partner."

"Anything else?"

"A chance to do some writing on your own."

I can tell that this class is going to be good. They pair up and go right to work on the Unit 1 exercises.

EXERCISE 1.1. Comparing Writeouts

Directions. You know from experience that some sentences "sound better" than others. Sometimes, this is related to *grammar or usage;* sometimes to *phrasing or sentence rhythm;* and sometimes to *sentence emphasis,* which depends on context and your writing intentions.

Compare the following writeouts on the basis of *grammar and usage:*

I have a goal.
The goal is learning to write better.

A. [SENTENCE FRAGMENT] *My goal, which is learning to write better.*
B. [GRAMMATICAL SENTENCE] *My goal is learning to write better.*

Listen to *phrasing and sentence rhythm* in the next writeouts:

I want to improve my sentences.
I want to improve my vocabulary.

A. [AWKWARD SOUNDING] *To improve my sentences and my vocabulary is my want.*
B. [NATURAL SOUNDING] *I want to improve my sentences and vocabulary.*

Now study the differences in *sentence emphasis.* The "better" writeout depends on what you want to say.

I have always avoided writing.
It is tough for me.

A. [ONE EMPHASIS] *I have always avoided writing because it is tough for me.*
B. [ANOTHER EMPHASIS] *Because I have always avoided writing, it is tough for me.*

The following exercises will help you develop your "sentence sense." Here are five steps for doing them:

1. Read the short sentences slowly; listen to what they say.
2. To hear differences, say the two writeouts aloud.
3. Check (√) the writeout that sounds better; make sure its meaning is the same as in the short sentences.
4. Compare your preference to the Answer Key (p. 275).
5. Create a writeout of your own; compare it with the one you have checked to see which sounds better.

1. The shark swallowed some piranha fish.
   The shark was terrifically hungry.

1-A. The shark swallowed some piranha fish that were terrifically hungry.

1-B. The shark, which was terrifically hungry, swallowed some piranha fish.

1-C. _____

_____

2. The convict was headed for prison.
   The convict wailed with regret.

2-A. Being headed for prison, the convict wailed with regret.

2-B. Beheaded in prison, the convict wailed with regret.

2-C. _____

_____

3. The students wired the skeleton together.
   They called the skeleton Bonaparte.

3-A. After wiring the skeleton together, the students called it Bonaparte.

3-B. The students wired the skeleton to-gether, and they called the skeleton Bonaparte.

3-C. _____

_____

4. The accountant was finally institu-tionalized.
The accountant was seriously off bal-ance.

4-A. The accountant, being seriously off balance, was finally institutionalized.

4-B. Seriously off balance was the finally institutionalized accountant.

4-C. _____

_____

5. Our burly coach is not too intelligent. He was named Throwback of the Year. A puny sportswriter named him.

5-A. Our burly coach was named Throw-back of the Year by a puny sports-writer, who is not too intelligent.

5-B. Our burly coach, who is not too intel-ligent, was named Throwback of the Year by a puny sportswriter.

5-C. _____

_____

6. Tucker was stuck in Winnemucca. Tucker was a trucker. The trucker was out of luck.

6-A. Tucker, an out-of-luck trucker, was stuck in Winnemucca.

6-B. Tucker, stuck in a Winnemucca, where he was a trucker who was out of luck.

6-C. _____

_____

7. Poor Myrtle definitely got a raw deal. Her hamburger was put on last. The barbecue had gone cold.

7-A. Definitely getting a raw deal by hav-ing her hamburger put on last, after the barbecue had gone cold, was poor Myrtle.

7-B. Poor Myrtle—whose hamburger was put on last, after the barbecue had gone cold—definitely got a raw deal.

7-C. _____

_____

8. Harvey worked as a chauffeur. He worked for many years. He now has nothing to show for it.

8-A. Although Harvey worked for many years as a chauffeur, he now has noth-ing to show for it.

8-B. Because Harvey worked for many years as a chauffeur, he now has noth-ing to show for it.

8-C. _____

_____

9. She sang a beautiful hymn. She sang in the church choir. She was called "amazing Grace."

9-A. After she sang a beautiful hymn in the church choir, she was called "amazing Grace."

9-B. After she was called amazing, Grace sang a beautiful hymn in the church choir.

9-C. _____

_____

10.   Betting causes divorces.
       The betting is on horses.
       The cause is sometimes.

10-A.   Betting on horses sometimes causes
         divorces.

10-B.   On horses, sometimes, betting causes
         divorces.

10-C.   _____
         _____

EXERCISE 1.2.   Proofreading Practice

Directions. Shown below are two problem
writeouts from Unit 1. Each has *two* mistakes
—in spelling, punctuation, capitalization, or
usage. Spot the errors and rewrite the sentences. Check with the Answer Key (p. 275).

REWRITE 1 _____
            _____
            _____

This approach transfers power.
The transfer is from speech.
The transfer is to writing.
This approach increases options.
The options are related to style.

PROBLEM 1   *With this approach, theres a*
             transfer of power from speech to
             writing; which increases the op-
             tions of style.

PROBLEM 2   *This approach, which transfers*
             power from speach to writing. It
             increases style options.

REWRITE 2 _____
            _____
            _____

EXERCISE 1.3.   Inner Voice

Directions. Combine the following clusters of
sentences so that they retain all the information. *You can delete words; you can change
the form of words; and you can add "connecting" words.* If you have trouble combining all
the sentences from a cluster into one writeout,
it's okay to make two.

1.   I stare at sentences.
2.   The sentences are short.
3.   The sentences appear in clusters.

4.   My brain combines them.

5.   The combining is almost automatic.

6.   The result is sentences.
7.   The sentences are longer.
8.   The sentences are more complex.
9.   The complexity is structural.

10.   Combining all clusters is not required.
11.   Some may be left as is.

12.   I explore structure.
13.   I explore options.
14.   I feel a sense of freedom.
15.   The freedom is stylistic.

16. An inner voice makes connections.
17. The connections are between sentences.
18. The sentences are short.
19. The voice spins out new ones.
20. These are more interesting.
21. They are more readable.

22. I read these sentences.
23. I can't help but combine them.

24. I am pulled from one cluster.
25. I am pulled to the next.
26. I whisper my writeouts.

27. I work my way through this cluster.
28. The cluster is final.
29. Distractions fade from consciousness.
30. Distractions are around me.

EXERCISE 1.4.   Sentence-Combining Dialogue

Directions. Here's an exercise that you'll enjoy. It's a back-and-forth "scripted" conversation between two students, X and Y. The combining is set up in sequential sentences rather than in lists of clusters.

MODEL

X. My brain can put sentences together. It is super-smart.
    My super-smart brain can put sentences together.

Y. Your brain can't put anything together. It is sleepy.
    Your brain, which is sleepy, can't put anything together.

Find a partner so that you can do this exercise *orally.* Then switch roles and put the sentences together in new ways. After you're comfortable with the combining, add gestures and other dramatic flourishes.

X. I can combine short sentences. The combining is without thinking.

Y. You have trouble even thinking. The thinking is about sentences.

X. For me, combining is a task. The task is effortless.

Y. But you bumble two-sentence clusters. The clusters are easy.

X. My speed is incredible. The speed is in sentence combining.

Y. Your speed is slow. Your slowness is incredible.

X. My skill has made me famous. My fame has spread throughout the school.

Y. Your lack of skill has made you notorious. Your notoriety has spread everywhere.

X. I can invent sentences. The sentences are new. They have never been spoken before.

Y. Your sentences are unspeakable. They are pitiful. They are worn-out.

X. For me, combining is natural. It is spontaneous. It is automatic.

Y. For you, combining is an attempt. The attempt is to conceal your ignorance.

X. I like making sentences. The sentences are complex. They flex my language muscles.

Y. But your sentences lack variety. They lack grace. They lack structure.

X. I like to experiment with syntax. I like to explore possibilities. The possibilities are stylistic.

Y. Your style is plain. Its plainness is painful. Your style is dull.

X. I appreciate your comments. The comments are friendly. They are about my skills. They are about my style.

Y. It has been my pleasure. The pleasure is sincere. The pleasure is to give you feedback. The pleasure is to give you encouragement.

X. Your criticism has been most helpful. It is unbiased. It has been informative. It has been constructive.

Y. My aim is to be positive. It is to be supportive. It is to build self-confidence. The self-confidence is in my friends.

EXERCISE 1.5   On-Your-Own Writing Options

Directions. Pick one of the following options. Use it as the focus for on-your-own writing related to Unit 1.

1. Imagine yourself as a student in the class you've been reading about in Unit 1. You can ask the instructor a question—any question. Put this question down on paper with quotation marks around it.

    Now on the next line *answer* the question in the instructor's voice. Put down what you imagine he or she would say, again with quotation marks.

    Is your question answered? If so, you can ask another related one. If not, you can demand a better, *clearer* answer—using quotation marks, of course.

    Try to keep this dialogue going—like a rally between John McEnroe and Bjorn Borg. Let these voices get *aggressive* with one another and zero in on "soft spots" in the other's statements.

    With this dialogue as your raw material, now *rework* the ideas. Put them into the form of a story or transform them into an essay. Each question and answer in the dialogue should be a separate paragraph. If you use the essay form, you'll find your new paragraphs acting as "magnetic poles"—pulling the ideas, like metal filings, from the dialogue.

2. One of the key ideas in Unit 1 is that when you're writing, you're talking to yourself and trying to imagine that you're a reader.

    As a reader, what is it that you find particularly irritating, distracting, or difficult in the writing of others? Try to be *specific* about this. Tell what you regard as "problem reading" and provide an example or two.

    Now think back to the difficulties that people have had with your writing. How have your readers (particularly teachers) responded to you? Provide an example or two. Then ask yourself whether you, as a reader, are *more* or *less* demanding than the people who read your prose.

3. Think back to both pleasant and unpleasant experiences you've had with writing.

    What are your early memories of learning to write? What is it like inside your head when you're writing? What steps do you usually go through to get a paper from conception to completion? What kinds of "blocks" do you sometimes encounter and how do you solve them?

    Choose *one* of these questions as the focus for a "reflective" personal paper. Talk about your writing "from the inside out," being as specific with examples as you can.

UNIT TWO
A CLOSER LOOK
AT COMBINING

The class assembles slowly, some people visiting quietly, others clustered around my desk to clear up questions. At the work table Nate has just handled Chico's arm-wrestling challenge.

"Let's talk about kernel sentences," I say to the class. "The short sentences that I've been asking you to combine are called *kernels*. Basically, they're unmodified sentences that occur over and over in English. There are only a few of these basic patterns altogether. Here are two sentences that show one pattern —probably the most common—in which there are an actor, an action, and an action-receiver. Even though the pattern and the words are the same in both sentences, the messages are quite different."

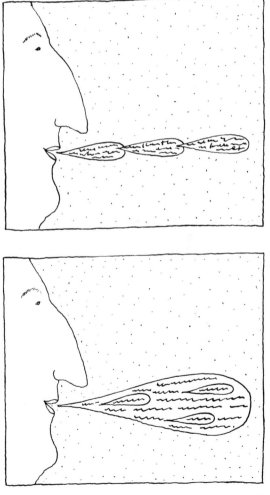

> Princesses kiss toads.
> Toads kiss princesses.

"What do you mean *unmodified?*" Maria asks.

"Just that no descriptive or qualifying words are added. You see, a *modifier* limits or restricts the meaning of a sentence. For example, modifiers such as *lonely, slyly, unsuspecting,* and *in the garden* could be added to the kernels."

Lonely princesses slyly kiss unsuspecting toads in the garden.

Lonely toads slyly kiss unsuspecting princesses in the garden.

"Not all sentences you'll be combining will be kernels in a strict technical sense," I continue. "Some will be slightly modified; others will be sentences that you wouldn't normally speak or write. But most will be very simple patterns such as these."

The princess smiles.
The princess is a teenager.
The princess is lonely.
The princess is in the garden.
The princess gives the toad a kiss.

Rob has a hand up. "Nobody I know really uses those short, choppy sentences."

"Good point. You've brought up the idea of *transforming*—the kernels changing form and hooking up with other kernels to form longer, more complex sentences."

The princess, a lonely teenager in the garden, smiles and gives the toad a kiss.

Rob looks pleased with himself.

"Transformations are mental operations," I tell the class. "They're processes that your brain computer uses to alter individual kernels, to join kernels, and to embed pieces of kernels into one another. It's transforming that enables you to generate billions of new, unique sentences from the basic patterns."

Here and there, notebooks click open.

"In other words," I add, "having a small number of kernel patterns and a limited number of transformations is really what makes language possible. Transforming helps you create and understand an almost infinite number of different sentences and the ideas behind them."

Randy has a hand up. "Example?"

"To get started, let's look at various transformations for a *single* sentence, not for clusters or kernels. Think about the kernel I gave you earlier: *Princesses kiss toads*. A transformation of this would be *Toads are kissed by princesses*. The idea is the same, but the style is different. You've been making transformations like this ever since you were a child—though you probably couldn't describe what you were doing."

"Does it work the same each time?" Kristin asks.

"As regular as clockwork. This one's called the *passive transformation*. It's deeply programmed into your language machinery, just like others we'll be studying. Take the *cleft transformation*, for example. By using it in

our original kernel sentence, *Princesses kiss toads,* you get another alteration in style: *What princesses do is kiss toads.*"

"Do some transformations change the meaning?" Peter inquires.

"Indeed they do. A good example is the *question transformation.* Make the kernel we've been studying into a question. Begin with the word *do.*"

Theresa volunteers an answer. "*Do princesses kiss toads?*"

"Right. Now make a *negative transformation.* Your key word is *not.*"

"*Princesses do not kiss toads,*" Eric says.

"Okay. How about a question transformation *plus* a negative transformation?"

The students are looking puzzled, so I put a hint on the board.

Princesses ———— ———— kiss toads, ———— they?

Is it true that princesses ———— ———— kiss toads?

"I get it," Paulo says. "The first one reads, *Princesses do not kiss toads, do they?* And the second says, *Is it true that princesses do not kiss toads?*"

"Good work. Now try *three* transformations: passive, question, and negative."

Toads ———— ———— kissed ———— princesses, ———— they?

Michelle calls out the answer. "*Toads are not kissed by princesses, are they?*"

"Only rarely," I reply.

"Question," Peter says. "Will we have to know *names* for different transformations?"

"Being able to *use* transformations doesn't mean that you have to label them. Our aim, remember, is to do *writing,* not learn terminology."

I put a transparency on the projector. "So much for transforming a *single* kernel," I continue. "With sentence combining, we'll practice transformations on *clusters* of related kernels. Our purpose is to explore stylistic options—the variety of ways to say something in English. Making different kinds of sentence choices will help you get more in control of your writing skills."

To introduce two of the most basic transforming processes for clusters of kernel sentences, I project definitions for the class to study.

ADDITION: Joining parts of kernel sentences *to* a base sentence with the connecting word *and.* The resulting writeout has *pairs* of words or phrases (compounding) or a *series* of words or phrases.

EMBEDDING: Putting parts of kernel sentences *into* a base sentence without using connecting words. The resulting writeout has words that *modify* the main words in the base sentence.

Twenty-six blank faces stare back at me. "Maybe we'd better look at some *examples* of these transforming processes," I say with a smile. "First, addition. Then embedding."

ADDITION

The princess sits in the garden.
The toad sits in the garden.

[ADDITION] *The princess and the toad sit in the garden.*

Both appear to be relaxed.
Both appear to be "laid back."

[ADDITION] *Both appear to be relaxed and "laid back."*

They listen to the quiet.
They feel the sun's warmth.
They enjoy an inner peace.

[ADDITION] *They listen to the quiet, feel the sun's warmth, and enjoy an inner peace.*

"Why doesn't the first one say, *The princess sits in the garden, and the toad sits in the garden?*" I ask the class.

"Because it sounds dumb that way," Terry says. "There's no point in repeating *sits in the garden.* The extra words don't add anything to the meaning."

"Right. So the addition process makes a compound subject instead, using the *and* connector. With another similar kernel in the cluster, the compounding can be extended into a *series.* The *and* connector is used between *chaperone* and *a toad*; and *sits* is changed to *sit* because you're talking about more than one sitter."

The princess sits in the garden.
Her chaperone sits in the garden.
A toad sits in the garden.

Your writeout goes here:

_____

_____

_____

"Addition works at both ends of the sentence," I continue. "Notice, in the second and third examples, you've got the same process—except that kernel parts are added to the predicate of the base sentence. These clusters can also be extended, of course."

They look at each other.
They listen to the quiet.
They feel the sun's warmth.
They enjoy an inner peace.

Your writeout goes here:

_____

_____

_____

_____

"*And* comes before the word *enjoy?*" Tony asks.

"That's right. The last word or phrase in a series gets the connector. Commas separate words or phrases in a series. Of course if only one addition is made, a comma is not needed."

I put up another transparency. "So much for addition," I conclude. "It happens when sentence parts are *added* to one another. Let's now look at a second basic operation, *embedding.*"

EMBEDDING

The princess kisses the toad
The princess is lonely.
The toad is sleeping.

[EMBEDDING] *The lonely princess kisses the sleeping toad.*

A smile plays across her mouth.
The play is sensual.
Her mouth is teenage.

[EMBEDDING] *A smile plays sensually across her teenage mouth.*

Then her fingers discover a wart.
Her fingers are outstretched.
Her fingers are trembling.
The wart is on her lip.

[EMBEDDING] *Then her fingers—outstretched, trembling—discover a wart on her lip.*

"With embedding, one-word or phrasal modifiers are put *into* a base sentence. These kernel parts usually come before the words they modify but can also come afterward."

"So, what's the *difference* between addition and embedding?" Carol asks. "They both add meaning, don't they?"

"Right. But whereas addition *adds on* to the base sentence, embedding really makes the base sentence more *specific* and *descriptive*. That's what the modifiers do, of course—*particularize*."

"Sounds technical," Eric says.

"But it's not. Here are two clusters that require embedding. Give them a try."

The toad touches his mouth.
The toad is half sleeping.
The touch is careful.
His mouth is tingling.

Your writeout goes here:

_____

_____

_____

_____

He finds a smile.
The smile is teenage.
The smile is sensual.
The smile is on his lips.
His lips are inexperienced.

Your writeout goes here:

_____

_____

_____

_____

"Embedding and addition are very *basic* transforming processes," I conclude. "You'll practice them to get the patterns down. And in the lesson that follows, you'll study two related processes—coordination and subordination."

"But *why?*" Tim interjects. "If we already know *how* to use them, what's the point in practice?"

"A basic purpose of combining is to see *options* in writing. By looking at various writeouts and thinking about *how* they express meaning, you make practical decisions about style. But that's not all. By practicing specific transformations and making more complex logical connections, you develop more maturity in your sentences."

"Another question," Carlos says. "Why even *try* to make longer sentences?"

"The goal isn't simply to make long sentences. It's true that increased sentence length is one feature of mature writing, but remember this: *Just because you're able to make long sentences doesn't mean that you have to.* Sometimes, shorter is better; sometimes not. You have to decide."

"You said *one* feature?"

"Right. Besides making longer sentences, we also tend to put more *into* them as we mature. We literally *say more* in fewer words." To explain this point, I put three kernels on the board.

> The students listened closely.
> They looked puzzled.
> They tried to understand their instructor.

"You see, as a child you might well have combined these to say, '*The students listened closely, and they looked puzzled, and they tried to understand their instructor.*' But now you'd probably say something like '*Listening closely and looking puzzled, the students tried to understand their instructor.*' The second way says more. It expresses a *connection* between listening and looking puzzled and the act of trying to understand."

"And this development happens naturally?" Kristin asks.

"Apparently so. Of course, studying sentences probably adds to your sentence growth just as studying words broadens your vocabulary. The basic point is this: *Being able to use more complex sentences and an expanding vocabulary helps you do higher-level thinking.*"

Carlos is not convinced. "But I don't know if making long sentences is *always* such a good idea."

"Good point," I reply. "A series of long, involved sentences can be as much a problem as a series of choppy ones. One style tends to confuse you or put you to sleep. The other sounds like a grade school primer. Remember, variety makes for interest. I'd therefore urge you to *mix up* sentence lengths. Change the structure. Experiment for effects."

"You mean we can choose how long to make the writeouts?"

"Absolutely. Sometimes you'll want to combine two clusters of kernels into one. But sometimes a cluster needs to be split up. You'll need to *listen* to what you write and follow your instincts. They'll get educated with combining practice."

The class feels more alert now.

"Let me emphasize one thing," I add. "Sentence combining looks easy at first—and it is. You're able to tap into your own language power without learning something new. Sooner or later, though, you'll probably make some disastrous transformations. Just don't panic. We'll work them out together. That's where the growing starts."

"What do you mean by *growing*?" Andrea asks.

"Trying things with words you haven't tried before. Sure, you'll make some mistakes, but that's how you learn."

"A little while ago, you said something about options in writing," Patsy says. "What happens in combining that'll show us options?"

"To answer your question, let's look at kernels from the end of Unit 1. I think you'll see that different transformations create different ways of saying the same thing."

Familiar kernel sentences flash up on the screen.

Sentence combining provides practice.
It provides feedback.
It leads to awareness.
The awareness is of skills.
The skills are in writing.

"Let's see how your writeouts differ," I say to the class, handing out clear plastic sheets and water-soluble pens. "Please do your transforming on a transparency."

The students begin transcribing their writeouts onto the sheets. Then I collect the transparencies and begin projecting them one by one, asking the class to focus on differences in phrasing and sentence rhythm.

STOP.   CHECK TO SEE IF YOUR SENTENCE FROM THE END OF UNIT 1 IS AMONG THESE WRITEOUTS. THEN RESUME YOUR READING.

A.   Sentence combining provides practice and feedback. It leads to an awareness of skills in writing.

B.   Sentence combining provides practice and feedback that lead to awareness of writing skills.

C.   Awareness off writing skills is provided by sentence-combining practice and Feedback.

D.   Providing practice and feedback, sentence combining leads to skill awareness in writing.

E.   Practice and feedback provided by sentence combing, this leads to skill awareness in writing.

F.   Sentence combining practice and feedback lead to an awareness of writing skills.

"We'll side-step proofreading problems for the moment. Which of these six is the right solution?"

Anne looks puzzled. "What do you mean by *right*? I mean, most of them sound good to me. What's different is the phrasing."

"Okay, you're on your toes. There are usually *lots* of ways to say something in English; yet we don't always see or hear the options. Being locked into one way of saying something can make for some pretty stiff, dull writing. That's the trap we're trying to avoid in this class." I then ask the students to cast a vote for the version they think "sounds best."

STOP. REREAD WRITEOUTS A THROUGH F. MAKE A CHECK MARK BESIDE THE SENTENCE THAT YOU PREFER. THEN RESUME YOUR READING.

The voting is quickly accomplished.

A. 4	C. 1	E. 0
B. 8	D. 6	F. 7

"Our opinions differ," I continue, "although we *do* seem to have some consensus, too. With a little practice you'll get more confident about your choices."

"How's that?" Terry asks.

"You'll begin to develop *reasons* for preferring one sentence over another. You'll make judgments about whether the sentence is grammatical. You'll ask yourself about clarity. You'll listen to sentence rhythm and differences in emphasis. In short, you'll become more articulate about *style*—the way meaning is expressed through words."

"So which one do *you* like?" Theresa asks.

"Yeah," Randy says. "Give us your vote."

"Fair enough. But remember this is just one person's opinion. I prefer an option that's not on the list."

G. Because sentence combining provides practice and feedback, it leads to an awareness of writing skills.

"It's different," Eric offers.

"Right. And stylistic differences are what we're considering today. I like it because it expresses a *causal* connection and because of its rhythm."

I flick off the projector. "So you'll be composing writeouts, listening to each other's sentences and making decisions. You'll be stretching yourself and trying new things with language. This is what growth in writing is really all about. It's taking risks and not playing it safe."

"This is a different idea to me," Nate says. "If we're here to learn writing, what do we use for a guide? I don't understand where we're going to get our rules."

"There are at least *two* kinds of 'rightness' in writing," I explain. "One kind is correct spelling, commas in the expected places, capital letters, making your subjects and verbs agree—that sort of thing. You could call it *good usage.* The other kind of 'rightness' is harder to talk about. It's choosing one word over another, varying the length of your sentences, rewriting a paragraph so that it moves from general to specific. It's making both logic and style right so that your writing does what you want it to."

"But how do we *know* what's right?"

"Mainly by checking, comparing, and reading sentences aloud," I reply. "Of course, there *are* standard resources like dictionaries and usage handbooks you can consult for the first kind of 'rightness.' These help if you've got a specific question—like how to spell a word or where to put a comma. But these books probably won't help improve the logic of your writing, for example. And they sometimes don't help much with style, either."

Nate smooths the corners of his mouth. "What you call good usage," he says, "will we be going into that?"

"We'll cover the mechanics of writing—where to punctuate, how to get modifiers in the right places—just as those problems come up in your combining. And later, of course, I'll give you lots of feedback on writing you do on your own."

"So you'll really be *telling* us what's right?" Laura asks.

"Sometimes, yes," I hedge. "But usually I'll *ask* you to solve problems that come up—both in mechanics and in style. You can learn a lot just by working with real day-to-day usage problems and trusting your own ear. That's why we'll often do combining aloud. And that's why I'll insist that you compare your writeouts with those that other students have done. This approach makes you think about *all* levels of writing decisions."

I pull out two transparencies used earlier. "To get some practice working together on usage, let's proofread two writeouts. We're not concerned with identifying the team that wrote these sentences. We're simply interested in how to *improve* the writeouts. The aim, remember, is to learn from mistakes."

C. Awareness off writing skills is provided by sentence-combining practice and Feedback.

E. Practice and feedback provided by sentence combing, this leads to skill awareness in writing.

STOP.   CIRCLE THE ERRORS IN THE ABOVE SENTENCES. THEN RESUME YOUR READING.

"Isn't *of* misspelled in the first one?" Randy asks.

"That's right. What's the other minor error?"

"*Skill* instead of *skills?*"

"No, that's not a problem."

"The word *feedback* is capitalized," Kim says.

"Good, you've spotted it. How about writeout E?"

Christopher's hand is up. "*Combing* instead of *combining.* And the punctuation's wrong, I think."

"Okay, but there's a problem in sentence structure that punctuation won't fix. How could it be rewritten?"

I transcribe two volunteered rewrites for writeout E.

Practice and feedback are provided by sentence combining; these activities lead to an awareness of writing skills.

Practice and feedback provided by sentence combining lead to skill awareness in writing.

STOP. CHECK (√) THE REWRITE THAT YOU PREFER. THEN RESUME YOUR READING.

"Both are good solutions. They solve the problem of a run-on sentence. Notice that the first rewrite makes *two* sentences by adding the word *are*, a semicolon, and the phrase *these activities*. The second rewrite deletes the comma and the pronoun *this*; it also changes *leads* to *lead* so that the compound subject agrees with its verb."

I flick on the projector again. "Now that you've mastered this cluster, let's attach it to another that you worked your way through in Unit 1. The task is to get both clusters into *one* writeout. In other words, you're going to *stretch* your combining skills."

This approach transfers power.
The transfer is from speech.
The transfer is to writing.
This approach increases options.
The options are related to style.

Sentence combining provides practice.
It provides feedback.
It leads to awareness.
The awareness is of skills.
The skills are in writing.

Paulo laughs. "You've got to be kidding."
"No way," Eric says.
"There are *lots* of ways. This is a very tough problem, but it can be solved if you really concentrate. Begin with the phrase *transferring power.* Or try making a series, using the process of addition."

STOP. COMBINE THE ABOVE SENTENCES INTO ONE GRAMMATICAL WRITEOUT. SOME ADDITIONAL "STARTERS":

As this approach . . .
This approach not only . . .
In addition to transferring . . .
Because this approach . . .

THEN RESUME YOUR READING.

The only noise in the classroom is the whirring of the projector fan. Ten seconds go by, then twenty, then thirty. Finally a full minute has passed. A few students have begun to scribble the writeout in their notebooks. Others look perplexed.

"Let's hear what you came up with," I say.

Tim fumbles with a notebook page. *"Transferring power from speech to writing and increasing stylistic options, this approach provides practice and feedback that lead to awareness of writing skills."*

"Beautiful. You did ten into one."

Maria, who has been quiet for some time, now raises her hand. "I think I may have it; I'm not sure."

"There's only one way to find out. Let's hear it."

She pauses, then reads her writeout: *"Sentence combining transfers power from speech to writing, increases options in style by providing practice and feedback, and thus leads to skill awareness."*

"Very well done. Being able to handle *that* kind of problem takes real skill."

"I tried it another way," Kristin says. *"This approach not only transfers power from speech to writing and increases style-related options, but it also provides practice and feedback that lead to skill awareness in writing."*

"Another fine solution. So let's try something else now. Combine these."

1.   These problems are a headache.
2.   The problems are in sentence combining.
3.   The headache is real.

4.   My brain is dissatisfied with solutions.
5.   The solutions are easy.

6.   It seeks writeouts.
7.   The writeouts are unusual.
8.   It explores all alternatives.
9.   The alternatives are stylistic.

10.   I approach a cluster.
11.   The cluster is kernels.
12.   I hear possibilities.
13.   The possibilities are numerous.
14.   The possibilities are for transformations.

15.   These battle with one another.
16.   The battle is for my attention.

17.   What results is a headache.
18.   The headache is from sentence combining.
19.   The headache has me mumbling.
20.   The mumbling is to myself.

Within a few moments, the class has agreed on writeouts for the clusters. I transcribe these onto the board.

A. These sentence-combining problems are a real headache.
B. My brain is dissatisfied with easy solutions.
C. It examines unusual writeouts and explores all stylistic alternatives.
D. I approach a cluster of kernels and hear numerous possibilities for transformations.
E. These battle with one another for my attention.
F. What results is a headache from sentence combining that has me mumbling to myself.

"So far, so good," I tell the class. "Now for the harder part. Put these six writeouts into no more than four sentences."

The room is a chorus of groans and laughter. "Remember," I add, "how can you develop your skills if you don't *stretch* them?"

STOP. COMBINE WRITEOUTS B AND C INTO ONE SENTENCE. DO THE SAME FOR WRITEOUTS D AND E. THEN RESUME YOUR READING.

The students, though under duress, set to work. Finally, the team of Theresa, Nate, and Paulo volunteers to read "condensed" writeouts to the class.

A. These sentence-combining problems are a real headache.
B. My brain, dissatisfied with easy solutions, examines unusual writeouts and explores all stylistic alternatives.
C. Approaching a cluster of kernels, I hear numerous possibilities that battle one another for my attention.
D. What results is a sentence-combining headache that has me mumbling to myself.

"Now for something harder—this time with no hints. Combine writeouts A and B into one sentence."

STOP. INSERT THE WORD *BECAUSE* BETWEEN WRITEOUTS A AND B. READ THE RESULT AND ASK YOURSELF WHETHER IT SOUNDS GRAMMATICAL. THEN RESUME YOUR READING.

Several students are having trouble. Two minutes later I'm asking whether anybody has courage enough to put a problem sentence before the class. The class gets still. Everyone looks reluctant.

Finally Chico raises his hand. "I've made some strange sentences before, but this one's really a mess. I need some help."

"That's what we're looking for. Put it on the board."

These sentence-combining problems are a real headache, my brain is dissatisfied with easy solutions, which seeks unusual writeouts and explores all stylistic possibilities.

"Suggestions from the class?" I announce. "How can we fix this sentence?"

"It's a run-on," Anne volunteers. "It's two sentences with a comma between them. The comma between *headache* and *my brain* needs to become a period, with *my* capitalized."

"Good. That solves the punctuation problem. But what if we wanted this to remain *one* sentence, not two?"

"Take out the comma and put in the word *because*," Michelle answers.

I read the corrected version aloud: "*These sentence-combining problems are a real headache because my brain is dissatisfied with easy solutions.*"

Andrea's hand goes up. "That sounds good so far. But isn't there something wrong with the next part? I mean, it says the *solutions* seek writeouts. The modifier is in the wrong place."

"You're a good reader. How should it be?"

"Isn't it the *brain* that seeks the writeouts?" Carlos says. "And the *brain* that explores the stylistic possibilities? I mean, the *solutions* don't do the exploring."

"That's right. Who's got a corrected version? How about you, Chico? Take out *which* and use the addition process."

Chico bites his lip and swallows, then reads aloud. "*These sentence-combining problems are a real headache because my brain is dissatisfied with easy solutions, . . . seeks unusual writeouts, . . . and explores all stylistic possibilities.*"

The class applauds his effort.

"That's thinking," I say to him. "Excellent work."

"I tried it another way," Eric announces.

"Put it on the board."

Eric comes forward and writes another "corrected" version.

These sentence-combining Problems are a real headache because my brain which is dissatisfied with easy solutions, seeks unusual writeouts and explore all stylistic possibilitys.

"*Almost* perfect," I respond with a smile. "You've solved the word order problem beautifully. But you've capitalized *problems* and misspelled *possibilities.* You also need a comma after *brain* and an *s* on *explore.*"

"Details." Eric grins.

"Agreed. The real skill is being able to combine nine kernels into one

sentence, as you did so nicely. But since you *can* do that, why not master the details, too? Taking care of the little things is mainly a matter of habit."

"But spelling's *always* been a problem for me," Eric complains.

"It's a problem for me, too. But in combining exercises, the words are already spelled for you. The main details are punctuation and capitalization."

"I get the message." His grin is self-conscious as he heads for his desk, glad to be off the hook.

"Well, actually, it's a message for *everybody*," I say to the class. "These 'little things' turn out to be very important for employers, teachers, and the people who process your application for a doughnut franchise. With just a little effort everyone can make big improvements in these basics. It's a matter of reading your sentences aloud, double-checking, taking time to look up or ask about spellings you're not sure of, and *caring* enough to fix minor problems. There's no reason to let careless errors bring down your grades in school or limit your opportunities in the world of work."

I look out over the classroom. The overhead lights, like suspended white egg cartons, make a soft fluorescent hum as I pause.

"All of this is simply a matter of personal *pride*, personal *power*," I add. "You with me?"

"Yeah," Nate says. "You want the power, you need the words."

"Okay, let's summarize: As long as your writeouts make sense and maintain basic usage conventions, they're *right* in a technical sense. But just because a sentence is mechanically right, you can't assume it's necessarily effective. In other words, some writing is grammatically correct but stiff and dull. So what we're after is writing that's correct but also interesting. That's why the emphasis on stylistic choices." I punctuate this paragraph with a pointed index finger.

"And now my final point: Sentence combining is only a skill builder for real writing. It'll give you practice in putting sentences and paragraphs together, rearranging parts, and learning how to edit. But it's not the same thing as on-your-own writing. It's not going to help you find a topic, invent something to say, get your ideas organized, express them intelligently, and make a final copy. Doing those things *right* takes time to learn. Since no one's yet invented an instant learn-to-write pill, we'll have to learn things from the inside out—by really doing them."

"Well, at least it's *interesting*," Rob says.

"Enjoy the Unit 2 exercises."

EXERCISE 2.1   Comparing Writeouts

Directions. In exercises from the previous lesson you made choices between two writeouts, checked with the Answer Key, and tried combining a third version of your own. The following exercises, set up in the same way, will further extend your sentence sense. As before, your decision about the better-sounding sentence may be based upon *grammar* or *usage*.

I don't always understand terminology.
The terminology is grammatical.
I can usually hear mistakes.

A. [NONSENSE SENTENCE] *Not always understanding grammatical terminology can usually hear mistakes.*

B. [GRAMMATICAL SENTENCE] *I don't always understand grammatical terminology but can usually hear mistakes.*

It may also be based upon *phrasing or sentence rhythm*.

I am now catching on to the exercises.
The exercises are in sentence combining.
I am even enjoying them a little.

A. [AWKWARD SOUNDING] *Now catching on to exercises in sentence combining, I am enjoying these exercises a little.*

B. [NATURAL SOUNDING] *I am now catching on to sentence combining exercises and even enjoying them a little.*

And finally, your choice may be determined by the logical relationships being expressed.

I am looking forward to the next exercises.
They are probably bizarre.
They are probably fun to do.

A. [ILLOGICAL SENTENCE] *Although I am looking forward to the next exercises, they are probably bizarre and fun to do.*

B. [LOGICAL SENTENCE] *I am looking forward to the next exercises because they are probably bizarre and fun to do.*

Follow the same five steps you used for doing Exercise 1.1.

1.   Some youth have gone to pot.
      This is according to statistics.
      The statistics are on marijuana usage.

1-A. According to statistics on marijuana usage, some youth have gone to pot.

1-B. To pot, according to statistics on marijuana usage, have some youth gone.

1-C. _____

      _____

2.   People are overweight.
      Jokes are sometimes made.
      The jokes are at their expanse.

2-A. If people are overweight, jokes are sometimes made at their expanse.

2-B. People are overweight if jokes are sometimes made at their expanse.

2-C. _____

      _____

3.   Old cigar butts are hard to light.
      They are soggy.
      They are cool to smoke.

3-A. Old cigar butts are hard to light and they cool to smoke, but they are soggy.

3-B. Old, soggy cigar butts are hard to light but cool to smoke.

3-C. _____

      _____

4.   A trainer is perhaps barking up the wrong tree.
      The trainer tries to reason with dogs.

The trainer tries to understand their hang-ups.

4-A. A trainer who tries to reason with dogs and understand their hang-ups is perhaps barking up the wrong tree.

4-B. Trying to reason with dogs and understand their hang-ups is a trainer, perhaps barking up the wrong tree.

4-C. ————————————————

————————————————

5. The police officers heard noises.
The noises were unusual.
The noises were from the parked car.
The officers used their spotlights.

5-A. When the police officers heard unusual noises from the parked car, they used their spotlights.

5-B. When the police officers used their spotlights, they heard unusual noises from the parked car.

5-C. ————————————————

————————————————

6. Becoming a nun requires a habit.
The habit is thinking.
The thinking is religious.
The habit is more than mere appearances.

6-A. More than mere appearances, thinking religiously, a habit which is required for becoming a nun.

6-B. Becoming a nun requires a habit of thinking religiously, which is more than mere appearances.

6-C. ————————————————

————————————————

7. Maxwell preened himself in front of a mirror.

The preening was loving.
The mirror was full-length.
He prided himself on his humility.

7-A. Maxwell lovingly preening himself in front of a full-length mirror, priding himself on his humility.

7-B. Maxwell lovingly preened himself in front of a full-length mirror, priding himself on his humility.

7-C. ————————————————

————————————————

8. Please remember something.
Punmanship can make your letters easier to read.
The punmanship is good.
The punmanship is clean.

8-A. Please remember that good, clean punmanship can make your letters easier to read.

8-B. It is to be remembered that your letters can be more easily read when your punmanship is both good and clean.

8-C. ————————————————

————————————————

9. Henry VIII was quite a figure.
The figure was cutting.
This was especially to women.
The women were unfortunate.
He married the women.

9-A. Henry VIII was quite a cutting figure, especially to the unfortunate women whom he married.

9-B. Henry VIII, a cutting figure, who married especially unfortunate women.

9-C. ————————————————

————————————————

10.   The banker was proud of his ancestry.
        The banker was masked.
        The banker rode a white stallion.
        The banker called himself "The Loan
        Arranger."
        His ancestry was Italian.

10-A.   The masked banker, riding a white
        stallion and calling himself "The
        Loan Arranger," was proud of his
        Italian ancestry.

10-B.   The masked banker rode a white stal-
        lion and called himself "The Loan Ar-
        ranger," which was proud of his Ital-
        ian ancestry.

10-C.   _____

        _____

        _____

EXERCISE 2.2.   Proofreading Practice

Directions. One writeout in each of the following exercises has two errors. Spot them,
make corrections, and check with the Answer
Key. Then make your *own* writeout for the
cluster of kernel sentences. Decide which version is stylistically preferable, in your opinion.
Compare your preferences with those of other
students.

1.   Her brother smiled.
        Her brother was tall.
        His smiling was with energy.
        The energy was vibrant.

1-A.   Her tall brother smiled; his energy
        was vibrant.

1-B.   Her brother, who was tall smiled with
        Energy that was vibrant.

1-C.   A smile of vibrant energy came from
        her tall brother.

2.   He rubbed his chin.
        The rubbing was impatient.
        The rubbing was brisk.
        The chin was covered with stubble.
        The stubble was tough.
        The stubble was unshaved.

2-A.   He rubbed his chin briskly and impa-
        tiently; it was covered with tough, un-
        shaved stubble.

2-B.   Impatiently and brisk, he rubbed his
        chin, which is covered with tough and
        unshaved stubble.

2-C.   He rubbed the tough stubble on
        his unshaved chin with brisk impa-
        tience.

3.   All the athletes stood for a band.
        The athletes were husky.
        The athletes were uniformed.
        Their standing was restless.
        The band played the national anthem.

3-A.   All the husky, uniform athletes stood
        with restlessness, the band played the
        national anthem.

3-B.   All the athletes, husky and uni-
        formed, stood restlessly as the band
        played the national anthem.

3-C.   Husky, uniformed, and restless, all
        the athletes stood for the band's play-
        ing of the national anthem.

EXERCISE 2.3.   Addition and Embedding

Directions. Combine the following clusters of kernels by making *both* addition and embedding transformations.

MODEL

Addition

We have grown dependent on oil.
We need to develop energy sources.

Embedding

The oil is from foreign lands.
The sources would be alternative.

[ADDITION AND EMBEDDING] *We have grown dependent on oil from foreign lands and need to develop alternative energy sources.*

Addition

1. Minorities have made progress.
    Women have made progress.

    Embedding

    The progress is social.
    The progress is in recent years.

    Addition

2. Our neighbors were cooing.
    They were kissing.

    Embedding

    The neighbors live next door.
    Their kissing was passionate.

    Addition

3. Harriet Tubman posed as a wanderer.
    She managed to lead slaves to freedom.

Embedding

The wanderer appeared hapless.
The slaves numbered 3000.

Addition

4. A marijuana cigarette contains carcinogens.
    It may therefore be hazardous to health.

    Embedding

    The carcinogens are equal to 22 tobacco cigarettes.
    The hazard may be extreme.

    Addition

5. Some bacteria synthesize magnetite.
    The bacteria use it to orient themselves.

    Embedding

    Magnetite is an iron/oxygen compound.
    The orientation is in the earth's magnetic field.

    Addition

6. Forests provide a habitat.
    Forests provide timber.
    Forests provide solace.

    Embedding

    The habitat is for animals.
    The timber is for construction.
    The solace is for the soul.

    Addition

7. The waiter approached the table.
    The waiter stumbled.
    The waiter dropped the platter.

    Embedding

    The waiter was dressed in a tuxedo.
    The tuxedo was elegant.
    The platter was steaming.

Addition

8. Navajos see the universe as animate.
    Navajos see the universe as ordered.
    Navajos see the universe as harmonious.

Embedding

The Navajos are traditional.
The universe is physical.
The harmony is spiritual.

Addition

9. Honesty was a promise.
    Candor was a promise.
    Budgeting was a promise.

Embedding

The promises were clever.
The promises were political.
The promises were untrue.

Addition

10. Death is among life's certainties.
    Taxes are among life's certainties.
    Inflation is among life's certainties.

Embedding

The certainties are few.
The taxes are unwanted.
The inflation is continuing.

EXERCISE 2.4.   Spelling Tune-Up

Directions. The following sentence-combining exercises involve words that sound alike or are sometimes confused. Many are sources of common writing errors. Do the combining as usual, but pay special attention to the meaning of these words in context. Focus on spelling in relation to different meanings.

MODEL

girl: a young female
grill: a stove, sometimes open

was: past form of *be*
saw: past form of *see*

one: a number
won: past form of *win*

One girl saw who won.
The girl was behind the grill.

One girl—who was behind the grill—saw who won.
Behind the grill was a girl who saw the winner.

1. *you're:* means "you are"
    your: indicates possession

    You're not going to confuse your spellings.
    The spellings are of *you're* and *your.*
    You're quick to catch on to your task.

2. *it's:* means "it is"
    its: indicates possession

    It's easy to confuse *its* with *it's.*
    It's has an apostrophe.
    It's means "*it is.*"

3. *threw:*   past tense of *throw*
    through: finished; in one side, out the other
    though: although; however

    Richard threw the Frisbee to me.
    He threw it through the trees.
    This was even though I was all through playing.

4. *two:* a couple, i.e., "2"
    too: likewise; also; more than enough
    to: a structure word usually indicating a direction or marking an infinitive verb

Two times is too many to misspell a word.
The word is simple.
The word is *to*.

5. *they're:* means "they are"
    their: indicates possession
    there: indicates place or is used as a sentence opener

There is no doubt.
They're doing sentences over there.
The sentences are theirs.

6. *all together:* everyone assembled
    altogether: entirely

We were working all together.
We were combining sentences.
The sentences were altogether bizarre.

7. *all right:* okay
    all write: everyone + write

It's all right with me.
You can all write on topics.
The topics are similar.

8. *will:* legal document; a helping verb, future tense
    we'll: contraction of *we will*
    well: hole; modifier meaning "in a good or proper manner"

We'll now read the will.
The will is of the deceased.
The deceased was a well-digger.
The deceased will be well remembered.

9. *picture:* visual image
    pitcher: one who pitches; a container for liquid

Picture a pitcher.
The pitcher is drunk.
The pitcher is throwing a pitcher.
The pitcher contains martinis.

10. *rapped:* slang for "talked"; hit with the knuckles
     wrapped: past tense of *wrap*

    axe: tool for cutting
    ask: to question

I rapped with the merchant.
I asked about the axe handle.
The axe handle had been broken.
It had been wrapped with tape.

11. *desert:* barren area; act of abandoning
     dessert: after-meal treat
     deserted: abandoned, left alone

They drove to a cafe.
The cafe was deserted.
The cafe was near the desert.
The drive was for a dessert.
The dessert was for after dinner.

12. *writing:* putting words on paper
     riding: being carried

    stationery: writing paper
    stationary: unmoving; stable

Writing is difficult.
The writing is while riding.
This is because stationery doesn't stay stationary.

13. *chief:* leader
     chef: cook

    diner: cafe
    dinner: meal

The chief didn't like his own dinner.
The chief was an Indian.
The chief had just become the diner's chef.

14.   *contract:*   to tighten; clench   I felt my stomach contract.
             contract: legal document   I signed a contract.
                                                      The contract was to fix a supper.
             super: great; outstanding   The supper would be super.
             supper: evening meal

EXERCISE 2.5.   On-Your-Own Writing Options

Directions. Pick one of the following options. Use it as the focus for on-your-own writing.

1. One of the main points of Unit 2 is that "just because you're *able* to make long sentences doesn't mean that you *have to*"—that sometimes "shorter is better." (The same idea would hold, of course, for word choice. Abstract, technical, or polysyllabic wording is *sometimes* appropriate and effective, but not always; simpler diction is often better.)

 Analyze the writing you did for Exercise 1.5 by following these steps:

 a. Read the paper aloud twice.
 b. On the first reading, identify any sentences that may be too long-winded or rambling.
 c. On the second reading, identify any choppy sentences that need to be combined with others.

 Rewrite the material, making the changes that "feel" right. Then ask someone in your class to read *both* versions and pick the better one. See what happens.

2. Your life style is often mirrored in your writing style. Here's an example.

 ### INSTRUCTOR'S JOURNAL

 I'm hungry, and it's been a long day. After some determined searching, I find two crusts of wheat bread and press them into the toaster; the machine hums and clicks in protest. I set out a half-quart of cold milk, a jar of peanut butter, and a juicy dill pickle. The pungent pickle brine makes my mouth flood with saliva.

 The toast pops up without having to be pried out, and I set to work quickly, smoothing peanut chunks and oil, making sure the goo spreads out to the edges of the bread. Then I slice the fat pickle lengthwise into four strips and lay them out neatly, one overlapping the other, like green terraces against a brown landscape. I ease the sandwich together. Crumbs are everywhere, and I sweep them to one side with the back of my hand.

 The milk makes a cold, sweet trail down my esophagus. Eying the sandwich, I smile. The room is utterly still and waiting. I close my eyes, and crunch the first bite. A few moments later, with my sandwich half eaten and peanut butter still on my fingers, I decide to close the day's journal entry with a short thought:

 The now we have is all there is;
 that's why I write these words.

 Focus on the reality of your present life style. What is its essence? Think of the details of the "now" that you're presently experiencing—its smells, sounds, sights, tastes, and textures. Try to capture it with a net of words, your *personal* writing style.

3. In the December 1975 issue of *Newsweek* magazine, the lead article was titled "Why Johnny Can't Write." Here is the first paragraph.

If your children are attending college, the chances are that when they graduate they will be unable to write ordinary, expository English with any real degree of structure and lucidity. If they are in high school and planning to attend college, the chances are less than ever that they will be able to write English at the minimal college level when they get there. If they are not planning to attend college, their skills in writing English may not even qualify them for secretarial or clerical work. And if they are attending elementary school, they are almost certainly not being given the kind of required reading material, much less writing instruction, that might make it possible for them eventually to write comprehensible English. Willy-nilly, the U.S. educational system is spawning a generation of semiliterates.

Focus on the last sentence of the paragraph. Do you agree or disagree? Use this statement as a springboard for an *articulate* statement of your own about "semiliteracy."

UNIT THREE
MAKING CHOICES FOR EMPHASIS

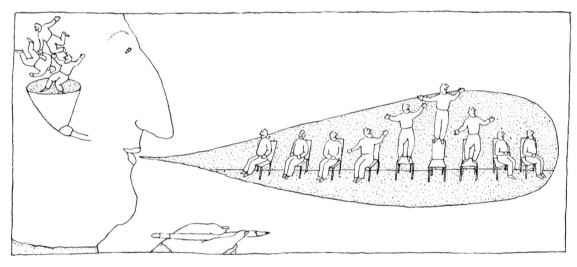

"Today's focus is *emphasis* in sentences. We've talked about how sentence combining forces you to make choices. Now let's consider the effects of those decisions. Our aim is to gain more conscious control of what's going down on paper."

The classroom whispering begins to drop off.

"Choices," I continue. "You make them all the time. Whether you're doing exercises or doing writing on your own, you're choosing *where* to put words. Each choice in a sentence creates a different emphasis." Switching on the projector, I present a cluster of kernel sentences.

I read sentences.
I transform them.
I sometimes feel puzzled.
I compare writeouts.
I try to decide on my preferences.

"To study how different kinds of emphasis are achieved, let's look at three different transformations. Each will use a different kernel for the base sentence. Notice how emphasis shifts."

A. *I read and transform sentences*, sometimes feeling puzzled as I compare writeouts and try to decide on my preferences.

B.   As I read and transform sentences, *I sometimes feel puzzled* in comparing writeouts and trying to decide on my preferences.

C.   Reading and transforming sentences—sometimes feeling puzzled as I compare writeouts—*I try to decide on my preferences.*

Anne raises her hand. "So the base sentence—the place where you begin—is really important."

"That's what combining *shows* you. Whatever you choose as the base sentence creates a particular emphasis. Why? Because everything gets embedded into or hooked onto it."

Another cluster goes up. I ask the class to select one kernel as a base sentence and do the transforming as usual.

Emphasis is personal.
I can select base sentences.
The base sentences differ.
I can use connectors.
The connectors differ.
I can choose word orders.
The word orders differ.

I watch Carlos quickly scan down the seven kernels and begin scribbling his writeout. I'm wondering what emphasis he has chosen as I put up another transparency to project three transformations, each of which is quite different from the others.

A.   Emphasis is personal: I can select differing base sentences, use differing connectors, and choose differing word orders.

B.   Selection of differing base sentences, connectors, and word orders creates a personal emphasis for me.

C.   It is not only that I can select differing base sentences; I can also use different connectors and word orders to make the emphasis personal.

"Brace yourself," I say. "We're going to analyze how these sentences differ in the *ways* they work."

The students are studying the three writeouts and glancing at their notebooks, making silent comparisons.

"In writeout A, there's a three-word *general* statement that's followed by *specifics*. The pattern is *statement-restatement*—or general-to-specific. So the emphasis is really on the first three words. The restatement *explains* the general idea."

I move on to writeout B. "The next one takes a different slant. In shortened form, the base sentence reads *selection—creates—emphasis.* Your attention rivets on those three words. But notice, too, that the focus is on what's being selected. Since the details are embedded up front—in the subject part of the sentence—that's where the emphasis is.

"Now to writeout C," I continue. "What's interesting here is the emphasis on two of the *specific* points—different connectors and different word order. The up-front use of the word *not* puts all the emphasis at the end. So this sentence is quite different from the other two."

Carlos raises his hand. "Okay, you're saying these different connectors make one part of the sentence more important?"

"That's it. Different connectors make for different kinds of emphasis—and so does the *position* of key ideas or sentence elements."

"Yeah, I can see the thing about position."

"How about your writeout? Is it like one of these three?"

"Mine's sort of different," he says.

"How about putting it up for study?"

After coming forward to print his sentence across the chalkboard, Carlos rereads it and inserts a missing comma.

D. Personal emphasis allows me to select differing base sentences, and it also permits me to use differing connectors and choose differing word orders.

"Well done. Tell us about the emphasis."

"I don't know how to explain it. But I know that *and* is the connector."

"Right. You've got a *balanced* emphasis here. This writeout nicely illustrates the technique of *coordination*. Instead of making one part of the writeout dependent on the other, you've balanced the two parts through use of a coordinating conjunction—the word *and*. In short, the sentence parts are logically and grammatically independent of each other. Both halves can stand alone as separate, complete sentences."

"Can you go through that again?" Patsy asks.

"Okay, study the first half of writeout D—*Personal emphasis allows me to select differing base sentences.* That part stands by itself as a complete base sentence. Now look at the second half, where the word *it* refers to *personal emphasis.* This part also stands by itself, grammatically speaking. It's not dependent on or subordinate to the first half of the writeout."

"Yes, but what about Unit 2? We used *and* for compounding and for putting things in a series."

"Coordination and addition are much the same process," I reply. "With coordination you're connecting complete, independent sentences; but with addition, you're connecting sentence *parts*—such as words and phrases."

"Example?" Andrea asks.

"Look at the second half of writeout D. You'll see addition in action, connecting the verbs *to use* and *to choose.* The word *and* is the conjunction."

She studies the writeout. "Okay, that helps."

"Back to coordination between sentences. You should realize that a coordinating conjunction isn't really *required* to make a balanced writeout. You can also take two sentences—independent, but closely related—and

separate them by a semicolon. The result is a coordinate-style sentence—another version of writeout D."

D.   Personal emphasis allows me to select differing base sentences; it also permits me to use differing connectors and choose differing word orders.

Eric's hand goes up. "Let me get this straight. One way to coordinate sentences is with a comma and a coordinating conjunction. The other way is with a semicolon."
"You've got it."

STOP.   MAKE A MARGINAL NOTE ON THESE PUNCTUATION PATTERNS FOR COORDINATION. THEN RESUME YOUR READING.

With *coordination* introduced, I call for another writeout so that we can study a different kind of sentence emphasis. Kristin volunteers to put her transformation on the board.

E.   Because I can select differing base sentences, use differing connectors, and choose differing word orders, my emphasis is personal.

"How about emphasis in this one?"
"The connector is *because*," Kristin says. "It hooks all the words in front to the base sentence at the end."
"So where's the emphasis?"
"At the end, I guess. This one isn't a balanced emphasis."
"That's right. Your writeout makes a causal statement and shows the technique of *subordination*. You've subordinated a series of kernel sentences to your base sentence and main idea—*my emphasis is personal.* In other words, you've used the subordinating conjunction *because* to make certain ideas at the beginning logically and grammatically dependent upon the idea in your base sentence."
"Grammatically dependent?" Theresa asks.
"To subordinate is for one part to limit, support, or explain the other. Here are some common patterns of this dependent connection."

Because a, therefore b.
Although a, nevertheless b.
When a, then b.
While a, also b.
If a, then b.

STOP.   MAKE A MARGINAL NOTE ON THIS PUNCTUATION PATTERN FOR SUBORDINATION. THEN RESUME YOUR READING.

"In other words," I continue, "subordination is a way of *modifying*."

"So it's sort of like embedding," Kristin observes.

"Indeed it is. But remember: Embedding puts one-word or phrasal modifiers into a sentence *without* the use of connecting words. Subordination is different. Subordination uses a variety of connecting words to make kernels —or parts of kernels—modify one another. Some connectors are of the *because, although, when, while, if* variety. Some are words like *who, whom, which,* and *that.* And some are prepositions—words like *by, in, before, after, through.* It's not essential that you label these different subordinating words. But it *is* important that you see how they work."

"All of these connectors do the same thing?" Tony asks.

"Basically, yes. They hook kernels together so that certain ones modify others." I hesitate for a moment.

"But they work in different ways?"

"Right. Even though they serve the same purpose—making one part of a sentence *depend* on another part—their patterns differ."

Hands start going up as people ask for more explanation.

"Okay, you've already seen the *because* connector in writeout E. This is one way of subordinating. Another way would be to shift from embedding, which Kristin used, to *that* connectors."

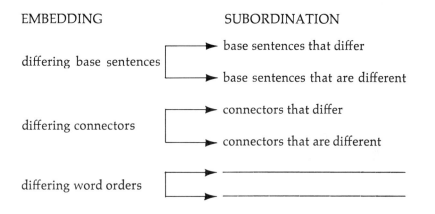

EMBEDDING   SUBORDINATION

differing base sentences ⟶ base sentences that differ
                         ⟶ base sentences that are different

differing connectors ⟶ connectors that differ
                     ⟶ connectors that are different

differing word orders ⟶ _____
                      ⟶ _____

"Notice that the meaning remains the same even though the style changes slightly. Another change happens as we shift from using the *because* connector up front to prepositions such as *by* or *in.* The overall pattern is still subordination, but the style is altered."

Because I can select . . . ⟶ By selecting . . .
                          ⟶ In the selection of . . .

"Here is Kristin's original writeout. Compare it with a version using a *by* preposition up front and *that* connectors."

[ORIGINAL WRITEOUT E] *Because I can select differing base sentences, use differing connectors, and choose differing word orders, my emphasis is personal.*

[REVISED WRITEOUT E] *By selecting base sentences that differ, using connectors that differ, and choosing word orders that differ, I have personal emphasis.*

STOP. CHECK (√) THE WRITEOUT YOU PREFER. THEN RESUME YOUR READING.

Carol has a hand up. "I have another version I like better." She comes forward and makes a quick series of changes.

[CAROL'S WRITEOUT E] *In the selection and use of base sentences, connectors, and word order—each choice differing—I create personal emphasis.*

STOP. COMPARE THIS WRITEOUT WITH THE ONE YOU JUST CHECKED. MAKE ANOTHER CHOICE (√). THEN RESUME YOUR READING.

Malee, one of the quieter foreign students, has a hand up. "This *coordination* and *subordination*," she says. "Why are we studying them?"

"Two reasons," I reply. "First, these ideas are basic tools for analyzing emphasis in sentences. In other words, they help you get more from your combining practice—and help you see what's happening in your *own* sentences. Second, coordination and subordination help you express complex ideas with precision and clarity. You *coordinate* when you're trying to give the same emphasis to items you're connecting. You *subordinate* when you're trying to limit or put conditions on a main idea."

"Sounds like something we'll be using," Eric says.

"The next unit on *signaled* combining is based on these ideas. So is the work we'll do later with sentence modeling. Over and over you'll come back to the basics of *coordination* and *subordination*."

With Malee's question answered, I project some examples for comparing writeouts. The students read them silently for a few moments.

COORDINATION AND SUBORDINATION

The room is quiet.
The teacher presents the first example.

[COORDINATION] *The room is quiet, and the teacher presents the first example.*

[SUBORDINATION] *The room is quiet as the teacher presents the first example.*

The second example flashes onto the screen.
Rob's eyes begin to droop.

[COORDINATION] *The second example flashes onto the screen; Rob's eyes begin to droop.*

[SUBORDINATION] *When the second example flashes onto the screen, Rob's eyes begin to droop.*

He struggles to stay awake.
Sleep has an attraction.
The attraction is powerful.

[COORDINATION] *He struggles to stay awake, but sleep has a powerful attraction.*

[SUBORDINATION] *Although he struggles to stay awake, sleep has a powerful attraction.*

It calls his name.
It beckons him to leave the class.
Things are dull there.
Things are routine there.

[COORDINATION] *It calls his name and beckons him to leave the class; things are dull and routine there.*

[SUBORDINATION] *Calling his name, it beckons him to leave the class where things are dull, routine.*

His name is used in an example.
He finally resists temptation.
He sits up straight.
He props open his eyelids.

[COORDINATION] *His name is used in an example, so he finally resists temptation, sits up straight, and props open his eyelids.*

[SUBORDINATION] *Because his name is used in an example, he finally resists temptation by sitting up straight, then propping open his eyelids.*

"I like that," Rob says. "You can really see how the emphasis changes."

"Right. Which brings us back to a basic point: Emphasis always pertains to your *intentions* in writing. The clearer you are about your writing *purposes,* the more likely your prose will be clear and emphatic."

Tony has his notebook open. "Uhm, could you review when to use coordination and subordination?"

"*Coordination* is appropriate when you're trying to show that things or actions are given *equal* value. You use it, as we've seen, to achieve the effect of balance. When you have more than two elements to coordinate, you put

the most important one last. That's the most emphatic position. Here's a cluster of kernels showing coordination."

COORDINATION

> Tony faked toward the sidelines.
> He took the handoff.
> He went straight up the middle.
> The crowd went wild.

[COORDINATION] *Tony faked toward the sidelines, took the handoff, went straight up the middle, and the crowd went wild.*

"Got it," Tony nods. "And subordination?"

"You use *subordination* when you're trying to show the *dependence* of ideas on one another. Details and unimportant ideas should always be subordinated. This highlights the more important *main* statements. You also use subordination to break up choppy writing—and to relieve the mental numbness that too much coordination sometimes causes. Here's a cluster showing subordination."

SUBORDINATION

> He spun away from tacklers.
> He twisted into the open.
> His head was down.
> His knees were churning.
> He didn't realize something.
> He was running the wrong way.

[SUBORDINATION] *As he spun away from tacklers—twisting into the open with his head down, knees churning—he didn't realize that he was running the wrong way.*

"What's more important," I continue, "is not the spinning and twisting or the description of running style. All of this is subordinate to the main fact of the sentence—that the ball carrier runs the wrong way. Notice, incidentally, how much *less* emphatic the sentence becomes when you make some other kernel the base sentence. Or try putting the base sentence up front to see how the emphasis changes."

Your writeout goes here:

_____

_____

"How about a list of connecting words for coordination and subordination?" Maria asks.

"Good idea. The coordinating words you've seen so far are called *coordinating conjunctions*."

COORDINATION

Coordinating Conjunctions

and	or
but	so
for	yet
nor	

"In Unit 4," I add, "you'll learn two other types of connectors for coordinate-style sentences. For now, though, just concentrate on *coordinating conjunctions* and the use of semicolons."

"And subordination?" Eric asks.

"I've already mentioned connectors like *who, whom, which,* and *that.* And you're also aware that prepositions such as *between, with, during,* and *into* make one part of a sentence modify another part. Therefore, the connectors you probably need to study are commonly used *subordinating conjunctions*."

SUBORDINATION

Subordinating Conjunctions

after	since
although	so that
as	unless
because	until
before	when
if	where
how	while

The class is still attentive, so I push on.

"Very shortly you'll practice both coordinating and subordinating conjunctions. But now let's shift attention to another aspect of emphasis—*sentence variety*."

"You mean mixing up sentence lengths?" Terry says.

"Not only sentence lengths. Their *structure*, too."

I move down a row of outstretched legs. "So far, we've studied sentences in *isolation* from each other. Why? So we could learn how they're put together. Now we're going to look at sentences in the context of *surrounding* ones. In choosing writeouts, we'll ask two questions: Which sentence is

clearest and most stylistically interesting? Which sentence 'fits' or 'sounds best'—next to the preceding one?"

I put up a transparency. "Here are four points to remember as you choose sentences in context."

1.   When sentences say basically the same thing, shorter ones are sometimes *clearer* than longer ones.
2.   Emphasis—and stylistic interest—often result from *varying* sentence patterns or moving the modifiers.
3.   To hear how a sentence "fits" in context, you must read the preceding one aloud, *then* read the one in question.
4.   Combining writeouts into longer sentences—or splitting writeouts into shorter ones—can *improve* the "flow" or "rhythm" of writing.

I begin handing out a combining exercise. "Your first task is familiar: make a writeout for each cluster. Your second task is something new: Instead of choosing the one you prefer and then making your own writeout, choose the writeout that 'sounds best' next to the writeout for a preceding cluster."

"Sounds easy enough," Randy murmurs.

"Your third task is to put your writeouts into a paragraph. You may wish to use coordinating and subordinating conjunctions to join sentences. Or you may want to split up certain writeouts."

"Just a matter of emphasis," Carlos says with a grin.

"Exactly. After finishing these tasks, you'll compare your style of writing to four other versions—*plain, coordinate, subordinate,* and *eclectic.* Then you can decide which style you prefer."

"Eclectic?" Jill asks.

"A mixture of the three other styles. The chances are that your style will also be eclectic. But maybe not."

"Sounds interesting," Nate says. "Like something for the book's readers to try."

The class sets to work. And so do you, I hope.

1.   The evening is humid.
     The evening is lit by neon.
     The neon is garish.

1-A.   The evening is humid and lit by garish neon.
1-B.   Garish neon lights the humid evening.

1-C.   _____

     _____

2.   Boys park their van.
     The boys are teenagers.
     They begin to drift downtown.
     They look for something to do.

2-A. Teenage boys park their van and begin to drift downtown to look for something to do.
2-B. With their van parked, teenage boys begin to drift downtown, looking for something to do.

2-C. _____

_____

3.   Tourists jam the sidewalks.
      Hawkers jam the sidewalks.
      The sidewalks are littered with paper.

3-A. Jamming the paper-littered sidewalks are tourists and hawkers.
3-B. The sidewalks, which are littered with paper, are jammed by tourists and hawkers.

3-C. _____

_____

4.   The gang shoulders through the crowd.
      The gang is like a ship cutting waves.
      The gang leaves a wake of faces.
      The faces are staring.

4-A. As the gang shoulders through the crowd like a ship cutting waves, it leaves a wake of staring faces.
4-B. The gang is like a ship cutting waves—shouldering through the crowd, leaving faces staring in its wake.

4-C. _____

_____

5.   Cars cruise by.
      Cars rev their engines.

5-A. Cars cruise by and rev their engines.
5-B. Cars cruise by, engines revving.

5-C. _____

_____

6.   The gang sneers with contempt.
      The contempt is cold.
      The sneering is at insults.
      The insults happen to pass.

6-A. The gang sneers at any passing insults; their contempt is cold.
6-B. To any passing insults, the gang sneers with cold contempt.

6-C. _____

_____

7.   Leather makes them intimidating.
The leather is black.
Looks make them intimidating.
The looks are tough.
The looks are snarling.

7-A.   Black leather and their looks—tough and snarling—make them intimidating.

7-B.   Their intimidation is based on black leather and tough, snarling looks.

7-C. _____

_____

8.   But swaggering adds to the effect.
The swaggering is in unison.
Their fists are tight.
Their shoulders are hunched.

8-A.   But a tight-fisted, shoulder-hunched unison of swaggering adds to the effect.

8-B.   But unified swaggering, with fists tight and shoulders hunched, adds to the effect.

8-C. _____

_____

9.   They hook their thumbs.
The hooking is through belt loops.
They head for their hangout.
Their hangout is a cafe.
The cafe is open all night.

9-A.   Hooking thumbs through their belt loops, they head for their hangout, which is an all-night cafe.

9-B.   With thumbs hooked through belt loops, they head for the all-night cafe, their hangout.

9-C. _____

_____

STOP. PUT YOUR PREFERRED WRITEOUTS INTO A PARAGRAPH. THEN COMPARE YOUR WRITING STYLE WITH THE FOUR VERSIONS THAT FOLLOW. CHECK (√) THE STYLE YOU PREFER.

VERSION 1: PLAIN ("SIMPLE") STYLE

The humid evening is lit by garish neon. Teenage boys park their van. Then they begin to drift downtown to look for something to do. The sidewalks are jammed with tourists and hawkers. The gang shoulders through the crowd like a ship cutting waves. This movement leaves a wake of staring faces. Cars cruise by and rev their engines. The gang sneers with cold contempt at any passing insults. Black leather makes them intimidating. So do their tough, snarling looks and swaggering. They tighten their fists. They hunch their shoulders. They hook their thumbs through belt loops. Then they head for an all-night cafe. This is their hangout.

VERSION 2: COORDINATE STYLE

The evening is humid and lit by neon. The van is parked, and teenage boys begin to drift downtown to look for something to do. Tourists and hawkers jam the paper-littered sidewalks; the gang shoulders through the crowd like a ship cutting waves and leaves a wake of staring faces. Cars cruise by and rev their engines, and the gang sneers coldly and contemptuously at any passing insults. Black leather and tough, snarling looks are the basis for their intimidation; but swaggering in unison—with fists tight and shoulders hunched—adds to the effect. They hook their thumbs through belt loops and head for an all-night cafe, their hangout.

VERSION 3: SUBORDINATE STYLE

After parking their van on a humid, garishly lit neon evening, teenage boys who are looking for something to do begin to drift downtown. Tourists and hawkers jam sidewalks that are littered with paper as the gang shoulders through the crowd. Like a ship cutting waves, they leave staring faces in their wake. As cars cruise by, engines revving, the gang sneers with cold contempt at any insults that happen to pass. Swaggering in tight-fisted, shoulder-hunched unison adds to their intimidation, which is based on black leather and tough, snarling looks. They hook their thumbs through belt loops, heading for their hangout, a cafe that is open all night.

VERSION 4: ECLECTIC ("MIXED") STYLE

Garish neon lights the humid evening as teenage boys park their van and begin to drift downtown, looking for something to do. Tourists and hawkers jam the paper-littered sidewalks. The gang, shouldering through the crowd like a ship cutting waves, leaves a wake of staring faces. Cars

cruise by, engines revving; the gang sneers with cold contempt at any passing insults. Black leather and tough, snarling looks make them intimidating. But swaggering in unison, with fists tight and shoulders hunched, adds to the effect. With thumbs hooked through belt loops, they head for their hangout, an all-night cafe.

EXERCISE 3.1.   Comparing Writeouts

Directions. The next combining extends the description you worked on in Unit 3. Continue the process of making and choosing writeouts, putting them into paragraphs, and comparing your writing style with four other versions.

1.   The gang surveys the scene.
The survey is with disdain.
The scene is inside the restaurant.

1-A.   It is with disdain that the gang surveys the scene inside the restaurant.

1-B.   Disdainfully, the gang surveys the restaurant scene.

1-C.   ————————————————

————————————————

2.   Nothing is happening.
This is as usual.

2-A.   It is as usual; nothing is happening.

2-B.   As usual, there is nothing happening.

2-C.   ————————————————

————————————————

3.   The boys take their places.
The places are at the counter.
They order hamburgers.
They order fries.
They order colas.
They then light up.

3-A.   At the counter, the boys take their places, order hamburgers, fries, and colas, and then light up.

3-B.   After taking places at the counter and ordering hamburgers, fries, and colas, the boys light up.

3-C.   ————————————————

————————————————

4.   Smoke swirls around them.
The smoke is from cigarettes.
The smoke is a cloud.
The cloud is gray.
The cloud is choking.

4-A.   Cigarette smoke—a gray, choking cloud—swirls around them.

4-B.   Swirling around them is a cloud of cigarette smoke—gray and choking.

4-C.   ————————————————

————————————————

5.   Other teenagers cram the booths.
The teenagers also try to look tough.
The teenagers also try to look cool.
The booths are orange.
The booths are covered with vinyl.

5-A.   Other teenagers, who are also trying to look tough and cool, cram the orange, vinyl-covered booths.

5-B.   Crammed into orange booths, covered with vinyl, are other teenagers, also trying to look tough and cool.

5-C.   ————————————————

————————————————

6.   The gang's hamburgers finally arrive.
The hamburgers drip condiments.
They ooze grease.

6-A.   The gang's hamburgers, which drip condiments and ooze grease, finally arrive.

6-B.   Dripping condiments and oozing grease, the gang's hamburgers finally arrive.

6-C.   ————————————————

————————————————

7.   These are their third burgers of the evening.
The burgers are cold.
They eat them anyway.

7-A.   These are their third cold burgers of the evening, but they eat them anyway.

7-B.   Although these burgers are cold—
and their third of the evening—they
eat them anyway.

7-C.   _____

_____

8.   They pay the price.
The price is for "visibility."
The visibility is social.
The visibility is on a Saturday night.
The price is indigestion.

8-A.   The price that they pay for social
"visibility" on a Saturday night is indigestion.

8-B.   For social "visibility" on a Saturday
night, they pay the price—indigestion.

8-C.   _____

_____

VERSION 1: PLAIN ("SIMPLE") STYLE

The gang disdainfully surveys the scene inside
the restaurant. As usual, there is nothing happening. The boys take their places at the counter. They order hamburgers, fries, and colas.
Then they light up. A gray, choking cloud of
cigarette smoke swirls around them. Other
teenagers cram the orange, vinyl-covered
booths. They too are trying to look tough and
cool. The gang's hamburgers finally arrive.
They drip condiments and ooze grease. These
are their third cold burgers of the evening.
They eat them anyway. They pay the price for
social "visibility" on a Saturday night—indigestion.

VERSION 2: COORDINATE STYLE

With disdain the gang surveys the restaurant
scene and finds, as usual, nothing happening.
The boys take their places at the counter and
order hamburgers, fries, and colas. Then they
light up, and cigarette smoke swirls around
them in a gray and choking cloud. Other teenagers cram the orange, vinyl-covered booths;
they too are trying to look tough and cool.
Finally, the gang's hamburgers arrive; they
are dripping with condiments and oozing
grease. These are their third burgers of the
evening, but they eat them anyway. There is
a price to be paid for social "visibility" on a
Saturday night, and that price is indigestion.

VERSION 3: SUBORDINATE STYLE

From their disdainful survey of the scene inside the restaurant, the gang sees that it is
just as usual: nothing is happening. After taking places at the counter, the boys order hamburgers, fries, and colas. Smoke swirls around
them in a cloud—gray and choking—as they
light up their cigarettes. Other teenagers, also
trying to look tough and cool, cram the
orange, vinyl-covered booths. Finally, the
gang's hamburgers arrive—dripping condiments, oozing grease. Although these cold
burgers are their third of the evening, they eat
them anyway. For social "visibility" on a Saturday night, they pay the price of indigestion.

VERSION 4: ECLECTIC ("MIXED") STYLE

Disdainfully, the gang surveys the restaurant
scene. It is as usual: nothing is happening.
Taking their places at the counter, they order
hamburgers, fries, and colas. Then they light
up, and a gray, choking cloud of cigarette
smoke swirls around them. Other teenagers
are crammed into orange, vinyl-covered
booths; they too are trying to look tough and
cool. By the time the gang's hamburgers finally arrive, dripping condiments and oozing
grease, they have gotten cold. These are their
third burgers of the evening, but the boys eat
them anyway. They pay the price for social
"visibility" on a Saturday night—indigestion.

EXERCISE 3.2. Proofreading Practice

Directions. Below is a writeout from Unit 3 that is correctly punctuated.

As I read and transform sentences, I sometimes feel puzzled in comparing writeouts and trying to decide on my preferences. It is not only that I can select different base sentences; I can also use differing connectors and word order to make the emphasis personal.

The writeouts that follow each have one or more punctuation errors. Spot these errors and do a rewrite; then check with the Answer Key, p. 275.

1. My writing style is unique.
    It is personal.
    It is like a fingerprint.

PROBLEM 1 *My writing style, like a fingerprint, is unique and personal.*

REWRITE 1 ——————————————

—————————————————

2. It may be bare.
    It may be modified.
    It may be direct.
    It may be indirect.
    It may be active.
    It may be passive.

PROBLEM 2 *It may be bare or modified direct or indirect active or passive.*

REWRITE 2 ——————————————

—————————————————

3. But my writing style is unlike a fingerprint.
    It can be consciously altered.

PROBLEM 3 *But, unlike a fingerprint my writing style can be consciously altered.*

REWRITE 3 ——————————————

4. I may decide to stress openers.
    The openers are for sentences.
    I may experiment with transformations.
    The transformations interrupt the flow.
    The flow is expression.
    The interruption is temporary.

PROBLEM 4 *I may decide to stress sentence openers, I may experiment with transformations that interrupt—temporarily—the flow of expression.*

REWRITE 4 ——————————————

—————————————————

—————————————————

5. Choices determine emphasis.
    The emphasis is in sentences.
    Choices force me to think.
    The thinking is about my habits.
    The habits are in writing.
    The habits are mostly unconscious.

PROBLEM 5 *Because choices determine emphasis in sentences they force me to think about my writing habits which are mostly unconscious.*

REWRITE 5 ——————————————

—————————————————

—————————————————

6. This awareness may not alter my experience.

This awareness may not alter my training.

The awareness is increasing.

It should help me.

The help will be to make decisions.

The decisions will be more informed.

The decisions will be about style.

PROBLEM 6   *This increasing awareness may*

not alter my experience or training but it should help me to make more informed decisions about style.

REWRITE 6 _____

_____

_____

EXERCISE 3.3.   A Very Sad Story, Versions 1 and 2

Directions. As you combine these clusters, choose the emphasis you want to get. After finishing both versions, pick the one you prefer and write an additional paragraph that will complete the story.

A VERY SAD STORY, VERSION 1

1.   The princess saw a toad.
2.   She was lonely.
3.   She was lovely.
4.   The toad was spotted.
5.   It squatted near a path.
6.   The path was in the garden.

7.   Her heart pounded.
8.   The pounding was in her chest.
9.   The pounding was excitement.

10.   She bent down.
11.   Her bending was quiet.
12.   She kissed the toad.
13.   Her kissing was gentle.
14.   The toad was ugly.
15.   It was sleeping.
16.   The sleeping was in the sun.

17.   There was a flash.
18.   It was blinding.
19.   It was sudden.
20.   There was a sound.
21.   It was thundering.

22.   The princess touched her mouth.
23.   She parted her lips.

24.   Her lips were sensuous.
25.   She murmured, "Ribbit, ribbit!"

A VERY SAD STORY, VERSION 2

1.   A toad sat near a path.
2.   He was green.
3.   He was warty.
4.   He was minding his own business.
5.   The sun warmed his body.
6.   The sun was in the afternoon.
7.   The sun was mellow.
8.   The sun relaxed his muscles.
9.   His body was hunched.
10.   He closed his eyes.
11.   The closing was languid.
12.   He let himself drift.
13.   The drifting was on a tide.
14.   The tide was sleep.
15.   The sleep was shimmering.
16.   A flash awoke him.
17.   The flash was crashing.
18.   The flash was sharp.
19.   The awakening was unexpected.
20.   He glanced up.
21.   He saw a princess.
22.   She was poised over him.
23.   She was wide-eyed.
24.   She was startled.
25.   Then the toad felt a tickle.
26.   The tickle was slight.

27. The tickle was in his throat.
28. The toad knew something.

29. He had contracted a cold.
30. A cold is the most basic social disease.

EXERCISE 3.4.   Coordination and Subordination

Directions. Combine the following clusters of kernels by using both *coordination* and *subordination* transformations. To find out how the sentence was *originally* transformed, check with the Answer Key, p. 275.

MODEL

    A man speaks with thought.
    A man acts with thought.
    The thought is pure.
    Happiness follows him.
    The following is like a shadow.
    The shadow never leaves him.
        —Buddha

[COORDINATION] *A man speaks or acts with pure thought, and happiness follows him like a shadow and never leaves him.*

[SUBORDINATION] *If a man speaks or acts with pure thought, happiness follows him like a shadow that never leaves.*

(In the above example, the *subordination* writeout is the sentence attributed to Buddha.)

1. Error will slip through a crack.
    Truth will stick in a doorway.
        —Josh Billings

2. Instruction ends in the classroom.
    Education ends only with life.
        —Frederick William Robertson

3. Being a woman is a task.
    The task is terribly difficult.
    It consists principally in dealing with men.
        —Joseph Conrad

4. Regret is a waste of energy.
    The waste is appalling.
    You can't build on it.
    It's only good for wallowing in.
        —Katherine Mansfield

5. Science is lame.
    The science is without religion.
    Religion is blind.
    The religion is without science.
        —Albert Einstein

6. A laugh gives one a dry cleaning.
    The laugh is hearty.
    A good cry is a wash.
    The wash is wet.
        —Puzant Kevork Tomajan

7. We read.
    We fancy we could be martyrs.
    We come to act.
    We cannot bear a word.
    The word is provoking.
        —Hannah More

8. Tempos invariably raise your pulse.
    Tempos invariably raise your respiration.
    Tempos invariably raise your blood pressure.
    The tempos are fast.
    Slow music lowers them.
        —Doran Kemp Antrin

9. We are all sculptors.
    We are all painters.
    Our material is our own flesh.
    Our material is our own blood.
    Our material is our own bones.
        —Henry David Thoreau

10. The discontent of God made the world.
     The discontent was splendid.

The discontent was with Chaos.
The world's best progress springs from discontent.

The discontent is man's.
              —*Ella Wheeler Wilcox*

EXERCISE 3.5.   On-Your-Own Writing Options

Directions. Pick one of the following options. Use it as the focus for on-your-own writing.

1. The following exercise is an introductory paragraph. Make your own transformation for each cluster; then choose the writeouts you prefer and put them into a paragraph. Tell about your "real strengths" in language in paragraphs that follow.

PERSONAL LANGUAGE STRENGTHS

1. People have strengths.
2. The strengths are in language.
3. The strengths differ.
4. The strengths depend on experience.
5. The experience is in the past.

A. The differing language strengths that people have depend on past experience.
B. Depending on past experiences, the language strengths of people differ.
C. People have differing language strengths; these depend on past experience.

D. _____

    _____

6. Some may be liars.
7. The liars are gifted.
8. Some may be con artists.
9. Some may be lovers.
10. The lovers are fast-talking.

11. Others are jokesters.
12. Others are conversationalists.
13. The conversationalists are good.
14. Others are poets.
15. The poets are sensitive.

A. Some may be gifted liars, con artists, or fast-talking lovers. Others are jokesters, good conversationalists, or sensitive poets.
B. Gifted liars, con artists, fast-talking lovers, jokesters, good conversationalists, sensitive poets—some may be one, others another.
C. Whereas some may be gifted liars, others are jokesters; and whereas some may be con artists and fast-talking lovers, others are good conversationalists and sensitive poets.

D. _____

    _____

    _____

16. My competence may be considerable.
17. The competence is personal.
18. The competence is in these areas.
19. My real strengths lie elsewhere.
20. The strengths are in language.

A. My personal competence in these areas may be considerable; nonetheless, my real language strengths lie elsewhere.
B. Although my personal competence in these areas may be considerable,

my real strengths in language lie elsewhere.

C. I may have considerable personal competence in these areas. Yet my real strengths lie elsewhere in language.

D. _____

_____

_____

2. Unit 3 points out that choices determine emphasis. In other words, your writing intentions and your characteristic way of expressing yourself produce a style of writing. Like a fingerprint, your writing style is different from everyone else's.

Reread the paragraphs you wrote at the end of Unit 3 and for Exercise 3.1. Ask yourself these questions:

a. *Do I favor short sentences or longer ones?* (Count the total number of words and divide by the number of sentences to get your average words per sentence.)

b. *Do I lean toward coordination or subordination?* (Compare the number of coordinating and subordinating conjunctions.)

c. *Do I prefer a plain, coordinate, subordinate, or eclectic writing style?* (Match your paragraph against Versions 1–4 to determine its style.)

Use these questions as the basis for writing about your own writing style.

3. Imagine that you have to explain in writing the meaning of *friendship* to two different audiences: (1) second- or third-grade students; and (2) students your own age. Develop at least one paragraph for each of these two audiences. Then go back and analyze the differences in your *content emphasis* (what you said) as well as your *stylistic emphasis* (how you said it). Under *content emphasis*, concentrate on items such as the examples you used; under *stylistic emphasis*, concentrate on items such as choice of words and length of sentences. Discuss these differences in analytical paragraphs.

UNIT FOUR
UMBRELLA AND MARGIN SIGNALS

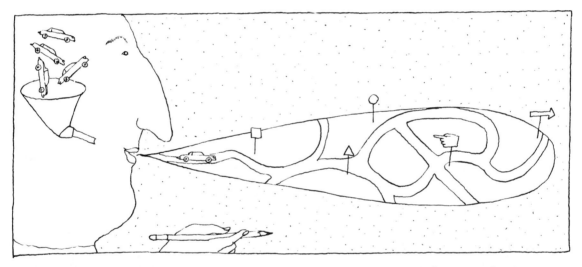

"So far, you've studied *open* sentence combining," I tell the class. "You've combined kernels in different ways to see how clusters hook together. You've explored different ways of saying the same thing and checked writeouts against options to see and hear the *range* of possibilities."

"What's for today?" Eric asks.

"This lesson takes up *signaled* combining. Unlike *open* exercises, these have a definite right answer. A signal tells you which specific transformation to apply."

"What good is that?" Maria asks. "Then everybody has the same answers. You can't compare."

"Right. But signaled exercises have a different purpose. They're a kind of calisthenics. Their aim is to strengthen your sentence-building skills in a disciplined way."

Kim glances at her notes. "These signaled exercises—do they work with addition and embedding? And coordination and subordination?"

"Indeed they do. Our aim is to get those processes working smoothly so they'll become part of your repertoire of skills."

I put a transparency on the projector. "Let's study the format of signaled exercises," I tell the class. "Notice first that the base sentence goes out to the left. Then notice that

the second kernel—the one that gets embedded into the base—has been indented. Finally there's the third kernel, which is indented even farther. Why? Because it modifies the second kernel, not the base sentence. This indentation helps you see what modifies what."

> The base sentence is set to the left.
> The sentence is for exercises.
> The exercises are signaled.

Writeout: The base sentence is set to the left for signaled exercises.

"That looks easy enough," Carol says.

"Indentation is simply a visual convenience for showing how sentence parts—the various kernels—relate to each other. But the base sentence won't always be the top one in a cluster. When one or more indented kernels come before the base sentence, the writeout will have modifiers in *front* of the base, usually separated from the base sentence by a comma."

"You mean sentence openers?" Christopher asks. "Subordination?"

"Exactly. Here's an example."

> Writers put modifiers up front.
> Writers can vary their sentences.
> The writers are resourceful.

Writeout A: As they put modifiers up front, resourceful writers can vary their sentences.

Writeout B: By putting modifiers up front, resourceful writers can vary their sentences.

"In the following example, you see that an up-front modifier can itself be modified. The indentation pattern signals this."

> Subordination is a technique.
> The subordination is up front.
> The technique is useful.
> Subordination can also be overused.

Writeout A: Although up-front subordination is a useful technique, it can also be overused.

Writeout B: A useful technique when used up front, subordination can also be overused.

"What else besides this indentation thing?" Chico asks.

"An insertion cue," I reply. "You'll occasionally see a slash mark (/) within a kernel sentence. This is a bit of extra help for tricky combining

problems. It shows *where* embedding or subordination should occur. In the next example it focuses your attention on a particular type of modifier—the kind that interrupts the flow of a sentence. Like indentation, it's there to help you see a pattern of modification."

> An interruption (/) can be signaled with a slash mark.
> An interruption is the addition of information.
> The information is modifying.

Writeout: An interruption—the addition of modifying information—can be signaled with a slash mark.

"So you combine just like usual?" Nate asks.

"Right. The insertion cue—the slash—is there simply to indicate *where* sentence parts go together. When the slash mark occurs in the middle of a kernel—as in the previous example—punctuation depends on the kind of transformation: You'll have either *two* punctuation marks or none at all. By the same token, when it occurs at the end of a kernel, the insertion cue will take either *one* punctuation mark or none at all."

Janet sighs. "I sure wish we had something more definite—a rule to follow on when to punctuate."

"The basic rule is to punctuate if you hear *pauses* for modifiers—and not to punctuate if the writeout reads smoothly. To get good at punctuation, you have to listen *closely* to your sentences."

Patsy wants to get back to the signals.

"How many combining signals will we learn?" she asks.

"We'll now study two types: the *umbrella signal* and the *margin signal*. In the next unit, we'll study the *footnote signal* in various forms."

"And these'll teach us new sentences?"

"*Different* sentences, perhaps. The aim at this stage is to practice transformations that you may not normally use. Signals make for a more disciplined kind of combining."

STOP. COMBINE THE FOLLOWING SENTENCES AND CHECK WITH THE ANSWER KEY, P. 275. THEN RESUME YOUR READING.

---

1. I go to work.
> The work is on exercises.
>> The exercises are simple.
>> The exercises are indented.

2.   A kernel appears before a base sentence.
> The writeout has a modifier.
>> The modifier is up front.

3.   A kernel is interrupted by a slash.
An internal modifier (/) interrupts the resulting writeout.
The modifier is sometimes set off by punctuation.

4.   I have already learned these two patterns (/).
One is introductory.
The other is interrupting.

The first example of the *umbrella signal* is projected. "The umbrella signal is a black line covering words to be embedded. Here, for example, you see words under three umbrellas. The task is simple: embed that information into other kernels."

UMBRELLA SIGNAL

The umbrella signal specifies words.
The words are for embedding.
The embedding is into layers.
The layers are deeper and deeper.

Writeout: The umbrella signal specifies words for embedding into deeper and deeper layers.

"Notice that *only* the words under the umbrellas are embedded. For purposes of combining, other words in the kernels are ignored. Try this exercise on your own."

This problem again uses the umbrella.
The problem is the second one.
The umbrella is used as a signal.
The signal is for sentence combining.

Laura's hand goes up. "*This second problem again uses the umbrella as a signal for sentence combining.*"
"Good. But you didn't do it in quite the way it's specified. Notice that the word *for* isn't under the umbrella. So it should read, *This second problem again uses the umbrella as a sentence-combining signal.* A *very* subtle difference, obviously."
A harder example is projected.

I am hoping to improve my skills.
I study the next example.
The example is of the umbrella signal.
I am uncertain of its writeout.

"Hoping to improve my skills," Eric volunteers, *"I study the next example of the umbrella signal, uncertain of its writeout."*

"You don't sound uncertain. You embedded modifiers before and after the base sentence with flawless ease. Let's try one more."

Embedding (/) can be overdone.
Embedding is like other transformations.
The transformations are major.
The transformations are for combining clusters.
The clusters are sentences.

The class is momentarily quiet.

"All the words under umbrellas go with the insertion cue?" Anne asks.

"That's right. Let's hear it."

"Embedding, like other major transformations for combining sentence clusters, can be overdone." She smiles. "As in this example?"

"That's right. Too many embeddings can make for overly complex, even snarled, writeouts. This is just a reminder."

STOP. COMBINE THE FOLLOWING SENTENCES AND CHECK WITH THE ANSWER KEY, P. 275. THEN RESUME YOUR READING.

---

5. I study the first exercise.
The exercise is for practice.
The exercise is for the umbrella signal.
I am whispering the words to myself.

6. I am feeling confident about my skills.
I then go on to the next exercise (/).
The exercise is a problem.
The problem is slightly more difficult.

7. These three exercises (/) have not been much trouble.
The exercises are all using umbrella signals.
The signals are for transformations.
The transformations are embedding.

I look the class over. "The *margin signal* is the second format we'll consider. It signals the processes of addition and coordination. How? By putting a coordinating conjunction in the left margin. Let's look at addition first, then coordination."

MARGIN SIGNAL

┌──The margin signal is for addition.

AND ──── It is also for coordination.

Writeout: The margin signal is for addition and for coordination.

"In this example, notice that *and* links the phrase under the umbrella to the base sentence. Previous examples had words *embedded* into a higher-level kernel; they *modified* something else. But here an element is being *added* to a base sentence, not as a modifier but as an independent item. As you learned in Unit 2, this transformation enables you to make a parallel series of words or phrases."

A second example goes up.

┌──The margin signal is easy to understand.

AND ──── The umbrella signal is easy to understand.

"Do you change *signal* to *signals?*" Paulo asks.

"That's right. You're talking about two signals, not one."

"*The margin and umbrella signals are easy to understand,*" he says.

"Good work. You changed *is* to *are* so that the subject and verb would agree. Try this."

┌── Peter studies the kernels.

├──── He thinks about the margin signal.

AND ──── He makes his transformation.

Peter swallows, then hesitates. "*Peter studies the kernels . . .*"

"So far, so good."

"*Thinks about the margin signal . . .*"

"Now the *and.*"

"*And makes his transformation.*"

"That's the idea. Here's one for Theresa."

┌── Theresa is taking her time.

AND ──── Theresa is whispering words to herself.

Theresa volunteers the next writeout.

Theresa blushes as she puts the kernels together. "*Taking her time and whispering words to herself, Theresa volunteers the next writeout.*"

"Good work. You're paying attention to signals and listening to your transformations."

STOP. FILL YOUR NAME INTO THE NEXT KERNEL SENTENCES AND DO THE COMBINING. THEN RESUME YOUR READING.

_____ (/) has figured out these signals.

    (Your name)

_____ is a student.

    (Your name)

    ┌────── The student is intelligent.

AND────── The student is hard-working.

Your writeout goes here:

_____

_____

_____

"So much for self-advertisements. Let's review what the margin signal does."

┌── The margin signal shows addition.

    The addition is within a sentence.

AND────── The margin signal also reveals coordination.

    The coordination is between base sentences.

"The margin signal shows addition within a sentence and also reveals coordination between base sentences," Chuck volunteers.

"Since you've got addition under control, we'll now turn our attention to coordination. Instead of joining words and phrases, we'll connect complete base sentences. Each base is set to the left as illustrated in the following examples."

┌── Coordination may sound complicated.

    The coordination is between base sentences.

BUT└── It's fairly easy to understand.

Writeout: Coordination between base sentences may sound complicated, but it's fairly easy to understand.

┌── Here the base sentences hook together.

    Hooking is with a conjunction.

AND   The conjunction is coordinating.

└── You do the combining as usual.

Writeout: Here the base sentences hook together with a coordinating conjunction, and you do the combining as usual.

STOP. MAKE A NOTE OF WHAT THE PUNCTUATION PATTERNS IN THE ABOVE WRITEOUTS ARE. THEN RESUME YOUR READING.

"I get it," Kristin says. "This set-up shows how base sentences are balanced."

"Exactly. Each half of the writeout consists of an independent base sentence with its own pattern of modification. Put together, the two parts make a *coordinate sentence.*"

Coordinate-style sentences are like others.
Coordinate-style sentences have modifiers.
BUT   The modifiers are in various positions.
They also have an emphasis.
The emphasis is balanced.

For a long moment, the class studies the two halves of the exercise. Then Randy volunteers a correct writeout. *"Like others, coordinate-style sentences have modifiers in various positions; but they also have a balanced emphasis."*

"For practice," I tell the class, "try this."

—————————————— (/) pretends to be asleep.
(Your name)
YET   —————————————— is a reader of this text.
(Your name)
He/she will undoubtedly make a writeout.
The writeout will be correctly punctuated.
The writeout will be coordinate-style.

Your writeout goes here:

———————————————————————————————————

———————————————————————————————————

———————————————————————————————————

———————————————————————————————————

"You've probably noticed that these sentences are using the coordinating conjunctions from Unit 3—*and, but, yet, or, so, for, nor.* But in addition to these, you'll come across two other types of conjunctions for coordinate-style sentences."

CORRELATIVE CONJUNCTIONS

both . . . and
either . . . or
neither . . . nor
not only . . . but also

CONJUNCTIVE ADVERBS

also	moreover
besides	nevertheless
consequently	nonetheless
furthermore	similarly
however	then
indeed	therefore
likewise	thus

"Let's now see how these other connectors function. Notice that the correlative conjunctions have two parts, each attaching to one of the base sentences. The *either* connector goes with the first base sentence, and *or* connects to the second."

EITHER

Tim will volunteer to transform this example.
 The example is devious.

OR — He will buy Cokes for everybody.
 The buying will be after class today.

Tim's response is unhesitating. *"Either Tim will volunteer to transform this devious example or he will buy Cokes for everybody after class today."*
"Skillfully done."
"Grace under pressure," he says.
Another example goes up.

NOT ONLY
BUT ALSO

This class is a joy to take.
 The class is for writing.
 The joy is educational.
It is a place out of the weather.

"The first connector goes with the first base sentence?" Carol asks.
"That's right. Give it a try."
"Do you start with the words *not only*?"
"There are two ways to make the transformation. Both involve some shifting of words to keep the writeouts idiomatic."
Hesitating, Carol whispers the words to herself, then says them aloud. *"Not only is this writing class an educational joy to take, but it is also a place out of the weather."*
"Good combining. The other choice is to embed the first connector into the base sentence: *This writing class is not only an educational joy to take, but it is also a place out of the weather."*
Taking a deep breath, I move into the last pattern for the margin signal.
"Since other correlative conjunctions work in the same basic way, let's shift attention to conjunctive adverbs. These also join related base sentences, but their combining patterns are different from what we've just

seen. Conjunctive adverbs either *introduce* a second base sentence or they're *embedded into* it. You'll see both patterns in the following example. Notice how punctuation is used with this type of connector. The *introductory* pattern requires a semicolon before the connector and a comma afterwards. The *embedded* pattern in this instance has commas on both sides of the connector, with a semicolon to separate the two base sentences."

STOP. MAKE A MARGINAL NOTE THAT *BOTH* PATTERNS REQUIRE A SEMICOLON. THEN RESUME YOUR READING.

HOWEVER
Conjunctive adverbs have a label.
    The label is technical-sounding.
    The label is even ominous.
They are not at all difficult to use.

Writeout [INTRODUCTORY PATTERN]: *Conjunctive adverbs have a technical-sounding, even ominous label; however, they are not at all difficult to use.*

Writeout [EMBEDDED PATTERN]: *Conjunctive adverbs have a technical-sounding, even ominous label; they are, however, not at all difficult to use.*

STOP. CIRCLE THESE TWO PUNCTUATION PATTERNS. THEN RESUME YOUR READING.

"Which way is better?" Terry asks.

"Both are perfectly acceptable. Your choice of patterns will be determined by the *emphasis* you want."

"How about embedding the word *however* at the end of the second base sentence?"

"That's fine, too. Once again, it's a matter of sentence emphasis—the rhythm you're after."

"I like it embedded in the middle," Andrea says. "That way the sentence sounds less choppy."

"Many writers agree with you," I reply. "But the other patterns are also correct. Once you know the options, the choice is yours."

STOP. THE TWO FOLLOWING WRITEOUTS ARE WITHOUT PUNCTUATION. MAKE CORRECTIONS AS NECESSARY AND CHECK WITH THE ANSWER KEY, P. 275. THEN RESUME YOUR READING.

THEREFORE
       Everyone seems to understand conjunctive adverbs.
              They are used as a margin signal.
       In this example we'll review patterns.
              The patterns will be punctuation.

Writeout [introductory pattern]: Everyone seems to understand conjunctive adverbs used as a margin signal therefore in this example we'll review punctuation patterns.

Writeout [embedded pattern]: Everyone seems to understand conjunctive adverbs used as a margin signal in this example therefore we'll review punctuation patterns.

"Not all embedded conjunctive adverbs are set off by commas," I add. "It depends on the connector and the sentence emphasis. You have to *listen* to get the punctuation right. Here, for example, you don't pause on either side of the *therefore* connector—so you don't need commas."

Writeout [embedded pattern]: Everyone seems to understand conjunctive adverbs used as a margin signal; we'll therefore review punctuation patterns in this example.

STOP. COMBINE THE FOLLOWING SENTENCES AND CHECK WITH THE ANSWER KEY, P. 275. THEN RESUME YOUR READING.

---

8.   New exercises confront me.
    AND   They demand my attention.
            The attention is intellectual.

9.   I am staring at kernels.
    AND   I am studying signals.
       I can hear writeouts.
            The writeouts are taking shape.

10.   I sometimes try to hold these sentences.
    BUT   The holding is in my mind.
       They quickly fade from consciousness.
            They are like whispers in the night.

11.   This "fading" occurs in exercises.
  NOT ONLY   The exercises are for combining.
  BUT ALSO It happens in situations.
            The situations are for note taking.

12. ┌── Language is elusive.
CONSEQUENTLY   The language is spoken.
     └──I need to capture it quickly.
          The capture is through transcription.
          The transcription is careful.

"That concludes today's work on signaled combining," I tell the class. "Be alert to punctuation patterns in the next exercises. And as you do open exercises, practice some of the transformations you've just learned."

"Any transformations in particular?" Tony asks.

"Try putting modifiers in front of the base sentence on occasion. Also, work with interrupted writeouts—putting special emphasis in the middle. Finally, you might focus on coordination patterns that use semicolons and various connectors. If handled well, these three structures can add a touch of class to your writing."

Eric is grinning. "A touch of writing class?"

The class groans at his pun.

Combine sentences in the following exercises (4.1–4.4) by using the signals that are provided. Refer back to the preceding text for help where necessary. Then check with the Answer Key on p. 275.

EXERCISE 4.1.   Signaled Format

MODEL

> We arrived at the hill.
>   The hill was steep.
> We found a problem.
>   The problem was frightening.
>   The problem was in the twilight.

Writeout: Upon arriving at the steep hill, we found a frightening problem in the twilight.

A.   A hole makes for a doughnut.
        The hole is large.
        The doughnut is small.

B.   The people are lifting weights.
        The people are muscular.
        The people are on the beach.
        The weights are fake.

C.   Our quarterback threw fifteen interceptions.
            The interceptions were perfect.
            The interceptions were in a row.
    Our quarterback was named their Most Valuable Player.

D.   Our neighbors (/) should probably pull their shades.
        They are a friendly couple.
        The couple has a house.
            The house is nearly all glass.

E.   I like all types (/).
        I like fat ones.
        I like foxy ones.
        I like sleek ones.

I like sexy ones.

F.   You drink goat's milk.
        The milk is fresh.
    You eat onions.
        The onions are raw.
    You might possibly live longer.

G.   The soldiers (/) seemed less than intelligent.
        The soldiers were bathing in a pond.
        The pond was small.
        The pond supplied their water.
            The water was for drinking.

H.   She had purchased oranges.
        The oranges were fermenting.
        The purchase was at an auction.
            The auction was for fruit.
    She decided to make wine.

I.   He wants to marry a person.
        The person fixes motorcycles.
            The motorcycles are greasy.
        The person wears chains.
            The chains are around her neck.

J.   The restaurant had a reputation.
        The reputation was world-famous.
    Our dinner party (/) could not order pizza.
        The party was a class reunion.
        The reunion was raucous.

EXERCISE 4.2.   Umbrella Signal

MODEL

> My term paper has no odor.
>> My term paper is trash-com-pacted.
>> The odor might be offensive.

Writeout: My trash-compacted paper has no offensive odor.

A. The cow sat on the mouse.
> The cow was discontented.
> The mouse was belligerent.

B. Wearing the hubcap can be an embarrassment.
> The hubcap is the wrong one.
> The embarrassment is outrageous.

C. The subway is a place.
> The place is swell.
> The place is for a picnic.
>> The picnic is at 5:00 P.M.

D. Something happened under the typewriter.
We found a waffle.
> The waffle was flattened.
> The waffle was decayed.

E. Your cigarette has a smell.
> The cigarette is hand-rolled.
> The smell is odd.
> The smell is sweet.

F. Let's use her toothbrush.
> The toothbrush is new.
> The use is for scrubbing bike spokes.
>> The bike spokes are tarnished.

G. I saw him at lunch.
I saw him dive.
> The dive was end over end.
> The dive was into the vat.
>> The vat was wine.

H. Something happens after class.
Nonsense makes sense.
> The nonsense is wild.
> The sense is complete.
> The sense is to you and me.

I. There are features to this suit.
> The features are unique.
> The suit is for business.
> The suit is made of plastic.
>> The plastic is form-fitting.

J. She flirts to amuse her friends.
> Her friends are giggling.
She flirts with her teacher.
> The flirting is sometimes.
> Her teacher is barrel-shaped.
> The teacher teaches shop.

EXERCISE 4.3.   Margin Signal

MODEL

> ⌐ Sales have recently sagged.
> **BUT**　　The sales are of balloons.
> ⌐ Hot air has kept morale high.
> 　　The morale is in the company.

Writeout: Balloon sales have recently sagged, but hot air has kept company morale high.

A. ⌐ Tony's tacos were awful.
> **YET**　　The tacos were jelly-filled.
> ⌐ His burritos were even worse.

B.
- You shouldn't bait your hook.
- **OR** The hook is for fishing.
- You may have to clean fish.

C. Most teachers frown upon threats.
- **AND** — The threats are blackmail.
- — The threats are extortion.

D.
- **HOWEVER** — One may dream about a cure.
- The cure is for hiccups.
- Finding it is something else.

E.
- — We enjoyed backpacking.
- **BUT** The backpacking was in Central Park.
- — We didn't have a permit. The permit would be for mugging.

F. Something happened after the game.
- — They demanded ice cream.
- **WHEREAS** The ice cream was chili-flavored.
- — I wanted dill pickles.

G.
- — Tonya should take a bath.
- **EITHER** The bath will be hot.
- **OR** The bath will be soapy.
- — She should sleep outside tonight.

H.
- — The rock group played a number.
- **NOT ONLY** The number was "heavy."
- **BUT ALSO** The number was for the senior citizens. The senior citizens were enthusiastic.
- — The rock group bought them cocoa.

I.
- — Grab your partner. The partner is your favorite.
- — Boogie over to the Union Hall.
- **AND** The Union Hall is downtown.
- — Stomp some grapes. The grapes are hand-picked.

J. She was turning with a smile. The smile was coy.
- — She lowered her eyelashes.
- **THEN** Her eyelashes were dark. Her eyelashes were thick.
- — She told him to get lost.

EXERCISE 4.4.   Proofreading Practice

Directions. The following rhymed sentences lack proper punctuation. Make corrections and check with the Answer Key, p. 275.

1. ┌────── Fried rice (/) is rather nice.
    YET   The rice is seasoned with spice.
    └────── I still prefer spuds.
             The spuds are with a glass of suds.
                 The suds are cold.

PROBLEM 1   *Fried rice seasoned with spice is rather nice yet I still prefer spuds with a glass of cold suds.*

REWRITE 1   _____

2.   Kent's fast (/) occurred at Lent.
             The fast was his last.
             His fast was a campout in a tent.
                 The tent was cramped.
                 The tent was damp.

PROBLEM 2   *Kent's last fast a campout in a cramped damp tent occurred at Lent.*

REWRITE 2   _____

3.   The quietness was in spite of a riot.
        ┌─── The class was quite quiet.
    THEN
        └─── People embraced.
             They were making words in space.
                 The words were weird.
                 The space was waste.

PROBLEM 3   *In spite of a riot the class was quite quiet then people embraced making weird words in waste space.*

REWRITE 3   _____

4. ┌──────── Some critters are spitting.
    AND──────── Some critters are hitting.
        ┌──────── Some critters are fighting.
    AND──────── Some critters are biting.
    Some critters turn babysitters into quitters.

PROBLEM 4   *Spitting and hitting fighting and biting some critters turn babysitters into quitters.*

REWRITE 4   _____

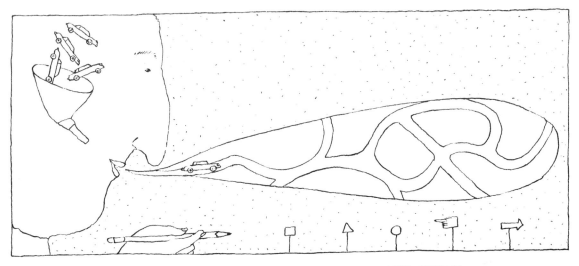

Chill, wind-blown rain buffets the classroom windows, making trickling rivers on the glass. We're under way again.

"Various forms of the *footnote signal* are very important," I tell the class. "They're the signals you'll probably practice most. Why? Because they're used to signal connecting words that make transitions and subordinate information. Not only that, they also make changes in word form. They're called footnote signals because they appear at the bottom of a cluster and serve as a reference point for combining."

"How do they work?" Maria asks.

To begin to answer Maria's question, I project three clusters for students to study.

THE FOOTNOTE SIGNAL

1. Let's study this example.
    2. The example shows two footnote signals.

1 FIRST OF ALL   2 THAT

Writeout: First of all, let's study this example that shows two footnote signals.

    3. That was painless.
4. Let's now look at this second example.
    5. The look will be brief.

3 SINCE   5 LY

Writeout: Since that was painless, let's now look briefly at this second example.

6.   SOMETHING is not surprising.
   7.   We'll learn even more about footnote signals.
   8.   We'll consider this third example.

6–7 IT . . . THAT   8 BY + ING

Writeout: It is not surprising that we'll learn even more about footnote signals by considering this third example.

"Each footnote signal has a number that corresponds to a preceding kernel sentence. You use the connecting word specified in the kernel, or you make a change in word form as directed. A connector in parentheses is optional; you can use it or ignore it when making your transformation."

"What kind of connectors?"

"The subordinating words and prepositions from Unit 3 are one group. Then there's also a large number of transition words and phrases. Some are conjunctive adverbs—the connectors such as *however, consequently,* and *moreover* that you learned with the margin signal; and some are words and phrases such as *hence, on the other hand, for example, in addition, of course, finally, in other words, to summarize,* etc. All these transitions help your sentences 'hang together,' so to speak. They're like signposts to direct your reader's attention."

"Can these transitions be either introductory or embedded?" Paulo asks.

"That's right. Just as you learned with the margin signal, it's your decision whether to put the transition connector into an introductory or embedded position."

"And the punctuation changes for the two patterns?"

"Right again. You have to *listen* for pauses and punctuate accordingly. Here are five examples of transition footnotes that reveal how things work."

TRANSITION FOOTNOTE SIGNAL

1.   Students in this class (/) are very inquisitive.
   2.   They are like readers of this book.

1 FIRST OF ALL

Writeout: Students in this class, like readers of this book, are first of all very inquisitive.

3.   Both groups will quickly master the system.
   4.   The system is for signaling.

3 AS A RESULT

Writeout: As a result, both groups will quickly master the signaling system.

5.   Connectors will take only a few illustrations.

6.   The connectors are for transitions.

5   FOR EXAMPLE

Writeout: Connectors for transitions, for example, will take only a few illustrations.

7.   Neither group should have problems.

8.   The problems are seeing punctuation patterns.

7   MOREOVER

Writeout: Moreover, neither group should have problems seeing punctuation patterns.

9.   Controlling their enthusiasm may be another matter.

10.   Their enthusiasm is for footnote signals.

9   HOWEVER

Writeout: Controlling their enthusiasm for footnote signals, however, may be another matter.

STOP.   CIRCLE THE PUNCTUATION PATTERNS FOR THE ABOVE TRANSITIONS. THEN RESUME YOUR READING.

"Seems pretty easy so far," Chico murmurs.

"All you do is attach the transition connector to the kernel sentence with the same number—in either an introductory or embedded way."

"Okay, how about *two* transitions for the same writeout?"

"Sure. You'll see that in what follows."

STOP.   COMBINE THESE CLUSTERS AND CHECK WITH THE ANSWER KEY, P. 275. THEN RESUME YOUR READING.

---

11.   ——————— has studied the examples.
   (Your name)

12.   The examples were preceding ones.

13.   He/she is able to use transitions.

14.   The use is in his/her writeouts.

13   NOT SURPRISINGLY + THEREFORE

15. He/she has paid attention to punctuation.

    16. The attention has been close.

15 IN ADDITION

17. These writeouts are correctly punctuated.

    18. The writeouts are for practice.

17 CONSEQUENTLY

"So much for transition footnotes. Now let's look at connecting words that subordinate. The first example of the *subordination footnote signal* shows the word *that* connecting the second kernel to the first one. The transformation is a simple and familiar one."

SUBORDINATION FOOTNOTE SIGNAL

1. We're now examining a new signal.

    2. The signal operates through footnotes.

        3. The footnotes are numbered.

2 THAT

Writeout: We're now examining a new signal that operates through numbered footnotes.

"You can have more than one footnote?" Paulo asks.

"That's right. The next example has two footnote signals, one in parentheses. As I mentioned earlier, parentheses mean that the connector is optional. Deleting an optional connector usually makes for a shorter, more readable transformation. Sometimes, though, you may prefer a sentence with more formal or emphatic rhythms—as in writeout B."

4. Connecting words can appear in many places.

       5. The connecting words make transitions.

AND

       6. The connecting words subordinate information.

5 THAT   6 (THAT)

Writeout A: Connecting words that make transitions and subordinate information can appear in many places.

Writeout B: Connecting words that make transitions—and that subordinate information—can appear in many places.

"I get it," Rob says. "The second *that* connector in Writeout A is understood—even though it's not used."

"That's because compounding lets one appearance of a word do the work of two. No need for a signal to cut through needless words. Just do it."

We move on to a slightly harder example.

   7.   Smart people make two transformations.
       8.   The people solve this problem.
       9.   The transformations use relative pronouns.

8 WHO   9 THAT

"Notice that *who* subordinates kernel 8, and *that* subordinates kernel 9."

Tim raises his hand. *"Smart people who solve this problem make two transformations that use relative pronouns."*

"That's it. Here's one with a different structure."

  10.   This sentence (/) is fairly easy to transform.
     11.   The sentence has two kernels.
       12.   The kernels are embedded.

11 WHICH   12 THAT

Janet makes a try at combining. *"This sentence is fairly easy to transform, which has two kernels that are embedded."*

"You've got the *which* and *that* part correct; just put it in the middle of the base sentence—where the slash appears—so that it makes sense. *Which has two kernels* modifies the word *sentence*."

She eyes the cluster again. *"This sentence, which has two kernels that are embedded, is fairly easy to transform."*

"Well, maybe *not* so easy the first time through, but you've got it now. Notice that the interrupting modifier has pauses—and therefore punctuation—around it. Next we'll see modifiers both before and after the base sentence."

     13.   These exercises look tricky.
  14.   You soon catch on to signals.
     15.   The signals use subordinating words.

13 ALTHOUGH   15 THAT

"I'm not sure how to start," Rob says.

"Begin at the top. Use the word *although*."

Rob is hesitant. *"Although these exercises look tricky . . ."*

"You soon catch on to signals that use subordinating words," Kim adds.

"Good teamwork. As usual, a comma separates the introductory, dependent part of the writeout from the base sentence. Here's a more difficult cluster set up in the same way."

16.   These signals specify connectors.
    17.   The connectors are <u>subordinating</u>.
18.   They enable you to make writeouts.
    19.   The writeouts are more structurally complex.

16 BECAUSE   19 THAT

Theresa's hand goes up. *"Because these signals specify subordinating connectors, they enable you to make writeouts that are more structurally complex."*

"Good. I think you're onto it."

STOP. COMBINE THESE CLUSTERS AND CHECK WITH THE ANSWER KEY, P. 275. THEN RESUME YOUR READING.

---

20.   Before me are exercises.
    21.   The exercises have footnote signals.

21 THAT

    ┌— 22.   I am weary.
AND
    └— 23.   I do my best to ignore them.
24.   I find myself scanning the kernels.

22 ALTHOUGH   23 (ALTHOUGH)

25.   My brain (/) clicks into action.
    26.   It cannot leave sentences alone.
        27.   The sentences are uncombined.

26 WHICH   27 THAT

    28.   I know what has happened.
29.   I have combined four writeouts.
    30.   The writeouts demonstrate my skills.

28 BEFORE   30 THAT

"Now that you've practiced subordinating connectors, we'll use the word *something* as a slot that you can put other information into. You'll see that *something* has been capitalized in the next example. This is a cue to put a kernel into that location."

"So *something* is sort of a placeholder," Christopher says.

"Right. We're using it to practice a different set of transformations called nominalization."

FOOTNOTE SIGNAL AND *SOMETHING*

   1.   Kristin thinks SOMETHING.
       2.   She is top dog.

2 (THAT)

Writeout: Kristin thinks that she is top dog.

"You see? Nothing to it. Put the second kernel into the *something* slot and use the optional footnote connector."

   3.   I therefore believe SOMETHING.
       4.   She would enjoy a hamburger. _____
           5.   The hamburger would be made from dog food.

4 (THAT)

Writeout: I therefore believe she would enjoy a hamburger made from dog food.

"With those examples as an introduction, let's go to work," I tell the class. "Here's a cluster using different connectors."

   6.   Laura tries to understand SOMETHING.
     ┌──7.   These signaled exercises work.
AND
     └──8.   They improve on-your-own writing.

7 HOW   8 WHY

Laura does the combining almost immediately. *"Laura tries to understand how these signaled exercises work and why they improve on-your-own writing.*

"Obviously, you've figured out *how* they work. Do you see why they might help your writing?"

"Well, they show you how to construct different sentences," she says.

"Exactly. These force you to make transformations that you might not think of by yourself. The next cluster illustrates this point because it puts the *something* slot up front in the base sentence. See if you can figure it out."

   9.   SOMETHING pleases some students.
      10.   Signaled exercises give guidance. _____
         11.   The guidance is in combining.

10 (THE FACT) THAT

Chuck makes a nervous try. *"The fact that something pleases . . ."*

"Not quite. The signal and indentation show that you embed the second kernel into the first."

"Oh, I see. *The fact that signaled exercises give combining guidance pleases some students.*"

"Right. You might also delete the part of the signal in parentheses: *That signaled exercises give combining guidance pleases some students.*"

"Sort of tricky," Maria says.

"Just at first. Once you get used to inversion—putting unusual emphasis at the front of a sentence—it's really not that difficult. Here's an example that has the *something* slot up front and subordination after the embedded sentence. The slash mark (/) shows where to subordinate."

12.   SOMETHING seems easy to predict.
  13.   This class will do something for homework (/).
    14.   The instructional session ends.

13   WHAT 14   WHEN

Paulo eyes the cluster. "Looks like the word *something* in kernel 13 isn't needed. Do you take it out to do the combining?"

"That's right. Delete unneeded words to keep your writeouts idiomatic. Trust your ear."

"*What this class will do for homework when the instructional session ends seems easy to predict,*" he says. "These signaled exercises?"

"Yes, indeed. But before we get to homework, let's try these."

STOP.   COMBINE THESE CLUSTERS AND CHECK WITH THE ANSWER KEY, P. 275. THEN RESUME YOUR READING.

---

15.   I tell myself SOMETHING.
  ┌─16.   I can resist temptation.
AND
  └─17.   I can ignore these exercises.

16   (THAT) 17   (THAT)

18.   But SOMETHING suggests otherwise.
  19.   I keep doing them.

19   THE FACT THAT

20.   I sometimes wonder SOMETHING.
  21.   I may have acquired an addiction.
    22.   The addiction is strange.
    23.   The addiction is to combining.

21   IF

24. SOMETHING is a puzzle.
    25. I want to work with them (/).
        26. I don't have to.

25 WHY   26 EVEN THOUGH

"So far, so good. Now let's look at a signal that's split into two, some-times three, parts. These parts work together in very systematic ways. The trick is to put *it* into the *something* slot before embedding other informa-tion. To help you do this, the *split footnote signal* appears as a unit. The three periods indicate where a kernel sentence goes."

SPLIT FOOTNOTE SIGNAL

1. SOMETHING seems easy to predict.
    2. This class will do something for homework (/).
        3. The instructional session ends.

1–2 IT . . . WHAT   3 WHEN

Writeout: It seems easy to predict what this class will do for homework when the instructional session ends.

"I get it," Michelle says. "The first two kernels work together with the split signal. First comes one, then the other."

"The main thing to remember is that *it* goes into the *something* slot and that the other connector is delayed. The effect of this transformation is to put emphasis at the end of a sentence. Here's another example."

4. SOMETHING is debatable.
    5. Eric is getting enough sleep.
        6. The sleep is outside of class.

4–5 IT . . . WHETHER

"I'm *not* sleeping," Eric protests, eyeing the transparency from his head-on-the-desk position.

"Your turn for combining, then."

"*Whether Eric is getting enough sleep outside of class is debatable,*" he says.

"A very good sentence—in fact, I prefer it to the one called for here. But you need to begin this writeout with the word *it: It is debatable whether Eric is getting enough sleep outside of class.*"

"Try me again." He grins.

"Okay, figure this out."

7. I want SOMETHING understood.

8.   Split footnote signals aren't too tricky (/).
   9.   One pays attention.

7–8 IT . . . THAT   9 IF

"Nothing to it: *I want it understood that split footnote signals aren't too tricky if one pays attention.*"

"One more for practice. Then we'll try a more difficult kind of split footnote."

10.   SOMETHING is not clear.
   11.   These students (/) are so obnoxiously confident.
      12.   The students have never seen signaled sentence combining.

10–11   IT . . . WHY   12 WHO

Hands are going up as Andrea calls out the transformation. "*It's not clear why these students, who have never seen signaled sentence combining, are so obnoxiously confident.*"

"Good work. Now think about *this* one."

13.   SOMETHING would be unlikely.
   14.   You solve this problem without help.
      15.   The problem is more difficult.

13–14 IT . . . FOR . . . TO

The class is quiet, puzzling over this three-sentence cluster. Then Malee's hand goes up. "*It would be unlikely* . . ."

"You're on the right track."

"*It would be unlikely for you to solve this more difficult problem without help,*" she says.

"Maybe not so unlikely. You did very well. Let's try another."

16.   SOMETHING seems impossible.
   17.   This teacher stumps the class.
      18.   The class is for writing.

16–17 IT . . . FOR . . . TO

"*It seems impossible,*" Terry begins, "*for* . . . uhmmm . . ."

"*For this teacher to stump the writing class,*" Christopher adds.

"Notice that *stumps* gets changed to *stump* in the writeout. This kind of regular switch is part of the grammatical idiom of English. It's a subtle but important kind of transformation—like changing *is* to *are* for agreement of subject and verb."

To throw the class a curve, I give them the same cluster with a different split signal.

19.   SOMETHING seems impossible.
   20.   This teacher stumps the class.
      21.   The class is for writing.

20   FOR . . . TO

The class looks perplexed. Few students have noticed that *it* is missing from this split footnote signal.

Finally, Kristin volunteers a correct transformation. *"For this teacher to stump the writing class seems impossible."*

"Well done," I respond with a nod. "Not having the *it* up front means that the second kernel gets embedded into the *something* slot—just like a regular footnote signal."

"Tricky," Carlos says.

"Let's conclude with subordination *plus* a split footnote signal."

   22.   SOMETHING is apparent.
      23.   These students are almost unstumpable.
24.   They will get some practice exercises.

22–23   BECAUSE + IT . . . THAT

Carol's hand goes up. *"Because it is apparent that these students are almost unstumpable, they will get some practice exercises."*

STOP. COMBINE THESE CLUSTERS AND CHECK WITH THE ANSWER KEY, P. 275. THEN RESUME YOUR READING.

25.   SOMETHING seems obvious.
   26.   I can kick my combining habit (/).
      27.   I really want to.

25–26   IT . . . THAT   27   IF

28.   But SOMETHING is not clear.
   29.   I should give up a process.
      30.   I find it so enjoyable.

28–29   IT . . . WHY   30   THAT

31.   SOMETHING is sometimes traumatizing.
   32.   An addict quits "cold turkey."

31   MOREOVER   32   FOR . . . TO

   33.   SOMETHING is undeniable.
      34.   There are worse things to be addicted to.
35.   Perhaps I should be thankful for my addiction.

33–34   SINCE + IT . . . THAT

"We'll conclude with footnote signals that change the *form* of words. These are interesting to play with and, like the others, push us in new directions with sentences. The idea is to take a word from under an umbrella, change it with a footnote signal, and then embed it."

WORD FORM FOOTNOTE SIGNAL

1.   This exercise calls for SOMETHING.
 2.   You change word form.

2   ING

Writeout: This exercise calls for changing word form.

"In this case, you take *change* from under the umbrella signal and add *-ing*. Then you put *changing word form* into the *something-ing* slot. The next example is only slightly more complicated. First, you add *-ly* to *incredible*. Then you add *-ing* to *solve*. The words *incredibly* and *solving word form problems* are then embedded, with *when* used as a connector."

3.   This class is arrogant.
 4.   Its arrogance is incredible.
  5.   This class solves word form problems.

4   LY   5   WHEN + ING

The class is quiet for a few moments; then Randy speaks up. *"This class is incredibly arrogant when solving word form problems."*
"Right. Try another."

  6.   We use word form signals.
 7.   We can explore stylistic options.
  8.   The exploration is systematic.

6   BY + ING   8   LY

Chuck is catching on. *"By using word form signals, we can explore stylistic options systematically."*
"Right again."

  9.   We play it safe.
10.   We'll try new things with sentences.
  11.   We'll listen for changes.
   12.   The changes are in emphasis.

9   INSTEAD OF + ING   11   ING

It's Andrea's turn to volunteer. *"Instead of playing it safe, we'll try new things with sentences, listening for changes in emphasis."*

    13.   Some people remember past experiences.

14.   Some people are reluctant to volunteer.

    15.   They have feelings.

       16.   They might fail.

13 ING   15 BECAUSE OF   16 THAT

"How about some new voices? Volunteers?"

Terry glances up, and seconds tick by. *"Remembering past experiences,"* he begins.

The class waits.

"Some people are reluctant to volunteer . . ."

"Why?" I ask.

"Because of feelings that they might fail," he concludes in a hoarse whisper.

"Good job. You're willing to risk—and you're therefore learning."

STOP. COMBINE THESE CLUSTERS AND CHECK WITH THE ANSWER KEY, P. 275. THEN RESUME YOUR READING.

---

    17.   I transcribe sentences.

      18.   The transcribing is tentative.

19.   I sometimes pause.

17 AFTER + ING   18 LY

20.   I can picture the book's author.

    21.   He reads over my shoulder.

      22.   His reading is silent.

21 ING   22 LY

23.   Writeouts are always perfect!

    24.   The writeouts belong to ——————————.

                         (Your name)

      25.   The perfection is flawless.

23 OF COURSE   24 ING   25 LY

"After you get familiar with footnote signals, you'll probably want to cover them up with a notecard," I tell the class. "Often you'll be able to *guess* the right connector from context—just by listening to the logic of

preceding writeouts. Of course, if you *do* need signals, they're at your fingertips, both for combining and feedback. You can get back on the transforming track with a glance."

"So what if I like my connector better?" Carlos asks. "For example, I put in *because,* and it's supposed to be *since.*"

"You're the decision maker. If you do the signaled writeout but still prefer your own set of transformations, trust your best hunches. The point is to *think about* the connectors you're using to combine sentences."

Carlos frowns. "I like the open exercises better. More free-wheeling, you know?"

"In later units, you'll see that not all signaled exercises are as structured as these. In fact, most are only *partly* signaled—a hint here and there about how to combine. These have been heavily signaled simply to teach you the system."

Students are turning to the Unit 5 exercises just as the buzzer sounds.

Combine sentences in the following clusters by using the signals provided. Refer back to the unit text if you need help. Then check with the Answer Key on p. 275.

EXERCISE 5.1.   Transition Footnote Signal

MODEL

    1. Transitions mark turns in logic.

    2. The turns are $\overline{\text{explicit}}$.

1   FIRST OF ALL

Writeout: Transitions first of all mark explicit turns in logic.

A.   3. They might be compared to signposts.

        4. The signposts guide the reader's attention.

3   IN OTHER WORDS

B.   5. Some signposts are more visible than others.

        6. Some signposts are more explicit than others.

5   OF COURSE

C.   7. The word *however* is a transition.

        8. The transition is $\overline{\text{quite obvious}}$.

        9. The transition points to contrast.

7   FOR EXAMPLE

D. 10. The phrase *of course* is a transition.

      11. The transition is $\overline{\text{more subtle}}$.

      12. The transition points to added emphasis.

10   ON THE OTHER HAND

E. 13. Transitions serve to advance writing.

14. The advance is $\overline{\text{from point to point}}$.

15. The advance is $\overline{\text{toward a conclusion}}$.

13   SECOND

F. 16. They show the building of ideas.

      17. The building is $\overline{\text{visible}}$.

      18. The building is $\overline{\text{cumulative}}$.

16   TO PUT IT ANOTHER WAY

G. 19. Words signal insistence.

      20. The words include *indeed*.

      21. The words include *in fact*.

19   THUS

H. 22. Words signal amplification.

      23. The words include *in addition*.

      24. The words include *furthermore*.

22   SIMILARLY

I. 25. Transitions are very important in writing.

     26. They mark turns in logic.

     27. They show the building of ideas.

25   IN CONCLUSION

J. 28. Writers pay attention to transitions.

     29. The writers are skilled.

     30. The attention is very close.

28   NOT SURPRISINGLY + THEREFORE

EXERCISE 5.2.   Subordination Footnote Signal

MODEL

    1. I am nervous.

  2. I stay away from snakes.

    3. The snakes speak with forked tongues.

1 WHEN   3 THAT

Writeout: When I am nervous, I stay away from snakes that speak with forked tongues.

A.   4. Bless the people.

      5. The people have a grasp on reality.

5 WHO

B. 6. You will hear a gasp.
　　7. The floor drops away.

7 AS

C. 　8. The windows are open.
　　9. The windows are not closed.

8 WHEN

D. 10. The college was led by men.
　　11. The men wore ties.
　　12. The men wore T-shirts.

11 WHO　　12 (WHO)

E. 13. We are hurried.
　14. We'll use the mistakes.
　　15. The mistakes were incorrectly published.

13 BECAUSE　　15 THAT

F. 16. The sadness occurs.
　　17. We leave the natives.
　　　18. The natives worship us.

17 WHENEVER　　18 WHO

G. 　19. Avocado is delicious.

20. I would not like it in my beard.
21. My beard is always well groomed.

19 ALTHOUGH　　21 WHICH

H. 22. Our boss (/) demands loyalty.
　　23. My boss is a perfectionist.
　　24. The loyalty is complete.
　　　25. She is not loyal to us.

23 (WHO)　　25 EVEN THOUGH

I. 　26. Winston hears the news.
　27. He turns it off.
　　28. It makes him informed.
　　　29. Being informed makes him uneasy.

26 WHEN　　28 BECAUSE　　29 WHICH

J. 30. Journalists (/) wrote articles.
　　31. They interviewed the football team.
　　　32. The team had not showered.
　　33. The articles were pungent.

31 WHO　　32 THAT

EXERCISE 5.3.　　Footnote Signal and *SOMETHING*

MODEL

　1. SOMETHING does not stop me from skiing.
　　2. My brains are scrambled.
　　　3. I crash into things.

2 THE FACT THAT　　3 BECAUSE

Writeout: The fact that my brains are scrambled because I crash into things does not stop me from skiing.

A. 4. I told him SOMETHING.
　　5. He shouldn't chase dogs with my truck.

5 THAT

B. 6. SOMETHING soon became clear to Reggie.
　　7. Wanda had something in mind.

7 WHAT

C.   8.   SOMETHING is no justification for your behavior.

9.   It is fun to mutilate a board.

9 THE FACT THAT

D.   10.   She complained SOMETHING.

11.   Watermelons made her lunch lumpy.

12.   They smashed her sandwiches.

11 THAT   12 (THAT)

E.   13.   He announced SOMETHING.

14.   He had swallowed a tooth.

15.   This turned out to be the truth.

14 THAT   15 WHICH

F.   16.   SOMETHING doesn't mean you can ignore her.

17.   She has breath.

18.   The breath curls your moustache.

17 JUST BECAUSE   18 THAT

G.   19.   It is a nice evening.

20.   I don't see SOMETHING.

21.   You should go skinny-dipping alone.

19 SINCE   21 WHY

H.   22.   Laboratory tests show SOMETHING.

23.   Women will not buy Pungent Cologne.

24.   They are moved by its fragrance.

23 THAT   24 EVEN THOUGH

I.   25.   We heard SOMETHING.

26.   Flying saucers had landed.

27.   We sent for the Welcome Wagon.

28.   It is sponsored by the Chamber of Commerce.

25 BECAUSE   26 THAT   28 WHICH

J.   29.   Mildred wanted to marry Horace.

30.   His mother (/) said SOMETHING.

31.   His mother loved her son dearly.

32.   She would have to tuck him in at night.

29 ALTHOUGH   31 WHO   32 THAT

EXERCISE 5.4.   Split Footnote Signal

MODEL

1.   SOMETHING was questionable judgment.

2.   Jim called the linebacker a chicken.

3.   The linebacker was surly.

4.   The linebacker was burly.

1–2 IT . . . FOR . . . TO

Writeout: It was questionable judgment for Jim to call the surly, burly linebacker a chicken.

A.   5.   Nurse Kathy thought SOMETHING strange.

6.   Her date howled at her window.

5–6 IT . . . THAT

B.   7.   SOMETHING seemed inevitable.
     8.   Throckmorton would make a fool of himself.

7–8 FOR . . . TO

C.   9.   SOMETHING seems reasonable.
    10.   You volunteer to wash your teacher's car.

9–10 IT . . . FOR . . . TO

D. 11.   SOMETHING was unclear.
    12.   The fraternity had something cooking.

11–12 IT . . . WHAT

E. 13.   SOMETHING doesn't matter.
    14.   You boycott the school's cafeteria.

13–14 IT . . . HOW OFTEN

F. 15.   SOMETHING comes as no surprise.
    16.   Scientists are investigating SOMETHING.
    17.   Kissing spreads germs.

15–16 IT . . . THAT   17 HOW

G. 18.   SOMETHING might be predicted.
    19.   Marriages will continue to occur.
    20.   The marriages are born of necessity.

18–19 IT . . . THAT   20 WHICH

H. 21.   SOMETHING is difficult to understand.
    22.   Today's fashions call for argyle socks.
    23.   The socks extend over the knee.

21–22 IT . . . WHY   23 THAT

I. 24.   SOMETHING would seem slightly presumptuous.
    25.   Howard (/) invites wedding guests.
    26.   Howard is not yet engaged.

24–25 IT . . . FOR . . . TO   26 WHO

J. 27.   SOMETHING was uncertain.
    28.   The weather (/) would worsen.
    29.   We watched it wistfully.

27–28 IT . . . WHETHER   29 WHICH

EXERCISE 5.5.   Word Form Footnote Signal

MODEL

    1.   The teachers ask students to write.
    2.   The writing is regular.
    3.   The writing is thoughtful.
    4.   The teachers claim to teach writing.

1 BY + ING   2–3 LY

Writeout: By asking students to write regularly and thoughtfully, the teachers claim to teach writing.

A.   5.   The Council declared itself incompetent.
     6.   The declaration was belated.
     7.   The Council restored public confidence.

5 BY + ING   6 LY

B.   8.   Richard did not want to face the dishes.
     9.   The dishes were piled high in the sink.

10. Richard stopped going back to his apartment.

8 ING   9 THAT

C. 11. SOMETHING is still difficult to understand.
    12. Hubert's gelatin was eaten.
    13. The eating was so insensitive.

11–12 IT . . . WHY   13 LY

D. 14. The defense rested its case.
    15. The defense insisted SOME-THING.
        16. The defendant had an honest face.

15 ING   16 THAT

E. 17. She attempted the impossible.
   18. She balanced on the high wire.
       19. Her balance was precarious.
       20. Her weight was supported by one toe.

17 ING   19 LY

F. 21. SOMETHING helps to explain SOMETHING.
    22. Snodgrass was absent.
        23. The absence was continual.
    24. He was fired.

22 THE FACT THAT   23 LY   24 WHY

G. 25. You grovel at our feet.
   26. You try to flatter us.
   27. You should consider bribery.
   28. The bribery is selective.

25 INSTEAD OF + ING   26 ING

H. 29. We assume SOMETHING.
       30. These figures are correct.
   31. Our company is now broke.
       32. This relieves us of worry.

29 ING   30 THAT   31 ING

I. 33. SOMETHING was clear.
       34. Manuel's attempt was doomed.
       35. The attempt was to train alligators.
   36. His friends (/) cheered him on.
       37. His friends did not want him to quit.

33–34 ALTHOUGH + IT . . . THAT   37 ING

J. 38. The committee argued for hours.
       39. The arguments were vociferous.
   40. The committee finally reversed itself.
       41. It decided to give itself a raise.
       42. The raise was enormous.

38 AFTER + ING   39 LY   41 ING

PART ONE
SINGLE-
PARAGRAPH EXERCISES

Each combining exercise that follows will result in a single paragraph. Your basic task is to combine sentences, check your writeouts for errors, study the "links" between sentences, and then write a paragraph that *connects* to the exercise. Starters for writing you do on your own are listed in the *Paragraph-Building Options* for each exercise.

Early exercises in this section involve "open" sentence combining. You'll see that each cluster of kernel sentences usually has several possible writeouts—and that clusters can sometimes be combined. Your job is to explore stylistic options by combining sentences into the most effective writeouts you can manage. You'll notice "signaled" combining being introduced later in this section. Refer to Units 4 and 5 if you need to review how the signals work. (Using a notecard to cover up footnote signals will force your brain to supply connecting words.)

After doing the combining and checking your writeouts for accuracy in spelling, punctuation, and basic usage, you should follow the instructions titled *Rereading Your Writeouts*. These instructions will show you how the paragraph is structured and teach you how sentences "hang together." Learning about intersentence "links" will do much to help the "connectedness" of sentences in your own writing. Do this rereading carefully.

To *apply* skills you've been learning, you then write one or more paragraphs that *connect* to the exercise. Quite often, "linking" sentences are provided to get you started. Your aim in developing one of these *Paragraph-Building Options* is to go *beyond* the exercise—to provide an example, pose another viewpoint, summarize a position, and so on. It's here that you not only exercise creativity and imagination but also compare your own writing with that of other students.

Let's say, for example, that an exercise asks you to write your own paragraph in response to a one-paragraph introduction. You'll probably begin by selecting a "linking" sentence from the *Paragraph-Building Options* or inventing one more to your liking. Then you'll brainstorm associations. From the words and phrases you're listing, natural connections will begin to occur. You'll group some thoughts and push others aside. Sentences will begin to follow, each developing a little more what you want to say. You'll then read back through your writing, tinkering here and adding there. The process is not an orderly one, and everyone works a little differently.

The final step is making sure that your own paragraph connects to the exercise paragraph. You read it aloud. Then you read it to someone else. When it works, it *feels* right.

TWO VOICES

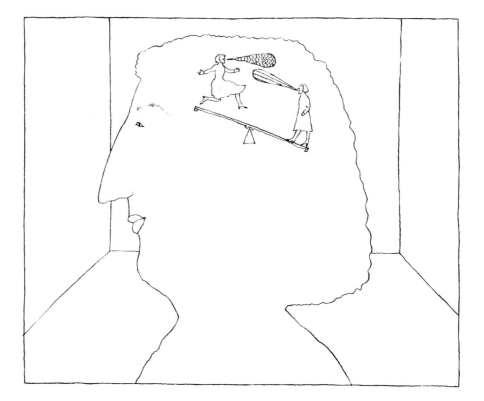

1. I have two voices.
2. The voices are inside me.

3. One voice is serious.
4. It is responsible.

5. The other voice is fun-loving.
6. It is carefree.

7. One voice is for study.
8. The other voice is for breaks.

9. One voice is for digging in.
10. The other voice is for dropping out.

11. One voice believes in self-discipline.

12. It believes in sacrifice for the future.

13. The other voice believes in self-expression.
14. It believes in "letting things happen."

15. The conflict is a real one.
16. The conflict is between these voices.

Rereading Your Writeouts: Notice how this paragraph works: A statement about one voice is balanced by a statement about the other voice. These contrasts unify the paragraph.

PARAGRAPH-BUILDING OPTIONS

The last sentence of the exercise—*The conflict between these voices is a real one*—helps provide a link to your writing.

Describe a specific, personal instance of conflict between "two voices" within you. Tell first what your serious, responsible voice says. Then say what your fun-loving, carefree voice argues in response. Here are some possible "starter sentences" that will link to the exercise.

1. *A vivid instance of such conflict occurred just recently for me.*
2. *My approach to _____ provides a good example of conflicting voices.*
3. *Consider, more specifically, the conflict between _____ and _____.*

FRISBEE AFTERNOON

1. Rob's motion is quick.
2. His motion is snakelike.

3. His flick sends the Frisbee into flight.
4. His flick is underhand.
5. His flick is sidearm.

6. It spins clockwise.
7. It rides a puddle of air.

8. It slices through sunlight.
9. It slices through shadows.
10. It glides across a clearing.
11. The clearing is grassy.

12. Then a breeze catches the disc.
13. The breeze makes it climb.
14. The breeze makes it dip.

15. The Frisbee hovers.
16. It follows the surface currents.

17. It whirls soundlessly.
18. It drops lower and lower.
19. It settles onto my index finger.
20. My finger is outstretched.

Rereading Your Writeouts: Notice that the pronoun *it* (Clusters 6–7, 8–11, 17–20) refers to *Frisbee* (Clusters 3–5, 15–16). Intersentence "links" between these words help unify the paragraph.

PARAGRAPH-BUILDING OPTIONS

1. Describe, as if in slow motion, your return toss: (1) what the Frisbee looks and feels like; (2) how you hold it and throw it; (3) the angle and appearance of the Frisbee in flight; (4) Rob's tumbling attempted catch. A possible linking sentence might be this one: *To make a running target, Rob takes off.*

2. Explain, *to someone who has never seen or thrown a Frisbee*, the following items: (1) what a Frisbee is; (2) what it looks like or might be compared to; (3) how it is usually thrown and caught; (4) why it is so popular. A possible linking sentence might be this one: *You may be wondering what a Frisbee is.*

PANIC

1. My throat was tight.
2. My stomach was clenched.

3. Adrenalin surged through my veins.
4. My muscles bunched into knots.

5. The panic was like a wave.
6. I felt the panic.
7. The wave was enormous.
8. The wave was crushing.

9. It lifted me.
10. It tumbled me head over heels.

11. My heart was pounding.
12. The pounding was loud in my ears.

13. I was intent on only one thing.
14. That thing was survival.

Rereading Your Writeouts: Notice how this paragraph narrows down to a topic sentence (Cluster 13–14).

PARAGRAPH-BUILDING OPTIONS

1. Describe an experience in which you felt raw panic. Open your story with a sentence that sets the scene for your reader. Then tell what happened. Make sure that the *last sentence* of your personal writing links with the *first sentence* of the exercise.

2. The word *survival* is a key link at the end of the exercise. Focus on this word in follow-up writing. Explain what your will to survive caused you to do. A linking sentence might go like this: *I acted quickly upon my survival plan.*

EMBARRASSMENT IN SCHOOL

1. Grade school is not always a pleasant place.
2. It is not always a happy place.

3. Its embarrassments are many.
4. Its embarrassments are varied.

5. You lose your notebook.
6. You sit on chewing gum.
7. You get sick after lunch.

8. You're denied your recess.
9. You're caught passing love notes.
10. You're shoved into the wrong rest room.

11. Some events are trivial.
12. Some events are traumatic.

13. But all make their impressions.

14. The impressions are indelible.
15. The impressions may be for better.
16. The impressions may be for worse.

17. Only one thing can be said about embarrassments.
18. The thing is good.
19. The embarrassments are in grade school.

20. They eventually fade away.
21. They can be objectively discussed.

Rereading Your Writeouts: Notice the "hourglass" shape of this paragraph. It begins with generalizations, narrows down to specific examples, and then becomes general again.

PARAGRAPH-BUILDING OPTIONS

The last sentence of the exercise—*They [the embarrassments] eventually fade away and can be objectively discussed*—helps provide a link to your writing.

Use the exercise to introduce a description of an embarrassing moment in grade school. Be specific about the time, place, and situation to help the reader understand how you felt.

Here are some possible "starters" that will link to the exercise:

1. *I remember, for example, an incident in the _____ grade.*
2. *Picture, for example, a scene in the _____ grade.*
3. *That day in the _____ grade, nothing went right for me.*

BEHIND THE MASK

1. I am like most people.
2. I wear a "mask."
3. The wearing is most of the time.

4. This "mask" is invisible.
5. It is still very real.

6. It shields my identity.
7. The identity is true.
8. The shield is from the world.

9. The "mask" shows appearances.
10. It does not show reality.

11. There is a difference.
12. The difference is between how things look.
13. The difference is between how things are.

14. I will briefly take off my "mask."
15. I will give an example.
16. The example is to clarify this point.

Rereading Your Writeouts: Notice that the word *mask* links five of the six clusters. Find another, less obvious link between Clusters 6–8, 9–10, and 11–13.

PARAGRAPH-BUILDING OPTIONS

The last sentence of the exercise—*I will briefly take off my "mask" and give an example to clarify this point*—helps provide a link to your writing.

Explain an *appearance* that you give to others as part of the "image" you project. Support the claims you make about your appearance by citing what others have said (or written) about you. Then explain how things *really* are behind the "mask" you wear. Here are some possible linking sentences on the lighter side.

1. *It takes considerable intelligence to project an image of stupidity.*
2. *Some people contend that I am only interested in sex.*
3. *At first glance, I appear to be a genetic mistake.*

INSTANT REPLAY

1. The quarterback stands behind the center.
2. He is the team's commander.
3. He glances down the line.

4. He barks out the signals.
5. He exhales puffs of breath.
6. The breath is foggy.

7. Then he is dropping back.
8. He is faking a hand-off.
9. The hand-off is to the fullback.

10. His body wheels to one side.
11. His body is half crouched.
12. His body is still retreating.

13. He cradles the ball between his palms.
14. He looks downfield.
15. He hunts for receivers.

16. The defense is coming hard.
17. He cocks his arm.
18. He pumps once.

19. Then the ball is lofting downfield.
20. The ball is like a bird unleashed.

Rereading Your Writeouts: Notice the tight sequence of action and the repetition of *he/his* pronouns. These features unify the paragraph.

PARAGRAPH-BUILDING OPTIONS

1. Describe the receiver's catch—or attempted catch—as it might be shown on "instant replay." Focus on a tight sequence of action and description. A possible linking sentence might be this one: *Meanwhile, the receiver is streaking downfield.*

2. Consider the possibility that "instant replays" are more real, for many people, than the actual events. Is a replay of a game's "highlights" the same thing as the game? If so, why watch the real game? A possible linking sentence might be this one: *Instant replays, endlessly repeated, are a familiar part of television.*

HEADING FOR DISASTER

1. I now look back.
2. I know something.
3. I should have known better.

4. I had built expectations.
5. The expectations were unreasonable.

6. My hopes soared high.
7. The height was dangerous.

8. My illusions swept me along.
9. The illusions were dreamlike.

10. I was heading for disaster.
11. I ignored common sense.

12. My story follows.
13. The story is sad.
14. The story is true.

Rereading Your Writeouts: Notice how the last cluster "announces" writing to follow, thereby making an interparagraph link.

PARAGRAPH-BUILDING OPTIONS

Use the exercise as an introduction for writing about a disaster—large or small, public or private—that you caused for yourself. As your story unfolds, make clear the time, place, and situation. You might open either with a scene-setting sentence or try one of these:

1. *Beating the odds had always intrigued me.*
2. *Unfortunately, I had a secret ambition.*
3. *It all began with a dare.*

A FAVORITE TEACHER

1. A teacher can make a difference.
2. The teacher cares about students.
3. I know.
4. I've had such an instructor.

5. This teacher took time to explain.
6. This teacher took time to clarify.
7. This teacher took time to praise.
8. This teacher took time to encourage.

9. He/she always showed an interest.
10. He/she was unlike some others.
11. The interest was genuine.
12. The interest was in my learning.

13. This teacher may not have been perfect.
14. He/she had much to offer me.

Rereading Your Writeouts: Notice the inter-sentence links: *such* (Cluster 3–4); *this* (Cluster 5–8); *he/she* (Cluster 9–12); *this* (Cluster 13–14). Each link refers back to the topic sentence (Cluster 1–2) and helps the paragraph "hang together."

PARAGRAPH-BUILDING OPTIONS

The last sentence of the exercise—*This teacher may not have been perfect, but he/she had much to offer me*—helps provide a link to your writing.

1. Create a character description of your favorite teacher, focusing on the person's appearance and personality traits. Identify the teacher's contribution to your education. A linking sentence might go like this: *Mr. Johnson, a senior English teacher, first of all offered me his love for words.*

2. Re-create an incident that will prove to your reader that your favorite teacher was indeed a good one. This scene should *show* your teacher in action. A linking sentence might go like this: *An incident from early in the year illustrates Mr. Johnson's approach to teaching.*

TRAIL'S END

1. It was late afternoon.
2. We decided to stop.
3. We stopped in a meadow.
4. The meadow overlooked the valley.

5. We had hiked for hours.
6. We had made our way up trails.
7. The trails were rocky.

8. The country around us was steep.
9. The country around us was rugged.
10. The sky was blue.
11. The blue was flawless.

12. Boulders were strewn over the landscape.

13. The boulders were granite.
14. The landscape was gently rolling.

15. The sunlight was warm.
16. The sunlight was golden.
17. The sunlight was the color of honey.

18. A wind moved through the aspens.
19. The wind was meandering.
20. The aspens were white-barked.
21. It shimmered their leaves.

22. Their shadows were long.
23. Their shadows were silent.
24. Their shadows were an echo for shapes.
25. The shapes were slender.

Rereading Your Writeouts: Notice that this paragraph moves from general, explanatory sentences (Clusters 1–4, 5–7) to specific, descriptive ones.

PARAGRAPH-BUILDING OPTIONS

1. Describe the sensation of sitting around a campfire or sleeping under the stars. Model your paragraph on the general-to-specific movement of the exercise. To link your writing to the exercise, try a linking sentence like this: *Later that evening, we slept under an open, cloudless sky.*

2. Describe what happens in setting up camp, trying to light a fire, and fixing supper. Develop a *contrast* between the postcard setting and things going wrong. To link your writing to the exercise, try a linking sentence like this: *Our problems started as the sun sank slowly over the western horizon.*

SPEAKING OUT

1. I am a person.
2. The person is generally good-natured.
3. The person is generally agreeable.

4. My approach is simple.
5. I strive to get along with others.

6. I see no point in hassle.
7. The hassle is needless.

8. I sometimes speak my mind.
9. I don't try to antagonize others.
10. The antagonism would be deliberate.

11. But I also see no point in hiding feelings.
12. I see no point in sidestepping conflicts.

13. I am angry.
14. I make my feelings known.

15. I have a complaint.
16. I verbalize it.

17. Paragraphs provide a case in point.
18. The paragraphs follow.
19. The case in point is clear.

Rereading Your Writeouts: Notice that the main idea—*I see no point in hiding feelings or in sidestepping conflicts*—appears in the *middle* of the paragraph.

PARAGRAPH-BUILDING OPTIONS

The last sentence of the exercise—*Paragraphs that follow provide a clear case in point*—helps provide a link to your writing.

1. Describe a past incident in which you vented your anger to someone else. After setting up the situation, tell what the issue was and how you handled it. A linking sentence might begin: *The problem started with. . . .*

2. Make an articulate complaint about some particular person, event, condition, or thing that is presently irritating

you. First, describe the problem; then tell how you feel about it. A linking sentence might begin: *My present problem relates to. . . .*

A PERSONAL VICTORY

1. There are those days.
2. The days are rare.
3. The days are remembered.
4. The days seem blessed by Providence.

5. The Fates smile upon you.
6. Nothing can go wrong.

7. You lead a life.
8. The life is charmed.

9. You are relaxed.
10. You are confident.
11. You are fully yourself.

12. You feel on top of things.
13. You feel in harmony with the universe.

14. You know something.
15. You are a winner.
16. You therefore behave like one.

17. Such are the days for victories.
18. Such are the days for triumphs.

19. You are programmed to succeed.
20. The programming is psychological.
21. You do so with style.
22. You do so with grace.

Rereading Your Writeouts: Notice how *parallel sentences* (Clusters 7–8, 9–11, 12–13, 14–16, 19–22) provide support for generalizations in the paragraph.

PARAGRAPH-BUILDING OPTIONS

The last sentence of the exercise—*You are psychologically programmed to succeed, and you do so with style and grace*—helps provide a link to your writing.

Use this paragraph to introduce a victory that means something to you. This triumph might be a key tackle you made, an argument you won, a decision you reached, a test you passed, an objective you achieved—or anything else important. Consider one of the following starters as a link to the exercise:

1. *I well remember my day of personal victory.*

2. *Picture, for a moment, the highlight of my life.*

3. *According to Emily Dickinson, "success is counted sweetest by those who ne'er succeed."*

HEROES AND HEROINES

1. Heroes embody a culture's values.
2. Heroines embody a culture's values.
3. Their behavior defines what is good.
4. Their behavior defines what is possible.

5.   They are recognizably human.
6.   They capture our imaginations.
7.   They become "larger than life."

8.   Their exploits are our fantasies.
9.   Their exploits are our dreams.

10.   Their minds are keener.
11.   Their muscles are stronger.

12.   Their wits are shrewder.
13.   Their willpower is deeper.

14.   They accomplish feats.
15.   The feats are impossible.
16.   They become models for emulation.

17.   Their style provides inspiration.
18.   Their grace provides inspiration.

19.   Their strength helps us persevere.
20.   Their courage helps us persevere.

Rereading Your Writeouts: Notice that Cluster 5–7 requires a *but* or *although* connector.

What connectors are logically required by Cluster 14–16?

PARAGRAPH-BUILDING OPTIONS

1.   Develop an example of a twentieth-century hero or heroine. This individual may be a well-known personality (sports figure, political leader, astronaut, etc.) or a mythical figure (character from television or literature). To link your writing to the exercise, try this sentence: *Consider, for example, a modern hero/heroine such as* —————.

2.   Argue persuasively that the twentieth century lacks heroes and heroines. Explain why well-known personalities or characters from television and literature do not serve as heroic models. To link your writing to the exercise, try this sentence: *Heroes and heroines are conspicuously absent from today's society.*

RUNNERS

1. They head out across the park.
2. They run with strides.
3. The strides are long.
4. The strides are even.

5. The pair moves in syncopation.
6. The pair is a man and a woman.
7. The syncopation is perfect.

8. Running is part of their routine.
9. The routine is protected.

10. They glide through sunlight.
11. They glide through shadows.
12. Their rhythms are always the same.

13. Yet their run is always different.
14. It changes with the seasons.
15. It changes with the day's mood.

16. Words are unnecessary.
17. They jog down a path.
18. The path is familiar.
19. They share a silence.
20. The silence is comfortable.

21. It is running that counts.
22. It is not talking that counts.

23. They are like other runners.
24. The runners number 25 million.
25. They enjoy many benefits.
26. The benefits are physiological.

27. But the payoffs are just as important.
28. The payoffs are psychological.

Rereading Your Writeouts: Notice that the word *they* (Clusters 1–4, 10–12, 16–20, 23–26) refers to *the pair, a man and a woman* (Cluster 5–7). This repetition helps link sentences in the paragraph.

PARAGRAPH-BUILDING OPTIONS

The last sentence of the exercise—*But the psychological payoffs [of running] are just as important [as the physiological benefits]*—helps provide a link to your writing.

1. If you're a runner, make a two-column list of running's positive effects—one titled *body*, the other *mind*. (If you're not a runner, interview someone who is and make the same two lists.) Use this information to write a paragraph that focuses first on the physiological (body) benefits, then on the psychological (mind) benefits. To link your writing to the exercise paragraph, you might use a transition sentence such as the following: *Let's consider both kinds of benefits as a runner expresses them.*

2. Read about running in magazines such as *Runner's World* or in books such as *The Complete Book of Running* by James F. Fixx (Random House, 1977) or *Running and Being* by George Sheehan (Warner Books, 1978). Focus exclusively on the *psychological benefits* of the sport. Use the information for a follow-up paragraph, making sure to use quotation marks for quoted information. Link your writing to the preceding paragraph with a transition sentence such as this one: *Let's examine the mental benefits of running in some detail.*

ROOT FOR JACKSON

1. The roots were very unusual.
2. The roots were gnarled.
3. Jackson had never seen anything like them.

4. They were packed in a box.
5. The box was wooden.
6. The box was imprinted with names.
7. The names were foreign.

8. SOMETHING was odd.
   9. They should be left in the alley.

8–9 IT . . . THAT

10. Jackson reached down.
11. Jackson touched one of them.
   12. He then picked it up.

10 ING

13. It was much heavier than he expected.
14. It was much softer than he expected.

15. It felt a little like flesh.
   16. The flesh was dead.

15 IN FACT

17. He smoothed its bumps with his thumb.
18. He smoothed its ridges with his thumb.
19. He then put it back.
20. He felt vaguely uneasy.

21. Its odor was strange.
22. Its odor was sweet.
23. Its odor was unfamiliar to him.

24. He wondered SOMETHING.
   25. The roots had been left in the alley.
      26. The alley was deserted.

25 WHY

27. His mouth felt dry.
28. He reached into the box again.
29. He picked up another one.
30. The one was smaller.

31. It too was pulpy.
32. It had the same smell.
33. The smell was pungent.

   34. He used a handkerchief.
35. He wrapped up the root.
   36. He put it in his windbreaker.

34 ING

37. He glanced over his shoulder.
   38. He did this.
      39. He suddenly had a feeling.
         40. The feeling was strong.
         41. The feeling was unmistakable.
         42. He was being watched.

38 AS   **39 BECAUSE**   **42 (THAT)**

Rereading Your Writeouts: Count the number of times that the words *it* (or *its*), *they*, *them*, and *one* are used to link sentences into a cohesive paragraph.

PARAGRAPH-BUILDING OPTIONS

The last sentence of the exercise—*He glanced over his shoulder as he did this because he suddenly had the strong, unmistakable feeling he was being watched*—helps provide an ominous link to your writing.

1. Tell the story of Jackson and his strange root. As you develop this narrative, make sure to *unfold* the answers to two questions: (1) Who was watching Jackson? (2) What was the purpose of the observation? A possible linking sentence might go like this: *When he got home and put the root in his bedroom, Jackson was feeling strangely detached from his body's functioning.*

2. Tell the story of the people who are watching Jackson from a distance. Describe their monitoring operation and gradually explain why they are conducting an experiment at Jackson's expense.

A possible linking sentence might begin in this way: *Across the street, a computerized replay of Jackson in the alley was being analyzed by technicians and transmitted to a distant control center.*

A REMEMBERED CONVERSATION

1. Sticks can break your bones.
2. Stones can break your bones.
3. Words can never hurt you.
4. This is according to a nursery rhyme.

5. This rhyme is stupid.
6. This rhyme is untrue.

7. It runs counter to most experience.
8. The experience is human.
9. The experience includes mine in particular.

10. I have learned something.
11. Words can be pleasurable.
12. Words can be painful.
13. Words can be helpful.
14. Words can be harmful.

15. Words are of course invisible.
16. The words are spoken.
17. Their effect lingers in memory.

18. Conversations can therefore be replayed.

19. The conversations are significant.
20. The conversations are from the past.

Rereading Your Writeouts: Notice that this paragraph works through a series of contrasts. Find the "opposites" that occur both within as well as between sentences.

PARAGRAPH-BUILDING OPTIONS

Use this exercise to introduce a "playback" of an important conversation in your life. Condense the conversation to its important facts and report their effects upon you. To create a link with the last sentences of the exercise, you might open as follows:

1. *I often replay one particularly significant conversation.*
2. *Consider, for example, this remembered conversation.*
3. *The effects of the following conversation are still being felt.*

ROAD TEST

1. She strapped herself into a sports car.
2. The car was low.
3. The car was open.

4. Starter gears whirred for a moment.
5. The exhaust belched a reply.
6. The exhaust was throaty.

7.   The reply was sharp.

8.   She checked the gauges.
9.   She shifted into low.
10. She wheeled out from under the trees.

11. The sun glistened on the car's paint.
12. The sun was red in the western sky.
13. The sun was swollen in the western sky.
14. The paint was highly waxed.
15. The paint was silver.

16. She pressed on the gas.
17. She accelerated onto the road.
18. The road was open.
19. Her car's whine ripped the desert quiet.
20. The whine was high-speed.

21. Heat waves wiggled on the horizon.
22. The horizon was sagebrush.
23. The horizon was asphalt.
24. The asphalt was black.

25. Fence posts flicked by.
26. They then diminished in the vibration.
27. The vibration was the rear-view mirror.

28. A smile was on her lips.
29. The smile was tense.
30. The smile was confident.
31. She approached a fork in the road.
32. The fork was dangerous.

33. She geared down to third.
34. The RPM needle leaped to 5200.

35. The car went into a slide.
36. The slide was controlled.
37. The car drifted as if on parallel tracks.
38. The car momentarily crossed the center line.

Rereading Your Writeouts: Notice the unity of this paragraph: All descriptions and narrations of action pertain to a single event. The repetition of pronouns (*she/her*) helps link the sentences.

PARAGRAPH-BUILDING OPTIONS

1. Write a paragraph to *precede* the one you just combined. Show *why* the woman driver puts the car through a high-speed road test. Ask yourself: What leads up to her getting in the car? Link the *conclusion* of your paragraph to the *opening* of the exercise.

2. What do you picture happening next as the woman puts the car into a four-wheel drift at high speed? Make this description the focus of your writing. Link your *opening sentence* to the *conclusion* of the exercise.

LATE EVENING IMAGES

Hold fast to dreams.   —*Langston Hughes*

1.   The time is evening.
    2.   The evening is late.
    3.   The world is going to sleep.

3   WITH

⌐4.   My room is folded in shadows.
BUT   5.   The shadows are hushed.
└6.   I am wide awake.
    7.   I am dreaming.

8.   Sounds are distant.
9.   Sounds are muted.

10. I listen to rain.
11. The rain is on the windows.
12. I glance at a clock.
13. The clock is softly ticking.
14. The clock is near my bedside.

┌ 15. The day has been busy.
│   16. The day has been filled with the
│   hustle.
BUT
│   17. The hustle is school routine.
└ 18. These moments are mine.
      19. They are to be savored.
      20. They are to be enjoyed.

21. This is like the changing of sea-
    sons.
22. This is an "in-between" time.
    23. Awareness is heightened.
    24. The awareness is personal.

23 WHEN

25. It gives me images.
26. The images are various.
27. The images are the future.
28. I can sort through the images.

29. These images provide me with direction.
    30. The images are mental.
    31. The direction is for my life.

29 IN TURN

    32. They are like signposts.
33. They point the way.
    34. The way is from present time.
    35. The way is toward my tomorrows.

Rereading Your Writeouts: Study how this paragraph moves from specific to general—

from description to explanation. Then trace the intersentence links created by *this* (Cluster 21–24), *it* (Cluster 25–28), *these images* (Cluster 29–31), and *they* (Cluster 32–35). Find the reference point for each word or phrase.

PARAGRAPH-BUILDING OPTIONS

The last sentence of the exercise—*Like signposts, they* [*images*] *point the way from present time toward my tomorrows*—helps provide a link to your writing.

1. Describe a *single* image—a vivid dream —that you have for your personal future. Be specific rather than general. Picture yourself in a situation. As details emerge in your imagination, put them down; these will stimulate other clarifying words. To open your paragraph, you might begin: *One image that I have for my future is a particularly vivid one.*

2. Make a "laundry list" of future images. (Backpacking across Europe does not necessarily conflict with setting up your own small business; it simply means that your personality has more than a single dimension.) You won't go into detail on these images but will simply group them into related categories. To introduce this paragraph, you might possibly begin like this: *Many images compete for my attention as I dream about the future.*

GOOD NEWS, BAD NEWS

1. Imagine being a passenger.
2. The passenger is on an aircraft.
3. The aircraft is commercial.

4. You have just finished your supper.
5. The supper was not-so-super.

6. The meat was water buffalo.
7. The meat was warmed by microwave.

8. The peas were pellets.
9. The pellets were cold.
10. The pellets were stamped from rubber.
11. The rubber was green.

12. The potatoes were a mixture.
13. The potatoes were mashed.
14. The mixture looked suspicious.

15. They tasted like glue.
16. The glue was white.
17. The glue was mixed with styrofoam.
18. The styrofoam was crushed.

19. The coffee smells like jet fuel.
20. The steward has just spilled it on you.

21. You wonder about its origin.
22. You watch it.
23. It begins to eat holes in your clothing.
24. Its eating is slow.

25. You are settling down.
26. You are preparing to enjoy the rest of your flight.
27. Your attention is roused by the co-pilot's voice.
28. The voice is raspy.

29. She thanks you for flying.
30. The flight is on Wing-and-a-Prayer Airlines.

31. She hopes something.
32. Your indigestion is bearable.

33. She comments on the fog.
34. The fog is heavy.
35. The fog is streaming by the windows.
36. The windows are plexiglass.

37. A pause follows.
38. The pause is hushed.
39. The pause is expectant.

40. You then notice something.
41. A child has dumped his potatoes.
42. The child is sitting next to you.
43. The potatoes have gone into your lap.

44. The child begins to whine.
45. The child begins to flick peas at you.

46. The co-pilot reports something.
47. She has some good news.
48. She has some bad news.

49. First comes the bad news.
50. This is as usual.
51. The aircraft is lost.

52. Then comes the good news.
53. The aircraft is making time.
54. The time is terrifically fast.

Rereading Your Writeouts: Notice that the specific details in Clusters 6–7, 8–11, 12–14, 15–18, 19–20, and 21–24 provide a "definition" of a "not-so-super supper" (Cluster 4–5).

PARAGRAPH-BUILDING OPTIONS

1. Link a "No News Is Good News" story to the exercise you have just completed.

In other words, extend the narrative so that it ends with a "twist." A possible linking sentence might go like this: *You settle back in your seat, contemplating the news.*

2. Tell a "Good News, Bad News" story of your own, making sure to set the scene as this exercise does. This narrative can be either real or fictional. Work for "connectedness"—a logical building—of your sentences and paragraphs.

PATHS NOT TAKEN

1. Life is a series of crossroads.
2. The crossroads involve decisions.
3. The decisions are about the future.

4. Some choices are inconsequential.
5. Others have effects.
6. The effects are far-reaching.

7. These decisions determine others.
8. The decisions are important.

9. Time does not flow backward.
10. Such choices are often irreversible.

11. One path leads to another.
12. The individual must accept the consequences.
13. The consequences are of past decisions.

14. Something happens as a consequence.
15. Paths not taken must go unexplored.

16. And yet a person *wonders* about paths.
17. The paths were alternatives.
18. The paths were in past decisions.

Rereading Your Writeouts: Notice how the paragraph develops an analogy between *crossroads* (or *paths*) and *decisions* (or *choices*).

PARAGRAPH-BUILDING OPTIONS

The last sentence of the exercise—*And yet a person wonders about alternative paths in past decisions*—helps provide a link to your writing.

Describe a single key decision in your life and speculate on what things would be like if you had chosen another path. To link your writing to the exercise, you might try a "starter" like one of these:

1. *For me, an important crossroads occurred when. . . .*
2. *I have often wondered, for example, about. . . .*
3. *In looking back it seems clear that. . . .*

REPLACING A BUTTON

1. Double a length of thread.
2. Pass it through the needle eye.
3. The passing should be loop first.

⌐4. Pull the loop of thread.
AND   5. Make all four strands the same.
└6. Knot the strands.

7. Place the button on the garment.
8. Bring the needle from underneath the fabric.
9. Bring it through one of the holes.
10. The holes are in the button.

11. Leave a space (/) between the button and the garment.
    12. The space is small.
    13. The space is called a "thread shank."

14. This reduces rubbing.
15. The rubbing is between the two.
16. It helps the thread last longer.

    17. The buttons are the two-hole kind.
18. Bring the needle up through one hole.
    19. Push it down through the second.

17 IF

    20. The button is the four-hole variety.
21. Move across the center of the button.
    22. Move down the opposite hole.

20 IF

23. Follow this pattern.
24. The pattern is for several loops.
25. Then repeat the pattern.
26. The repetition is with the other holes.

27. The strands will cross the center.
28. The strands are thread.
29. The button has a center.
30. They will make an "X."

    31. Several loops have been made.
32. Push the needle down through the button.
    33. Don't go into the fabric.

31 AFTER

34. Wrap the thread around the shank.
    35. The wrapping should be several times.

36. Then go into the fabric.

34 INSTEAD

37. Pull the thread tight.
38. Push the needle under the thread loops.
39. Do this two times.
40. Cut the thread.

41. This button is very well secured.
    42. It is in the wrong place.

42 ESPECIALLY IF

    43. A job is well done.
44. Take the afternoon off.

43 WITH

Rereading Your Writeouts: Notice that sentences beginning with verbs are substeps of a larger process. A consecutive time order links these steps into a paragraph.

PARAGRAPH-BUILDING OPTIONS

Use the preceding exercise as a model for writing focused on a single process. (Do not use the pronoun *you* in this piece of writing.) Make sure the steps are in chronological order so that they link together to make a cohesive paragraph. Here are some possible topics for process writing:

1. Changing an oil filter.
2. Making a home-made pizza.
3. Turning correctly on alpine or cross-country skis.
4. Registering for a new semester's classes.
5. Getting a teacher to change a low grade.
6. Creating a personal budget.
7. Changing messy diapers.
8. Grafting the branch of a fruit tree.
9. Looking good on the disco floor.
10. Writing a paragraph on "process writing."

BUS STATION

1. The terminal is almost deserted.
2. The terminal is a way station.
3. The way station is echoing.
4. The way station is somber.

5. A janitor moves through the gloom.
6. The janitor is shuffling.
7. The janitor has a pushbroom in hand.
8. A typewriter clicks.
9. The typewriter is muffled.
10. The typewriter is behind scarred doors.

11. A young man watches.
12. The wall clock's hand advances.
13. The advancing is minute by minute.
14. The advancing is click by click.

15. He sits alone on a bench.
16. The bench is oak.
17. The bench is long.
18. His arms are crossed.
19. A cap is pulled low over his eyes.

20. A backpack rests beneath his legs.
21. A bedroll rests beneath his legs.
22. His legs are outstretched.

23. He is dressed in jeans.
24. The jeans are new.
25. The jeans are stiff.
26. He is dressed in a jacket.
27. The jacket is denim.
28. The jacket has not yet been washed.

29. His glance flicks to the schedule board.
30. The flicking is once again.

31. He eyes the departure time.
32. The time is for his bus.

33. And then he feels a touch.
34. The touch is soft.
35. The touch is feminine.
36. The touch is on his shoulder.

Rereading Your Writeouts: Study how this paragraph moves from a *general* opening (the setting) to *specific details* that describe the young man. Imagine a camera lens shifting its focus from "long shots" to "close-ups."

PARAGRAPH-BUILDING OPTIONS

The last sentence of the exercise—*And then he feels a soft feminine touch on his shoulder*—helps provide a link to your writing.

Develop a paragraph describing the physical appearance of the person who has unexpectedly entered the bus station scene. Then, in *no more than* ten lines of dialogue, answer these questions that your reader will have: (1) Is this someone the young man knows? (2) Why the touch? (3) What is going to happen? Here are some possible linking sentences to introduce your description:

1. *The (young woman's/old woman's) face is a familiar one.*
2. *The stranger is (smiling/frowning) at him.*
3. *Her appearance is (attractive/unattractive).*

WRITING ABOUT TALK

1. Talk is generally an easy matter.
2. The talk is informal.
3. The talk is about a topic.
4. The topic is familiar.

5. The message is what counts.
6. Words take care of themselves.

7. Attention is usually unnecessary.
8. The attention is conscious.
9. The attention is to word order.

10. There is a message.
11. The message needs to be communicated.
12. Words come together naturally.
13. Words come together almost spontaneously.

14. They form phrases.
15. They form sentences.
16. These in turn link together.
17. These create a web of meaning.

18. The person revises in process.
19. The person is talking "off the cuff."

20. There may be many repetitions.
21. There may be many self-interruptions.
22. There may be many afterthoughts.
23. There may be many contradictions.

24. Content is foremost in the speaker's mind.
25. Form is not foremost in the speaker's mind.

Rereading Your Writeouts: Notice that Clusters 5–6 and 10–13 can take *causal connectors* such as *because, since, therefore,* and *consequently.* Double-check your punctuation when using these connectors.

PARAGRAPH-BUILDING OPTIONS

1. Develop an example for the exercise by tape-recording and transcribing a piece of spontaneous, sustained talk. (Your example should contain *at least* six continuous—i.e., uninterrupted—sentences.) Your linking sentence will probably read like this: *Unfortunately, transcribed talk usually makes for poor writing.*

2. Contrast the act of writing about a familiar topic with the act of talking discussed in the exercise. Your linking sentence is probably self-evident: *Writing about a familiar topic is generally more difficult than talking about it.* Explain why this is so.

WRITER-TO-BE

1. He imagined himself living in a cabin.
2. The cabin was small.
3. The cabin was in the wilderness.
4. The cabin was high in the mountains.

5. Something would happen each morning.

6. He would wake up.

7. He would stare at ceiling beams.
8. The ceiling beams were rough.
9. He would stare at the fireplace stone.
10. The stone had been hauled from the creek bed.

11. It would be cool.

12. It would be shadowed.
13. He would dress slowly.
14. He would put on the coffee.
15. He would lace his boots.

     16. Something would happen with the bluejay's cry.

17. His brain would be working.
     18. It would spin out images.

19. Then he would sit down at a table.
     20. The table was oak.

AND

     21. The table was scarred.
22. The words would be there.

23. He would follow his instincts.
24. He would trust his imagination.
25. His imagination would make him a living.

     26. Something would happen in the afternoons.

27. There would be fishing in places.
     28. The air was green.

AND   29. The air was dark.
     30. Light webbed the trees.

28 WHERE   30 (WHERE)

31. His line would flick across pools.
     32. The flicking was like a whisper.
     33. The pools were still.
     34. The fly would be drifting with the current.

35. Life would be harmony.
36. The harmony would be pure.
37. The harmony would be simple.
38. It would be a dream made real.

Rereading Your Writeouts: Trace the three-part development of this paragraph: *waking up, going to work, taking a break.* Notice that each "section" is introduced with a similar kind of sentence.

PARAGRAPH-BUILDING OPTIONS

1. Describe the "underside" of the writer's dream: mosquitoes, leaky roof, hauling water from the creek, and rejection slips. In your follow-up paragraph, maintain the same verb tense as the exercise—the use of *would*. To link your writing to the exercise, try an opener like this: *What he failed to imagine was the darker side of the dream.*

2. Contrast the writer's dream with his present reality as a student who is trying to learn the art and craft of writing well. Describe the surroundings—your present *real* surroundings—as accurately as you can. Your opening sentence, a link with the exercise, might say this: *Now, however, he was simply trying to survive a writing course.*

ELIZABETH

1. Elizabeth's appearance was elegant.
2. Elizabeth's appearance was reserved.

3. She was a woman.
4. The woman was black.
5. The woman was tall.
6. Her manner was always poised.
7. Her manner was always self-assured.
8. Her self-assurance was quiet.

9. Her features were dominated by her eyes.
10. The features were facial.
11. The features had no trace of edge.
12. The eyes were almond-shaped.
13. The eyes were intelligent.

14. She wore her hair in a style.
15. The style was natural.
16. The style was closely cut.
17. The style showed accents of gold.
18. The accents were glinting.
19. The accents were at her ears.

20. Her cheekbones were high.
21. Her nose was proud.

22. She carried herself with grace.
23. The grace was feline.
24. The grace was a kind of authority.
25. The authority was feminine.

26. She moved.
27. People watched.

28. She spoke.
29. People listened.

30. Her words were always clear.
31. Her words were always direct.
32. Her words were never terse.
33. Her words were never unfeeling.

Rereading Your Writeouts: Notice that repeated pronouns (*she/her*) link sentences into a cohesive paragraph.

PARAGRAPH-BUILDING OPTIONS

1. Link a paragraph of *action* to the description in the exercise. Tell what Elizabeth did with her "feminine authority." Record her "clear and direct" words in your narrative.

2. Create a character description of a real person modeled upon sentences in "Elizabeth." You may find that seeing someone *clearly*—and capturing his/her essence—is a little like meditating. Just when you think you've got it, you don't.

JESS

1. Jess was a man.
2. The man was gangling.
3. The man was slump-shouldered.
4. The man had hands.
5. The hands were gnarled.
6. The hands were arthritic.

7. His face was broad.
8. His face was angular.
9. His face was almost chiseled.

10. Eyes were set beneath eyebrows.
11. His eyes were steel-gray.
12. His eyebrows were heavy.

13. A scar crossed his left temple.
14. The scar was whitish.
15. The scar was like a wrinkle.
16. The wrinkle was thin.

17. His hair was now thin.
18. His hair was now wispy.
19. His hair had once been thick.
20. His hair had once been full of color.
21. The color was reddish blond.

22. It was parted in the middle.
23. It was combed straight back.

24. Years showed on his face.
25. The years were of work.
26. The work was in railroad yards.
27. His face was lined.

28. Now he endured his pain.
29. The endurance was with courage.
30. The courage was old-fashioned.
31. The endurance was with no bitterness.

32. His mouth seemed always on the edge of smiling.
33. His mouth was tight-lipped.
34. His mouth was soft-spoken.

Rereading Your Writeouts: Notice how the description moves from general (Cluster 1–6) to specifics (Clusters 7–9, 10–12, 13–16, 17–21, 22–23, 24–27)—all statements concentrating on Jess's head.

PARAGRAPH-BUILDING OPTIONS

1. Link a paragraph of explanation to the description in the exercise. Tell about the pain that Jess endured "with old-fashioned courage and no bitterness." Explain, too, why his mouth "seemed always on the edge of smiling."

2. Create a character description of a real person modeled upon sentences in "Jess." You may find that although a picture is worth a thousand words, no picture can *say* what words can. Words give *meaning* to appearances.

BURGER AND FRIES

1. Lunch arrived in a basket.
2. The basket was yellow.
3. The basket was plastic.
4. The basket was lined with wax paper.

5. The hamburger (/) was sandwiched between slices of toast. _____

    6. The hamburger was a slab of meat.

       7. The slab was thick.

       8. The slab was grayish.

       9. The meat was underdone.

    10. The toast was wheat.

    11. The toast was cut diagonally.

12. Juice had soaked the lower piece of bread.

13. Juice was from the meat.

14. Juice had turned it into near paste.

15. Mustard and cheese (/) oozed out of the sandwich. _____

    16. This was a glue for lettuce.

       17. The lettuce was shredded.

    18. This was a glue for onion.

       19. The onion was chopped.

    20. This was a glue for a relish.

       21. The relish was made from pickles.

22. The fries were lengths of potato.

23. The length was wedge-shaped.

24. The potato was freshly cut.

25. The fries were speckled with salt.

    ┌ 26. They were limp with heat.

AND   27. The heat was oily.

    └ 28. They were tinged golden-brown.

29. They exuded a breath.

    30. The breath was steamy.

31. Their outsides were crisp.

32. Their insides would be soft.

33. Their insides would be white.

34. Their insides would be chewy.

Rereading Your Writeouts: Notice that the paragraph moves from a general statement (Cluster 1–4) to three descriptive sentences about the hamburger, three about fries. Imagine a movie camera moving from a long shot to specific close-ups.

PARAGRAPH-BUILDING OPTIONS

1. Describe the milkshake or soft drink that arrives with the burger and fries. See it clearly. What is its container— glass, styrofoam, or something else? Any designs? Moisture on the outside? How about the drink? Foam on top? Color, appearance, and texture? A simple linking sentence for your paragraph might go like this: *The milkshake arrived next.*

2. Describe eating the burger and fries. Focus on details of smell, taste, and appearance. What is the overriding flavor? What is the texture of melted cheese against your tongue? How about the chunks of relish and onion? What does the cross section of hamburger meat look like? How about the fries— with catsup or not? How does the catsup arrive? A linking sentence for your paragraph might go like this: *With my mouth watering, I took a bite of the hamburger.*

SKID ROW

1. The day dawns (/) along skid row.
2. The day is cold.
3. The day is quiet.

4. Streets are full of shadows.
5. The streets are deserted.
6. Nothing is moving.
    7. One drives through this place.
8. One wonders about men and women.
    9. Men and women live here.

7 ING   9 WHO

    10. They are lucky.
11. They sleep in bunks.
    12. They don't sleep under bridges.
    13. They don't sleep in doorways.

10 WHEN   12 RATHER THAN

14. Do they dream about a childhood?
    15. The childhood was bright with hope.
    16. The childhood was full of promise.

17. Do they remember days?
    18. The days unfolded with laughter.
    19. The days unfolded with love.

20. Do they recall relationships?
    21. The relationships were with a family.
    22. The family was close-knit.

23. A newspaper tumbles in the wind.
24. It is tattered.
25. The tumbling is aimless.
26. It cartwheels toward a horizon.
27. The horizon is smudged.

28. One begins to wonder SOMETHING.
    29. Things went wrong for them.

28 WHY

30. Was it an event?
    31. The event was traumatic.
    32. The event shattered their hopes.

33. Was it a weakness?
    34. The weakness was personality.
    35. The weakness was character.

36. Was it simply circumstances?
    37. The circumstances were "bad luck."

38. Wine bottles stand vigil.
39. The vigil is silent.
40. The vigil is in doorways.
41. The doorways are to cheap hotels.

42. Windows flank a stillness. ·
43. The windows are faceless.
44. The stillness is concrete.
45. The stillness is in the streets.

46. One then wonders SOMETHING.
    47. Perhaps a force is at work.
        48. The force is unseen.
        49. The working is silent.
        50. The force chooses victims at whim.

47 IF   49 LY   50 ING

Rereading Your Writeouts: Notice how descriptive sentences are used to introduce unanswered questions so that the paragraph builds toward its final sentence (Cluster 46–50).

PARAGRAPH-BUILDING OPTIONS

The last sentence of the exercise—*One then wonders if perhaps an unseen force is silently at work, choosing victims at whim*—helps provide a link to your writing.

Choose *one* of the following sentences as a link to the exercise. Then explore its idea at some length.

1. *The "unseen force" is, of course, Satan.*
2. *Obviously, there is no "unseen force."*
3. *What seems like an "unseen force" is more likely predestination.*

4. *The "unseen force" is, quite simply, a disease called alcoholism.*
5. *A society that does not provide education, employment, and support services is the "unseen force."*

A PERSONAL VALUE

1. Values are standards.
2. A person uses the standards.
3. The standards are for judging worth.
4. The standards are for judging desirability.
5. The standards are for judging beauty.

6. These principles are learned.
7. These principles are not inherited.

8. They result first from teachings.
9. The teachings are direct.
10. The teachings are indirect.
11. The teachings are in the home.
12. The teachings are in social institutions.

13. They result from messages.
14. The messages are blatant.
15. The messages are subtle.
16. The messages are in the mass media.

17. And they result from experiences.
18. The experiences are positive.
19. The experiences are negative.
20. The experiences are in day-to-day life.
21. The experiences strengthen beliefs.
22. The experiences weaken beliefs.

23. Every person develops values.

24. The person grows up normally.

25. I am no exception to this process.
26. The process is natural.
27. The process is learning.

Rereading Your Writeouts: Notice that this paragraph moves from a definition (Cluster 1–5) to a three-part statement on how values are acquired (Clusters 8–12, 13–16, 17–22).

PARAGRAPH-BUILDING OPTIONS

The last sentence of the exercise—*I am no exception to this natural learning process*—helps provide a link to your writing.

Use this paragraph to introduce writing about *one* of your values. First, *name* the value—for example, patriotism, honesty, competition, helping others, etc. Then *explain* why and how this deep-seated principle is important in your life. As a possible link to the exercise, consider one of these "starters":

1. *My upbringing strongly emphasized the value of—*
2. *Perhaps the central value in my life is—*
3. *Over the years I have come to value—*

LONELINESS

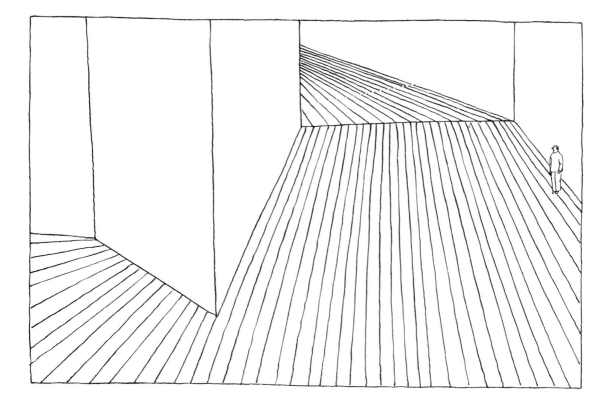

1. Loneliness is an experience.
2. The experience is common.
3. It is a part of growing up.
4. It is a part of being human.

5. It is a feeling.
6. The feeling is flat.
7. The feeling is gray.

8. Loneliness is like rooms.
9. The rooms are empty.
10. Loneliness is like beaches.
11. The beaches are deserted.
12. The beaches are windswept.

13. It is a feeling.
14. Something is missing.

15. Loneliness is tree branches.
    16. The branches are bare.
   17. Loneliness is photographs.
    18. The photographs are old.

AND
   19. The photographs are discarded.
   20. Loneliness is poems.
    21. The poems are written on napkins.
    22. The napkins are crumpled.

23. It is the sound of footsteps.
24. The sound is hollow.
25. The footsteps are shuffling.

26. Loneliness is lint.
27. The lint is in corners.
28. The corners are undusted.

29. Its evidence is shoulders.
30. The shoulders are sagging.
31. Its evidence is smiles.
32. The smiles are downturned.
33. Its evidence is eyes.
34. The eyes are vacant.

Rereading Your Writeouts: Notice that the repetition of the words *loneliness* and *it* ties the sentences together. Notice, too, that Clusters 5–7, 8–12, 15–22, 23–25, and 26–28 use *figures of speech* to "define" the feeling of loneliness.

PARAGRAPH-BUILDING OPTIONS

1. Describe the loneliest time that you can remember. To introduce this paragraph and link it to the exercise, your first sentence might say: *I well remember my loneliest time.* Tell about the circumstances that caused your loneliness and how you dealt with your feelings.

2. Write a paragraph modeled upon "Loneliness," but dealing with another common feeling such as joy, excitement, suspense, love, anger, fear, or relief. Your linking sentence might go like this: *A second common experience—a part of growing up and being human—is irritation.* Your follow-up sentences can *directly parallel* the ones in "Loneliness."

LAUNDROMAT FIELD TRIP

1. A Laundromat is the armpit.
2. The armpit is the universe's.

 3. It is crowded.
 4. It is noisy.
 5. It is poorly lit.
┌─6. It is hot as a steam bath.
├OR
└─7. It is drafty as a night train.
 8. The train is en route to Siberia.

9. It is a shambles.
10. The shambles is machines.
11. The machines are half-working.
12. The machines consume money.
13. The consumption is voracious.

14. Its walls (/) are covered with posters.
 15. The walls are faded gray.
 16. The walls are in need of cleaning.

17. The posters are stained.
18. The posters are dingy.

19. Its decor is garbage cans.
20. They overflow with boxes.
21. They overflow with bottles.
22. They overflow with paper.
23. They overflow with scraps of food.
24. The food is half-eaten.

25. It is a place.
 26. Not much happens there.

26 WHERE

┌─27. One can watch the machines.
│ 28. The machines turn their loads.
├OR
│ 29. The turning is endless.
└─30. One can watch the people.
 31. They pace the tiles.

32. The tiles are broken.
33. They try to relieve their boredom.

34. There are housewives.
35. They are frazzled.
36. They are sagging with weariness.

37. There are students.
38. They are unable to study.

39. There are cowboys.
40. They are transient.
41. They are anxious to get rolling.

42. There are working girls.
43. They are sharing their first apartment.

44. There are bachelors.
45. They are newly divorced.
46. They are just learning to fold clothes.

47. There are kids off the street.
48. They are looking for coins.

49. There is all of this.
50. There is more.
51. It is beneath the pallor.
52. The pallor is neon.

53. The Laundromat is a place.
    54. The place is thoroughly uncongenial.
    55. It is almost guaranteed to make one depressed.
        56. The depression is spiritual.

53 IN BRIEF   **55 THAT**   **56 LY**

Rereading Your Writeouts: Notice that this paragraph "hangs together" because of *parallel (i.e., repeated) sentences.* First, several sentences begin with the pronoun *it* (or *its*). Then several sentences begin with the word *there*.

PARAGRAPH-BUILDING OPTIONS

The last sentence of the exercise—*The Laundromat is a thoroughly uncongenial place that is almost guaranteed to make one spiritually depressed*—helps provide a link to your writing.

1. Discuss an antidote to the "almost guaranteed" depression caused by being in a Laundromat. List the *attitudes* and *behaviors* that you see as essential in overcoming the problem. Your linking sentence, opening the new paragraph, might go like this: *And yet by adopting certain attitudes and behaviors, most people can survive—perhaps even begin to enjoy—the time spent in a Laundromat.*

2. Focus on a place that is "almost guaranteed" to have the *opposite* effect of being in a laundromat. Describe the place in close detail and use *parallel (i.e., repeated) sentences* modeled upon those in the exercise. Your opener, a link to the Laundromat paragraph, might be similar to this: *On the other hand, _____ is almost guaranteed to make one feel spiritually uplifted and energized.*

PINBALL MEMORY

Nothing can be in the intellect that was not first in the senses.

—Aristotle

1. The brain has often been compared to a computer.
    2. We all possess a brain.

2   THAT

3. It has a capacity.
4. The capacity is astonishing.
5. The capacity is for processing experience.
6. The capacity is for making sense of it.
7. The capacity is for storing the information.
8. The capacity is for then using it.

9. But it might also be compared to a pinball machine.
10. This is in its memory function.

11. Experts know SOMETHING.
    12. Stimulating brain areas can trigger reactions.
        13. The stimulation is electric.
        14. The areas are specific.
    15. The reactions are behavioral.
    16. The reactions are emotional.

12   THAT   13   LY

17. Many therefore conclude SOMETHING.
    18. All our experience is "beneath the surface."
        19. It is mostly unremembered.
        20. It is mostly untapped.

18   THAT

21. This view would suggest SOMETHING.
    22. We never truly "forget" anything.

22   THAT

23. We may "go blank."
24. We are trying to recall a name.
25. The information is still there.

23   ALTHOUGH   24   WHEN

26. We are like the pinball machine.
27. We are simply waiting for the right stimulus.
    28. The stimulus will trigger associations.
    29. The stimulus will trigger connections.
    30. The associations and connections are called "memory."

26   IN OTHER WORDS

31. The stimulus is strong enough.
32. Experience will click on the scoreboard.
    33. The experience is remembered.
    34. The scoreboard is called "consciousness."

31   WHEN

Rereading Your Writeouts: Focus on the intersentence links in the first three clusters (*brain/it/it*) and then the next three clusters (*Experts/many/this view*). These are "glue" for the paragraph.

PARAGRAPH-BUILDING OPTIONS

The last sentence of the exercise—*When the stimulus is strong enough, remembered experience will click on the scoreboard called consciousness*—helps provide a link to your writing.

1. Play some records or tapes that you haven't listened to for a long time—or listen to old songs on the radio. Un-

doubtedly, some will bring back memories. Jot down the specific details of a remembered "scene." Then shape these details into a recollection. One link to the last sentence of the exercise follows: *Consider, for example, the stimulus of music.*

2. Find some spice bottles or tins in the kitchen. Close your eyes and smell. If this experience does not evoke clear memories, let your imagination "flash" on strongly pleasant or unpleasant smells: brewing coffee, a Big Mac hamburger, sweat socks, chalk dust on your hands. Jot down specifics of a remembered scene and put these into a paragraph. Link your paragraph to the exercise, perhaps like this: *For example, a smell such as _____ evokes clear recollections.*

BEACHCOMBING

1. Come with me.
2. We'll wander the beach.

3. We'll go for a walk in the fog.
4. The fog comes at early morning.
5. The fog ghosts the coastline in gauze.
6. We'll study the silhouettes of clam diggers.
7. The clam diggers are hunched in the wind.
8. The wind is damp.

9. We'll have breakfast at a cafe.
10. The cafe is small.
11. The cafe is weatherbeaten.
12. The cafe has varnished countertops.
13. The cafe has knotty pine walls.

14. Then we'll walk along the dunes.
15. The dunes are grassy.
16. We'll watch the sun begin to break through.
17. The sun peels away the fog cover.
18. The sun exposes houses.
19. The houses are gray-shingled.
20. The houses are half-hidden by coast pine.

21. You'll point to clouds.
22. The clouds are piling up to the south.

AND

23. Their bottoms are gray.
24. Their bottoms are on the horizon.
25. I'll notice seabirds.
26. The seabirds are working against the wind.
27. The seabirds are out beyond the waves.
28. The waves are mottled.

29. We'll hear the roar of swells.
30. The roar is white.
31. The swells are rolling over rocky outcroppings.
32. The outcroppings are covered with barnacles.
33. We'll see a trace of foam.
34. The trace is muffled.
35. The foam whispers along the sand.

36. You'll write messages with your toes.
37. The messages will be secret.

38. We'll climb piles of logs.

39. The logs are sandy.
40. The logs are bleached by sun.
41. The logs are bleached by salt.

42. There will be the smell.
43. The smell is brown.
44. The smell is kelp.
45. The smell is clams.
46. The smell is fish.

47. And we'll hear the cries of gulls.
48. The cries are sharp.
49. The gulls are soaring overhead.
50. The gulls are wheeling overhead.

Rereading Your Writeouts: Notice the inter-sentence linkage that occurs as sentences are written in parallel form, often repeating the pronoun *we*.

PARAGRAPH-BUILDING OPTIONS

1. Extend this description by describing to a friend what will be "left behind" by wandering on the beach. Remember: Your goal is to persuade your friend to join you. List a variety of real-life unpleasantries in the form of *parallel sentences.* To open this paragraph and make a link to the exercise, you might write: *You can leave behind all kinds of troubles.*

2. Create a description, modeled upon "Beachcombing," that invites a friend to join you at a favorite get-away place. Focus on specific sights, sounds, smells, and textures to persuade your friend to join you. To open this paragraph and make a link to the exercise, you might write: *Or, better yet, come with me to* _____.

PART TWO

SENTENCE STYLISTICS

UNIT SIX
SENTENCE-MODELING
WORKSHOP

When the students come into the room, they see a list of names on the board.

THE PLAYERS

Men

GRAYSON GOFERIT
a hill-climbing, gusto-grabbing dirt-biker

RICK ("QUICK-KICK") O'SHEA
a taller scholar-athlete specializing in field goals

CASEY SPACEY
an aspiring astronomer with head in the clouds

J. TROY PLAYBOY
a poor, but handsome, campus dreamboat

Women

SALLY RALLY
a peppy, high-stepping, gum-snapping cheerleader

BRIDGET BOUTIQUE
a fashion-blessed, well-dressed, perma-prest model

WENDY WAFFLESTOMPERS
a granola-toting backpacker with her own yogurt maker

GERTRUDE GOTTALOTTABUCKS
a rich, but homely, husband-hunting heiress

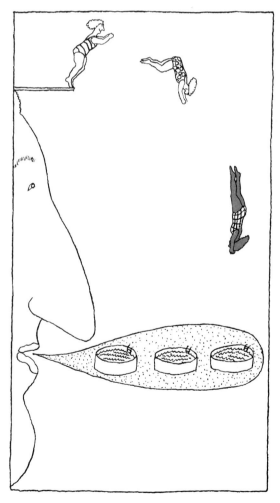

"Today, we'll have some fun with caricatures. These characters are for today's work on *sentence modeling.* A model is a pattern for imitation."

"Still sentence combining?" Theresa asks.

"Right. But now we're going to move sentence parts around to extend what you've already learned about sentence structure. These parts are called *additions*—or *free modifiers.* They're clusters of words that can be added to a base sentence to give it more detail and specificity."

"There are different kinds of free modifiers?" Tony asks.

"Four different types to be specific."

FOUR TYPES OF ADDITIONS

1. Verb Clusters
2. Noun Clusters
3. Adjective Clusters
4. Absolutes

"Understanding and *using* these various free modifiers doesn't mean that you have to memorize their grammatical labels," I add. "On the other hand, don't let the terms panic you."

"You had us worried for a minute," Nate says with a pained expression on his face.

"Here's a chart showing examples of free modifiers. Study it for a few moments."

FOUR TYPES OF ADDITIONS

Verb Clusters		*Noun Clusters*	
-ing type	smiling coyly picking his teeth	*simple*	a motorcyclist, Grayson Sally, the rally queen
-ed type	dressed by noon slumped in a chair	*expanded*	Rick, one strange and hassled athlete
-en type	swollen with pride forgotten by friends		Wendy, earnest advocate of the ecology movement

Adjective Clusters		*Absolutes*	
shows *detail*	green and golden blunt and rounded- smooth	*noun + noun*	his face a mask his smile an in- vitation

Adjective Clusters		*Absolutes*	
		noun + adj	her lips friendly
			her eyes nervous
shows	glossy like satin		
likeness	still as death	*noun + verb*	their anger mounting
		form	voices sharpened
shows	anxious for revenge	*noun + like*	the leaves like birds
quality	alert and eager to begin		the wind like a whisper

"Why even study these additions?" Malee asks.

"Actually they're nothing new. You've been using them during the past units. We're discussing them now because of their potential for increasing sentence variety and reader interest."

"How do they work?"

"Additions attach to base sentences in three different places."

THREE PLACES FOR ADDITIONS

1. Before the base sentence
2. Middle of the base sentence
3. After the base sentence

"What's interesting," I continue, "is that free modifiers don't need co-ordinating and subordinating connectors to hook on to base sentences. We'll look at four illustrations that make this point. Each shows how free modifiers work in comparison with coordination and subordination. Notice, incidentally, the punctuation patterns for these additions."

VERB CLUSTER ADDITION

Wendy wanted to be natural.
Wendy wore no make-up.
Wendy ate lots of yogurt.

[FREE MODIFIER] *Wanting to be natural, Wendy wore no make-up and ate lots of yogurt.*

[COORDINATION] *Wendy wanted to be natural and therefore wore no make-up and ate lots of yogurt.*

[SUBORDINATION] *Because Wendy wanted to be natural, she wore no make-up and ate lots of yogurt.*

NOUN CLUSTER ADDITION

Rick enjoyed being the team's blocking dummy.
Rick was an incredible hulk.
Rick was seven feet tall.

[FREE MODIFIER] *Rick*—an incredible hulk, seven feet tall—*enjoyed being the team's blocking dummy.*

[COORDINATION] *Rick was an incredible, seven-foot hulk; he enjoyed being the team's blocking dummy.*

[SUBORDINATION] *Since he was an incredible hulk who was seven feet tall, Rick enjoyed being the team's blocking dummy.*

ADJECTIVE CLUSTER ADDITION

Sally was giggly.
Sally was bright-eyed.
Sally was loved by home crowds.

[FREE MODIFIER] Giggly and bright-eyed, *Sally was loved by home crowds.*

[COORDINATION] *Sally was giggly, bright-eyed, and loved by home crowds.*

[SUBORDINATION] *Whenever Sally was giggly and bright-eyed, she was loved by home crowds.*

ABSOLUTE ADDITION

Troy moved through the cafeteria.
His swagger was cool.
His swagger was practiced.

[FREE MODIFIER] *Troy moved through the cafeteria,* his swagger cool and practiced.

[COORDINATION] *Troy moved through the cafeteria; his swagger was cool and practiced.*

[SUBORDINATION] *As Troy moved through the cafeteria, his swagger was cool and practiced.*

STOP. COMBINE THE FOLLOWING SENTENCES AND CHECK WITH THE ANSWER KEY, P. 275. THEN RESUME YOUR READING.

Verb Cluster Addition

  1. Grayson stood astride his motorcycle.
      2. He revved the engine.

2 ING

Noun Cluster Addition

  3. The sound (/) filled his ears.
      4. The sound was a bark.
          5. The bark was harsh.
          6. The bark was spiraling.

Adjective Cluster Addition

     7. He was tense.
BUT
     8. He was sure of himself.
  9. He eyed the steep hill.

Absolute Addition

10. His stomach was clenched.
    11. His heart was pounding.

"Any questions?" I ask.

"Punctuation," Randy says.

"One comma is required when there's an addition either *before* or *after* the base sentence. A pair of punctuation marks is required when the addition appears in the *middle* of the base sentence."

"How movable are these free modifiers?" Carol asks. "Can they attach anywhere?"

"To answer your question, let's look back at a free modifier for the cluster on Sally Rally and compare it with two other possibilities."

Giggly and bright-eyed, Sally was loved by home crowds.

Sally—*giggly and bright-eyed*—was loved by home crowds.
Sally was loved by home crowds, *giggly and bright-eyed.*

Paulo grins. "Oh, yeah. The last writeout sounds like the crowds are giggly and bright-eyed. That changes the meaning."

"Exactly. So you see that free modifiers don't just attach anywhere in a base sentence. You need to put the addition *near* what it refers to. If you get it too far away, the sentence becomes confused. We'll see more examples of this later when we talk about misplaced and dangling modifiers."

Kim raises her hand. "I'm having trouble with absolutes," she says. "They sound like run-on sentences to me."

"Absolutes are a bit tricky," I reply. "They're a type of addition that modifies the entire base sentence, not just a part of it. In the next example, compare the absolute to a run-on sentence by reading aloud."

[ABSOLUTE ADDITION] *Troy moved through the cafeteria,* his swagger cool and practiced.

[RUN-ON SENTENCE] *Troy moved through the cafeteria, his swagger was cool and practiced.*

"You see, the absolute deletes the word *was.* What's left—a noun plus modifiers—can then be attached to the base sentence with a comma or dash. But the run-on is two independent sentences hooked together with a comma. Changing the comma to a semicolon would fix the run-on. Still, though, you wouldn't have a free modifier as you do in the first writeout."

"Okay, another question," Carlos says. "Why have an absolute for that last cluster? Couldn't you make it into some other type of addition?"

"Sure. Here are writeouts that transform the same kernels into the three other kinds of additions. Each creates a different emphasis."

[ABSOLUTE] His swagger cool and practiced, *Troy moved through the cafeteria.*

[VERB CLUSTER] *Troy moved through the cafeteria,* swaggering in a cool and practiced way.

[NOUN CLUSTER] *Troy*—a cool, practiced swaggerer—*moved through the cafeteria.*

[ADJECTIVE CLUSTER] Cool and practiced, *Troy's swaggering was a movement through the cafeteria.*

"Notice, too, that these examples show the three locations for additions."

"What about having *two* kinds of additions attached to a base?" Kristin asks.

"It's quite common. Study this example."

VERB CLUSTER + NOUN CLUSTER ADDITIONS

Troy was not interested in schoolwork.
Troy still enjoyed fellowship.
The fellowship was of a fraternity.
The fraternity was called the "Culture Vultures."

[FREE MODIFIERS] Not interested in schoolwork, *Troy still enjoyed the fellowship of a fraternity,* the "Culture Vultures."

[COORDINATION] *Troy was not interested in schoolwork, but he still enjoyed the fraternal fellowship of the "Culture Vultures."*

[SUBORDINATION] *Although he was not interested in schoolwork, Troy still enjoyed the fellowship of a fraternity, which was called the "Culture Vultures."*

"In the first writeout you have two additions—an *-ed verb cluster* up front and a *noun cluster* at the end. Notice once again that such additions are an *alternative* to coordinating and subordinating conjunctions."

STOP. COMBINE THE FOLLOWING SENTENCES AND CHECK WITH THE ANSWER KEY, P. 275. THEN RESUME YOUR READING.

Verb Cluster Addition

  1. Bridget stood near Grayson.
      2. Bridget shouted "Go for it!"

2 ING

Noun Cluster Addition

  3. Her outfit (/) caught his attention.
      4. The outfit was a checkered jumpsuit.
  5. The jumpsuit was tucked into Gucci boots.

Adjective Cluster Addition

      6. Grayson was now aware of her presence.
  7. Grayson was unable to concentrate on the hill.

Absolute Addition

8.   His mind went blank.

     9.   His senses went numb.

Verb Cluster + Noun Cluster Additions

    10.   He waved to her.

11.   He released the motorcycle's clutch.

    12.   The release was unthinking.

       13.   This was a mistake.

        14.   The mistake was disastrous.

10 ING   12 LY

"Let's now return to the idea that additions need to be *near* the word they modify. When they're not, they're called *misplaced* or *dangling modifiers*. Read the following pairs of writeouts. You'll see why you have to be careful in attaching additions to a base sentence."

MISPLACED/DANGLING MODIFIERS

1.   Casey stared at posters.
       The posters hung on the wall.
       The posters pertained to space.

1-A.   *Hanging on the wall, Casey Spacey stared at space posters.*

1-B.   *Casey Spacey stared at space posters hanging on the wall.*

2.   His mother knocked on the door.
       The mother was an astrologer.
       She wore a housecoat.
       The housecoat was flowered.

2-A.   *His mother—an astrologer—knocked on the door wearing a flowered housecoat.*

2-B.   *Wearing a flowered housecoat, his mother—an astrologer—knocked on the door.*

3.   Casey huddled in the corner.
       He raised his voice.
       He said something.
       Astronomers didn't believe in astrology.

3-A.   *Huddled in the corner, Casey's raised voice said that astronomers didn't believe in astrology.*

3-B.   *Huddled in the corner, Casey raised his voice, saying that astronomers didn't believe in astrology.*

"As you can see, these misplaced and dangling modifiers aren't hard to spot if you *listen* to what you're writing. Here, writeouts 1-A, 2-A, and 3-A are ones with problems. The first has Casey hanging on the wall. The second has the door wearing a housecoat. The third has Casey's voice huddled in the corner."

I begin handing out exercise sheets. "Okay, you understand that we're looking at four different additions—*verb clusters, noun clusters, adjective clusters,* and *absolutes.* And you also understand that these free modifiers attach to a base sentence in *three* different places. Let's practice moving the additions around. These modeling exercises show one writeout already completed. Your task is to move free modifiers to the other two positions— if possible. Sometimes it's not."

"What if we move the modifier and it doesn't sound right?" Janet asks.

"Don't write sentences that sound wrong. And remember to be alert for any misplaced or dangling modifiers similar to what we've just studied."

STOP. DO COMBINING TO FILL IN THE FOLLOWING EXERCISE. THEN RESUME YOUR READING.

Rick was proud of his meanness.
He was a defensive punter.
He was also a human being.
The human being was offensive.

A. *Addition before the base sentence:*

_____

_____

_____

B. *Addition in middle of base sentence:*

Rick—a defensive punter and offensive human being—was proud of his meanness.

C. *Addition after the base sentence:*

_____

_____

_____

"The first position is easy," Tim volunteers. "*A defensive punter and an offensive human being, Rick was proud of his meanness.*"

"Well done. Notice, though, that if you move the addition *after* the base, it doesn't sound right."

"How can you change it?" Eric asks.

"Try another kernel sentence as your base. Switch the parts around. See what happens."

Eric eyes his worksheet and whispers his way through the transformation. "Yeah," he says. "It works." He dictates a sentence for me to transcribe.

> Rick was a defensive punter and also an offensive human being, *proud of his meanness.*

"In the first two solutions, the additions are *noun clusters.* But Eric's changed things so that an *adjective cluster* comes after the base sentence."

Maria's hand goes up. "I did it differently. I put a noun cluster up front and an adjective cluster at the end."

> *A defensive punter,* Rick was also an offensive human being, *proud of his meanness.*

"Skillfully done. I think you're ready for something trickier."

STOP. DO COMBINING TO FILL IN THE FOLLOWING EXERCISE. THEN RESUME YOUR READING.

> Sally became a little bored.
> She studied Rick's collection.
> The collection was of football photos.
> The collection was of football statistics.

A.   *Addition before the base sentence:*

_____

_____

_____

B.   *Addition in middle of base sentence:*

Sally, studying Rick's collection of football photos and statistics, became a little bored.

C.   *Addition after the base sentence:*

_____

_____

_____

Terry's hand goes up, and I transcribe his writeout.

Studying Rick's collection of football photos and statistics, it was a little boring for Sally.

A ripple of snickers goes through the class.
"What's wrong?" Terry asks.
"*Listen* to what your sentence says. Focus on the word *it*."
Terry breaks into a grin. "Sounds like *it* is doing the studying."
"Okay, let's fix this dangling modifier."
Carol volunteers a corrected version.

Studying Rick's collection of football photos and statistics, Sally became a little bored.

"Okay, we've got that problem straightened out. What about a position *after* the base sentence?" I take down Rob's two writeouts.

Sally became a little bored, *studying Rick's collection of football photos and statistics.*

It was a little boring for Sally, *studying Rick's collection of football photos and statistics.*

"I don't know," he says. "I don't like those as well as the other sentences. They're sort of awkward."
"In that case you might decide *not* to use free modifiers. Here are two possibilities."

Sally became a little bored as she studied Rick's collection of football photos and statistics.

It was a little boring for Sally to study Rick's collection of football photos and statistics.

"Those sound better," Rob decides. "Clearer."
The class moves on to another exercise.

STOP. DO COMBINING TO FILL IN THE FOLLOWING EXERCISE. THEN RESUME YOUR READING.

Troy had one goal.
The goal was to "be mellow."
He was suave.
He was well-groomed.

A. *Addition before the base sentence:*

Suave and well-groomed, Troy's one goal was to "be mellow."

B.   *Addition in middle of base sentence:*

_____

_____

_____

C.   *Addition after the base sentence:*

_____

_____

_____

"The middle position is no problem," Chico says. *"Troy—suave and well-groomed—had 'being mellow' as his one goal."*

"How about *after* the base sentence?"

"I don't know," Michelle says. "It doesn't sound right."

"To make the sentence technically correct, we'd need to invert it: *Being mellow was the one goal of Troy—suave and well-groomed.*"

STOP.   DO COMBINING TO FILL IN THE FOLLOWING EXERCISE. THEN RESUME YOUR READING.

Gertrude's appearance was hardly conventional.
Her expression resembled that of a bulldog.
The bulldog was fierce.

A.   *Addition before the base sentence:*

_____

_____

_____

B.   *Addition in middle of base sentence:*

_____

_____

_____

C.   *Addition after the base sentence:*

Gertrude's appearance was hardly conventional, her expression resembling that of a fierce bulldog.

"Once again we've got an addition called an absolute," I explain. "It's made from a noun cluster—*her expression*—and a verb cluster—*resembling that of a fierce bulldog.* Now let's move it around."

Theresa and Paulo volunteer two writeouts.

> *Her expression resembling that of a fierce bulldog,* Gertrude's appearance was hardly conventional.

> Gertrude's appearance—*her expression resembling that of a fierce bulldog*—was hardly conventional.

"How about an *adjective cluster* up front? Focus on the word *conventional* to get started."

Jill dictates a version for me to transcribe.

> *Hardly conventional,* Gertrude's facial expression resembled that of a fierce bulldog.

"You changed the absolute into your base sentence. Nice work."

I click off the projector.

"In the next exercises you'll practice making the four kinds of additions in the three positions. Of course, real writing isn't saturated with additions as these worksheets are. These are just skill builders for on-your-own writing."

EXERCISE 6.1   Making Additions

Directions. Follow the combining signals in order to add free modifiers to base sentences. Then ignore the signals and practice other kinds of additions. Check with the Answer Key, p. 275.

RICK O'SHEA:
VERB CLUSTER ADDITIONS

1. Rick sat alone at his training table.
    2. He was deeply depressed about his grades.

    3. He was confused by hard assignments.
AND
    4. He was confused by big words.
5. He was having a hard time in school.

6. These worries (/) were taking their toll.
    7. They were aggravated by a losing season.
    8. They were aggravated by no pro offers.
    9. They were aggravated by strained pectoral muscles.

10. Even his attempts at cheating had failed.
    11. They were fumbled first in the planning.
AND
    12. They were further bobbled in the coverup.

    13. He was heavy-hearted.
    14. He was humbled by circumstances.
15. Rick worked at a huge steak.
    16. He considered the situation.
    17. He decided to go look for trouble.

WENDY WAFFLESTOMPERS:
ADJECTIVE CLUSTER ADDITIONS

1. Wendy (/) jogged across campus.
    2. She was late for class.

    3. She was breathless.
AND
    4. She was disheveled.
5. She opened the classroom door.
    6. She slipped inside.

7. So did her dog.
    8. The dog was mangy.
    9. The dog was flea-bitten.
    10. The dog was hyperactive.

    11. Wendy was angry with her instructor's directive.
    12. The directive was to put the dog outside the door.
13. She protested loudly in class.

14. She contended SOMETHING.
    15. Her dog had educational rights.
    16. The rights were natural.
AND
    17. The rights were therefore irrevocable.

15   THAT

SALLY RALLY:
NOUN CLUSTER ADDITIONS

    1. Sally was a spark plug for the team.
2. Sally sprang to her feet.

3. The pep assembly (/) went wild.
    4. The assembly was mostly boys.
    5. The boys were enthusiastic.

6. Noise (/) crashed through the gymnasium.

7. The noise was a wave of shouts and whistles.
8. The gymnasium was a domelike structure.

9. Sally called for silence.
10. The silence was a moment of quiet.

11. Then the school band struck up the fight song.
AND 12. The fight song was familiar.
13. She did her award-winning routine.
14. The routine was a "rally ballet."

CASEY SPACEY:
ABSOLUTE ADDITIONS

1. Casey lounged on his bed.
   2. The bed was unmade.

3. His eyes were glazed.
AND
4. His eyes were dilated.

5. One hand was outstretched.
   6. The other was clenched.

7. Stereo music (/) burbled in his ears.
8. Its sounds were milky.
9. Its sounds were swirling.
10. Its sounds were distant.

11. His mood was relaxed.
12. His thoughts were vacant.

13. His mantra was echoing in his ears.
14. He rocked slowly back and forth.

EXERCISE 6.2   Sentence Modeling

Directions. Practice making additions, using skills you have learned. Complete the following writeouts and check with the Answer Key, p. 275.

1. Gertrude sat in a study hall.
Gertrude thumbed slowly through *Brides* magazine.

1-A. Sitting —————————,
Gertrude —————————.

1-B. Gertrude —————————,
thumbing —————————.

2. She was eager to get married.
She was preoccupied with finding a man.

2-A. Eager —————————,
she —————————.

2-B. Preoccupied —————————,
she —————————.

3. Her fantasies centered on Troy.
Troy was the campus dreamboat.

3-A. Her —————————,
the —————————.

3-B. Troy —————————,
a center —————————.

4. She pictured herself with him.
She imagined their lives being joined.

4-A. She ——————————,

their lives ——————————.

4-B. She ——————————,

imagining ——————————.

EXERCISE 6.3   Proofreading Practice

Directions. Shown below are writeouts that contain misplaced or dangling modifiers. Spot the errors and rewrite the sentences. Check with the Answer Key, p. 275.

1.   Bridget strolled with Grayson.
          She was dressed in a pinafore.
          The pinafore was frilly.
          The pinafore was eye-appealing.

PROBLEM 1   *Bridget strolled with Grayson, dressed in a frilly, eye-appealing pinafore.*

2.   The promenade was illuminated by moonlight.
          The promenade was nearly deserted.
          The moon shone softly through the trees.
          The trees were leafy.

PROBLEM 2   *Shining softly through leafy trees, the nearly deserted prome-*
nade was illuminated by moonlight.

3.   Casey Spacey leaned over the balcony.
          The balcony was above the boardwalk.
          He watched the couple.
          The couple paused to embrace.

PROBLEM 3   *The couple who paused to embrace, leaning over the balcony above the boardwalk, was watched by Casey Spacey.*

4.   They were unaware of Casey's presence.
          They struggled to untangle their braces.
          The struggle was in vain.
          The braces were on their teeth.

PROBLEM 4   *They were unaware of Casey's presence, struggling vainly to untangle the braces on their teeth.*

EXERCISE 6.4   Rewriting Choppy Sentences

Directions. The following two paragraphs are choppy. Rewrite them so that the sentences flow smoothly and logically from one to another. You may delete words, change the form of words, or add connecting words. (*Practice making additions to base sentences.*)

TRUCK STOP: Paragraph 1

Grayson was inside the cafe. He looked over the situation. Two boys lounged in a corner booth. They had bad complexions. They watched him. One puffed on a cigarette. His

breath made a fog. The fog was smoke rings. The other slouched against the red vinyl. He sipped a cola. At the jukebox were two girls. One was bent over the bubbled shield. The shield was plastic. She chewed a piece of gum. She punched buttons. The other combed her hair in the neon reflection. Her hair was silky. It was sun-bleached. The reflection was made by the jukebox. She jiggled her looped earrings. The earrings were wire. She kept time to the music. The music was country-western. It had a heavy beat. It had an insistent beat.

TRUCK STOP: Paragraph 2

He sat at the counter. The counter was a well-wiped surface. The surface had a pattern. The pattern was wood grain. The pattern looked like butcher block. Down the counter was a trucker. The trucker was balding and pot-bellied. The trucker leaned forward over a piece of chocolate cake. One hand smoothed his stomach. The hand was large. He sipped his coffee. Behind the counter was an aisle. The aisle was cluttered with cartons. The cartons were empty. The cartons were refuse from the day's work. Shelves near the kitchen displayed leather belts. They displayed jewelry. They displayed an assortment of signs. They displayed cigarettes. They displayed boxes of candy bars. The candy bars were brightly packaged. A collection of ceramics was near the windows. The ceramics were novelty items. The novelty items were odd-shaped. The windows were neon-lit. The windows were in need of washing.

UNIT SEVEN
TWO-LEVEL AND MULTI-LEVEL SENTENCES

"In the previous unit you learned about four types of additions. And you also learned that additions attach to a base sentence in three different places. Today we'll build on those principles by introducing the idea of *levels of modification* within a sentence."

"Levels?" Carol asks.

"The base sentence is usually at a *general* level. The free modifiers, though, are usually more *specific*. By numbering the levels—from general to specific—you can see the relationship of sentence parts."

"You mean how the parts go together."

"Exactly. What you'll now see is a series of general base sentences, each followed by a more specific addition. Notice that the base sentence is numbered with a 1, the additions with a 2."

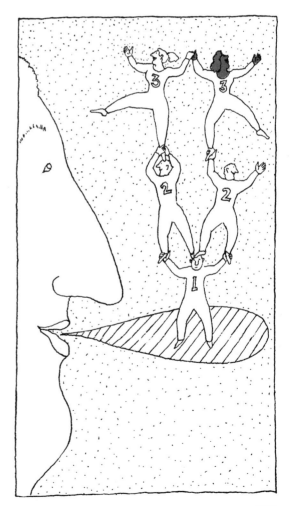

> At noon the rain was falling.
> The rain was cool.
> The rain was steady.

> 1   *At noon the rain was falling,*
>   2   *cool and steady.*

> Rick had his books.
> The books were under his arm.
> He jogged down the footpath.
> The footpath was puddled.

2   *With books under his arm,*
1   *Rick jogged down the puddled footpath.*

He was headed for the cafeteria.
The cafeteria was a room.
The room was grim.
The room was greasy.
The room was in the student center.

1   *He was headed for the cafeteria,*
    2   *a grim, greasy room in the student center.*

He ran in his form.
The form was legendary.
He left students along his route.
The students were mud-spattered.

1   *He ran in his legendary form,*
    2   *leaving mud-spattered students along his route.*

"In each of these examples, you see the same pattern: The base sentence is like a photographic 'long shot'; the second-level additions are like 'close-ups.' Seeing how general and specific go together gives you more *control* in your writing."

Eric has a hand up. "What about *more* than one addition?"

"What we'll study first is a pattern with a series of free modifiers—all the same kind—attached to a base sentence. This we'll call a *two-level sentence*. Then we'll look at a pattern with different types of free modifiers attached to the base sentence. This we'll call a *multi-level sentence*. Here's a quick preview of these two patterns."

Rick pushed through the lunch line.
His pushing was aggressive.
He piled his tray high.
He rippled his muscles for effect.

TWO-LEVEL SENTENCES

1   Rick pushed aggressively through the lunch line,
    2   piling his tray high,
    2   rippling his muscles for effect.

1   Rick pushed aggressively through the lunch line,
    2   his tray piled high,
    2   his muscles rippling for effect.

MULTI-LEVEL SENTENCES

     2   With his tray piled high,
1   Rick pushed aggressively through the lunch line,
         3   rippling his muscles for effect.

1   Rick pushed aggressively through the lunch line,
     2   piling his tray high,
            3   his muscles rippling for effect.

"What's the point?" Carlos asks.

"The point is this: Once you understand the *patterns* for two-level and multi-level sentences, you'll find it much easier to write such sentences on your own."

Carlos shrugs in his wait-and-see way.

"Let's look more closely at examples of a *two-level sentence*," I continue. "Each example is a writeout from a cluster of kernels. The base sentence, level 1, is more general. The additions, level 2, are more specific. Remember: For this to be a two-level sentence the additions have to be the *same kind* of free modifier."

TWO-LEVEL SENTENCES: VERB CLUSTERS

Grayson tried to look cool.
He smiled at Bridget.
He combed back his hair.
His hair was unwashed.

A.   *Additions before the base sentence:*
Smiling at Bridget and combing back his unwashed hair, Grayson tried to look cool.

     2   Smiling at Bridget and
     2   combing back his unwashed hair,
1   Grayson tried to look cool.

B.   *Additions in middle of base sentence:*
Grayson—smiling at Bridget, combing back his unwashed hair—tried to look cool.

    1   Grayson—/—tried to look cool.
    /2/   smiling at Bridget,
    /2/   combing back his unwashed hair

"Here you see two versions of the same basic sentence," I continue. "Notice that the additions—the second levels—are both *-ing* verb clusters

that modify the base sentence, which is more general. In Writeout B, the slash marks indicate that free modifiers appear in the middle of the base sentence."

"How many second levels can you add?" Tony asks.

"Well, you have to end the sentence at *some* point," I hedge. "And making a huge two-level sentence isn't an intelligent end in itself. But the truth is, there's no structural limit to the number of second-level additions you can attach. The trick is to make sure they're the same type."

"How do you do that?"

"First, ask yourself whether they *look* alike. With *-ing* verb clusters, for example, you see a repeated grammatical unit. If you're still in doubt, trust your ear. Read aloud. You'll *hear* the additions that belong together."

Eric is frowning. "Why even *bother* with levels? They look like something else to get confused about."

"Think of levels as blueprints for sentence structure. They reveal recurring *patterns* in sentences. And they help you see what's general and what's specific."

Anne gets my attention. "Let me see if I understand. You can add as many second levels as you want, just as long as they're the same type? And you can move them around—put them in the three positions."

"That's it. You need to remember that these lower levels add *specificity* to the base sentence. That's why they're so important. They're like close-ups that focus on a *specific* action or a *particular* detail."

"So the base sentence is usually general and the additions tend to be specific."

"Right again. Here's an example to clarify this point."

STOP. DO COMBINING TO FILL IN THE FOLLOWING EXERCISE. THEN RESUME YOUR READING.

TWO-LEVEL SENTENCES: VERB CLUSTERS

Bridget ignored Grayson's overtures.
She put on her make-up.
She winked at Troy.
She tried to look available.

A.   *Additions before the base sentence:*
     2   Putting on her make-up,
     2   winking at Troy, and
     2   trying to look available,
  1   Bridget ignored Grayson's overtures.

B. *Additions after the base sentence:*

1   As Bridget ignored Grayson's overtures, she tried to look available—

2   _____

2   _____

"How about additions for Writeout B?"

"*Put on her make-up* and *winked at Troy,*" Randy offers.

"No, that's not quite it. Let me show you why." I transcribe his sentence onto the chalkboard.

1   As Bridget ignored Grayson's overtures, she tried to look available, put on her make-up, and winked at Troy.

"You see? This is a fine grammatical sentence, but it's all at level 1. Why? Because it uses compounding rather than free modifiers. You have to change the verbs into an *-ing* form if you want second-level additions."

"You mean *putting on her make-up* and *winking at Troy?*"

"Exactly. Here's how the sentence would look in levels."

1   As Bridget ignored Grayson's overtures, she tried to look available—
2   putting on her make-up,
2   winking at Troy.

STOP.   DO COMBINING TO FILL IN THE FOLLOWING EXERCISE. THEN RESUME YOUR READING.

TWO-LEVEL SENTENCES: VERB CLUSTERS

Grayson misread these signals.
He stood up abruptly.
He bumped against the table.
He spilled his cola.

A. *Additions before the base sentence:*

2   _____ ,
1   Grayson stood up abruptly, bumped against the table, and spilled his cola.

B. *Additions in middle of base sentence:*
1   Grayson—/—bumped against the table and spilled his cola.

/2/ —————————————————————————————————,

/2/ —————————————————————————————————.

C. *Additions after the base sentence:*
  1 Because he misread these signals, Grayson stood up abruptly.

  2 —————————————————————————————————,

  2 —————————————————————————————————.

Students work together, quickly coming up with options for two-level sentences. Possible answers go up on the screen.

  2 Misreading these signals,
1 Grayson stood up abruptly, bumped against the table, and spilled his cola.

1 Grayson—/—bumped against the table and spilled his cola.
  /2/ misreading these signals,
  /2/ standing up abruptly

1 Because he misread these signals, Grayson stood up abruptly,
  2 bumping against the table,
  2 spilling his cola.

"Let me reemphasize a point," I continue. "These are two-level sentences because the additions—*misreading, standing up, bumping, spilling*—are the same type of modifier. They're verb clusters. But the two-level principle applies to *other* additions, too. We'll look at absolutes in the next example."

"Absolutes?" Chuck asks. "I was absent for that."

"An absolute is a kernel sentence with a key word deleted. Like other free modifiers, it attaches to a base sentence but can't stand by itself."

KERNEL ————————————————→ ABSOLUTE

KERNEL	ABSOLUTE
The toothpick was in his mouth.	*toothpick in his mouth*
His eyelids were lowered seductively.	*his eyelids lowered seductively*
A bike chain was hanging around his neck.	*a bike chain hanging around his neck*

"These absolutes work as free modifiers in the following exercise."

STOP. DO COMBINING TO FILL IN THE FOLLOWING EXERCISE AND CHECK WITH THE ANSWER KEY, P. 275. THEN RESUME YOUR READING.

TWO-LEVEL SENTENCES: ABSOLUTES

>He swaggered across the room toward Bridget.
>The toothpick was in his mouth.
>His eyelids were lowered seductively.
>A bike chain was hanging around his neck.

A.   *Additions before the base sentence:*

   2   _____ ,

   2   _____ ,

   1   He swaggered across the room toward Bridget with a bike chain hanging around his neck.

B.   *Additions after the base sentence:*

   1   He swaggered across the room toward Bridget—
   2   toothpick in his mouth,

   2   _____ ,

   2   _____ .

"Just like verb clusters, absolutes help you describe the details of an action," I tell the class.

"What about describing how characters or scenes look?" Tim asks.

"Generally speaking, for description of a character or scene you'll find more adjective and noun clusters hooked to base sentences. The next exercise, for example, gives a character description."

STOP. DO COMBINING TO FILL IN THE FOLLOWING EXERCISE AND CHECK WITH THE ANSWER KEY, P. 275. THEN RESUME YOUR READING.

TWO-LEVEL SENTENCES: ADJECTIVE CLUSTERS

>Bridget seemed frozen where she sat.
>She was pale.

She was panicked.
She was unable to speak.

A. *Additions before the base sentence:*

    2 _____,

    2 _____,

    1 Bridget seemed frozen where she sat and unable to speak.

B. *Additions in middle of base sentence:*

    1 Bridget—/—seemed frozen where she sat.

      /2/ _____,

      /2/ _____,

      /2/ _____

C. *Additions after the base sentence:*

    1 Bridget was pale and panicked,

    2 _____,

    2 seemingly frozen where she sat.

"Here you've got adjective clusters. They're focused on Bridget's *appearance* rather than on action. Next you see noun clusters describing a situation. Your sexist language detectors should be activated by this exercise."

STOP. DO COMBINING TO FILL IN THE FOLLOWING EXERCISE AND CHECK WITH THE ANSWER KEY, P. 275. THEN RESUME YOUR READING.

TWO-LEVEL SENTENCES: NOUN CLUSTERS

His chain was brandished before her.
The chain was greasy.
It was a "macho" symbol.
It was a gesture of bravado.

A. *Additions before the base sentence:*

    2 _____,

    2 _____,

    1 his greasy chain was brandished before her.

B. *Additions in middle of base sentence:*

1 _____,
  /2/ a "macho" symbol,
  /2/ a gesture of bravado.

C. *Additions after the base sentence:*

1 His greasy chain was brandished before her as a "macho" symbol,

2 _____.

"Hey," Rob laughs. "That Grayson is quite a mover."

Carol and several others look aghast.

Kristin has a hand up. "You've shown us four types of additions in the three positions. And you've said that additions have to stay the same in each position. What happens when additions *don't* stay the same?"

"You mean when you have different types of additions in the same sentence?"

"Right. That's my question."

"Then you move from a *two-level* sentence to a *multi-level* one. 'Multi-level' is a way of saying that some additions modify the base sentence from different positions—and that other additions modify each other."

"Sounds complicated."

"Multi-level sentences are a bit more difficult. But if you understand how two-level sentences work, you have a good foundation for what follows. Let's look at a multi-level example that completes the story of Bridget and Grayson."

MULTI-LEVEL SENTENCE:
ADDITIONS BEFORE AND AFTER BASE SENTENCE

Bridget's lashes were lowered.
Color was rising to her cheeks.
Bridget grabbed the bike chain.
She then threw it across the room.
She chased Grayson out the door.
She shouted, "Come back when you grow up."

  2 Her lashes lowered,
  2 color rising to her cheeks,
1 Bridget grabbed the bike chain and threw it across the room,
    3 chasing Grayson out the door,
    3 shouting, "Come back when you grow up."

Theresa, Anne, and Carol seem pleased with this turn of events.

"Notice that there are *two* kinds of additions in this multi-level example

—absolutes in level 2, verb clusters in level 3. Each set of additions is grouped together just as we've seen earlier. But because they're different *types* of additions, we change the numbering. Here both sets of additions modify the base sentence, but they do so from different positions. One group of free modifiers comes before the base sentence; the other group comes after."

Chico shrugs. "Seems easy enough."

"To practice this kind of multi-level sentence, here's an exercise that opens a new story involving Gertrude Gottalottabucks and J. Troy Playboy."

STOP. DO COMBINING TO FILL IN THE NEXT EXERCISE. THEN RESUME YOUR READING.

MULTI-LEVEL SENTENCE:
ADDITIONS BEFORE AND AFTER BASE SENTENCE

This next courtship tale is somewhat sad.
This next courtship tale is somewhat funny.
This next courtship tale will engage your interest.
It will tease you to read on.
It will stimulate your imagination.

2 _____ ,

2 _____ ,

1   this next courtship tale will engage your interest,

    3 _____ ,

    3 _____ .

Hands are up all over the room as I put Andrea's multi-level sentence on the chalkboard.

  2   Somewhat sad,
  2   somewhat funny,
1   this next courtship tale will engage your interest,
    3   teasing you to read on,
    3   stimulating your imagination.

"Once again, you see two sets of additions modifying the base sentence from different positions. It's also possible to condense the content in each addition and still have a multi-level sentence. Here's what I mean."

  2   Somewhat sad but funny,
1   this next courtship tale will engage your interest,
    3   teasing you to read on as it stimulates your imagination.

Eric raises a hand. "You mentioned earlier that sometimes the additions modify each other, not the base sentence."

"That's what we'll see in this next example. Two writeouts illustrate this point."

MULTI-LEVEL SENTENCES:
ADDITIONS BEFORE AND AFTER BASE SENTENCE

Gertrude was pointedly uncongenial.
This was particularly when she snarled.
She had only one thing going for her.
That thing was an inherited fortune.

    2   Pointedly uncongenial,
        3   particularly when snarling,
1   Gertrude had only one thing going for her—
        4   an inherited fortune.

    2   With only one thing going for her—
        3   an inherited fortune—
1   Gertrude was pointedly uncongenial,
        4   particularly when snarling.

"Notice that when a free modifier has a different grammatical structure from preceding ones, you shift down to another level. The numbers and indentation show this downshifting, step by step. What's interesting in both examples is that level 3 modifies level 2, which in turn modifies level 1, the base sentence. You can hear these levels as you read both sentences aloud."

"Do lower levels always modify the next level up?" Carlos asks.

"Not always. That's what makes multi-level sentences more complicated. Sometimes a lower-level addition modifies the base sentence, not the preceding free modifier. You have to *listen* to hear how the additions go together. The aim, remember, is to see *how* free modifiers attach to base sentences."

"So, actually, getting the numbers exactly correct isn't that important."

"Right. Our *real* aim is to see and hear the different levels of specificity."

STOP. DO COMBINING TO FILL IN THE FOLLOWING EXERCISE. THEN RESUME YOUR READING.

MULTI-LEVEL SENTENCE

Gertrude yearned for a husband.
The husband would be a man.

The man would take care of her.
She had tried computerized dating services.
She had tried the want ads.

A.   *Additions before the base sentence:*

2   _____ —

     3   a man who would take care of her—

1   _____

_____.

B.   *Additions before and after base sentence:*

2   _____,

1   Gertrude yearned for a husband,

     3   _____.

Students help each other with writeouts as I move up and down the rows. Then I project answers for the two exercises.

     2   Yearning for a husband—
       3   a man who would take care of her—
1   Gertrude had tried computerized dating services and the want ads.

     2   Having tried computerized dating services and the want ads,
1   Gertrude yearned for a husband,
       3   a man who would take care of her.

"I think we're catching on," Carlos chortles. "How about something more challenging?"

"Fair enough. Let's try a more complex exercise."

STOP. DO COMBINING TO FILL IN THE FOLLOWING EXERCISE. THEN RESUME YOUR READING.

MULTI-LEVEL SENTENCE

Then something happened one evening.
The evening was dark.
The evening was a time of despair.
Her phone rang unexpectedly.
The ring brought a voice.
The voice was low.

The voice was crooning.
The voice was an answer to her want ads.

A. *Additions before and after base sentence:*

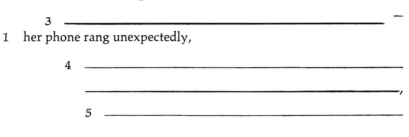

Students work in groups to experiment with free modifiers. Afterwards, three sample sentences go on the board.

> 2 Then one dark evening—
>   3 a time of despair—
> 1 her phone rang unexpectedly,
>   4 bringing a low, crooning voice,
>   5 an answer to her want ads.

> 2 Then one evening—
>   3 dark and despairing—
> 1 her phone rang unexpectedly,
>   4 bringing a voice,
>   5 its low croon an answer to her want ads.

> 2 Then one evening—
>   3 a time of darkness and despair—
> 1 her phone rang unexpectedly,
>   4 bringing a voice, /, to answer her want ads.
>   /5/ low and crooning.

"All of these are elegant, controlled sentences," I tell the class. "They work because you're *listening* to what you write—making sure that the additions fit together as they should."

"How about free modifiers in all three positions?" Tony asks.

"That takes even more control."

"But it works in the same way we've been studying?"

"Right. The principles are the same. Here's an example of the sentence you're asking about."

MULTI-LEVEL SENTENCE

She was nervous.
She was happy.
Her eyes were like glazed marbles.
She pursed her lips.
She bared her canine teeth in the mirror.
She then inspected her complexion.
She hoped to make a good impression on tonight's date.

A.   *Additions before, in the middle of, and after the base sentence:*
    2 Nervous and happy,
       3 her eyes like glazed marbles,
 1 she pursed her lips—/—and then inspected her complexion,
       /4/ baring her canine teeth in the mirror
          5 hoping to make a good impression on tonight's date.

"This example shows a multi-level sentence with additions in all three positions. Here's how it reads: *Nervous and happy, her eyes like glazed marbles, she pursed her lips—baring her canine teeth in the mirror—and then inspected her complexion, hoping to make a good impression on tonight's date.* The sentence has 33 words—9 in its base, 24 in its additions. It reads easily because the levels are logically interlocked. You certainly wouldn't want a *series* of such sentences, but an occasional one in the right place can be very effective."

A final worksheet goes before the class.

STOP. DO COMBINING TO FILL IN THE FOLLOWING EXERCISE AND CHECK WITH THE ANSWER KEY, P. 275. THEN RESUME YOUR READING.

MULTI-LEVEL SENTENCES

Meanwhile, Troy stood in front of another mirror.
He eyed his own image.
He wondered what his date would look like.
His hair was fluffed.
His moustache was trimmed.

A.   *Additions before the base sentence:*
    Meanwhile,

  2 _____ —

      3 his hair fluffed,

3 ———————————————————————— —
1   Troy eyed his own image and wondered what his date would look like.

B.   *Additions in middle of base sentence:*
1   Meanwhile, Troy stood in front of another mirror, /, and wondered what his date would look like.

/2/ ———————————————————————— —
/3/   fluffy hair and a trimmed moustache—

C.   *Additions after the base sentence:*
1   Meanwhile, Troy stood in front of another mirror,
2   wondering what his date would look like as he eyed his own image—

3 ————————————————————————,

3 ————————————————————————.

D.   *Additions before and after base sentence:*
Meanwhile,

2 ————————————————————————,

1 ————————————————————————,
3   his eyes on the image of his fluffy hair and trimmed moustache.

"Notice some of the style possibilities here. You can have absolutes— *his hair fluffed, moustache trimmed*—or you can transform the same information into noun clusters—*fluffy hair, a trimmed moustache.* You can have a verb cluster—*eyeing his own image*—or an absolute such as *his eyes on his own image.* How about another sentence that's different from these four?"

Carol raises a hand and comes to the board to transcribe a different multi-level sentence.

1   Meanwhile, Troy stood in front of another mirror,
2   eyeing his own image—
3   fluffed hair,
3   a trimmed moustache—
2   wondering what his date would look like.

"I get it," Peter says. "Even if there's an interruption, you can go back— like from 3 to 2."

"That's it. You change numbers whenever you shift to another level. But you can also use an addition of an earlier kind to backtrack."

The class is quiet, rereading Carol's sentence.

"You should remember three things about levels," I conclude. "First, when the additions stay the same, so does the numbering of levels. Second, when you get a *different* type of addition, you shift down to another level. Third, you number the levels consecutively."

I turn off the projector.

"As you do the exercises on two-level and multi-level sentences, don't worry about naming the various parts. And don't fuss too much with differences in numbering. What's most important is that you *do* the combining and experiment with structure. The numbers are just a *tool* for learning, not the learning itself."

Notebooks click shut. "And a final point," I add. "These two-level and multi-level sentences shouldn't be used all the time in your writing. You can of course overdo them. Your real goal is sentence variety, not simply long sentences. In other words, just because you're *able* to make long, nicely structured sentences doesn't mean that you're *obliged* to write them one after another. You need balance—some short sentences, some longer ones."

EXERCISE 7.1   Two-Level Sentences

Directions. Shown below are clusters of kernels that you can transform into two-level sentences. Check the Answer Key, p. 275, after you are finished.

CASEY SPACEY:
TWO-LEVEL SENTENCES

> Casey's mother rapped at his door.
> She was apparently upset.
> She was somewhat bewildered.

1   Casey's mother—/—rapped at his door.

/2/ _____ ,

/2/ _____

> Her questions were met with silence.
> The silence was Casey's refusal to talk.

1   _____ ,

2   Casey's refusal to talk.

> Her eyes were narrowed.
> Her face was pinched.
> She pleaded with him.
> The plea was to switch from astronomy to astrology.

2   _____ ,

2   her face pinched,

1   _____ .

> The door arced open slowly.
> It creaked on its hinge.
> It revealed the murkiness.
> The murkiness was of his observatory.
> The observatory was star-filled.

1   _____ ,

2   creaking on its hinge,

2   _____ .

> He stumbled down the stairs.
> He was unwilling to argue.
> He was seemingly full of despair.
> He checked her biorhythm charts.

1   He stumbled down the stairs—/—and checked her biorhythm charts.

/2/ _____ ,

/2/ _____

RICK O'SHEA:
TWO-LEVEL SENTENCES

> Rick still felt a little queasy.
> He was bandaged.
> He was limping badly.

1   _____ —/— _____ .

/2/   bandaged,

/2/ _____

> His head was pounding.
> His muscles were aching.
> His muscles were convulsed.

1   His head was pounding,

2   _____ .

> He vaguely remembered his last stand.
> The stand was on the goal line.
> The stand was a scene of violence.
> The stand was an occasion of contact.
> The contact was bone-crushing.

1   _____ —

2   a scene of violence,

2   _____ .

> It had been primitive.
> It had been violent.
> It had been emotionally satisfying.
> It had been a free-for-all.
> The free-for-all was complete.

2   _____ ,

2   _____ ,

2   _____ ,

1   it had been a complete free-for-all.

169

Now he was in the cafeteria.
He was nursing his wounds.
He was thumbing the sports section.
He was looking for his name in print.

1   ——————————————— ,

   2   ——————————————— ,

   2   ——————————————— ,

   2   looking for his name in print.

EXERCISE 7.2   Multi-Level Sentences

Directions. Shown below are clusters of kernels that you can transform into multi-level sentences. Check the Answer Key (p. 275) after you are finished.

WENDY WAFFLESTOMPERS:
MULTI-LEVEL SENTENCES

Wendy had a full backpack.
Wendy trudged up a hiking trail.
Her trudging was weary.
She was trying to have fun.

   2   With her backpack full,

1   ——————————————— ,

     3   trying to have fun.

She paused for a moment.
She was sweaty.
She was discouraged.
She asked herself, "Why do this?"

1   ——————————————— —

   2   sweaty and discouraged—

     3   —————————————— .

Something happened without warning.
Grayson roared up beside her.
He was jazzing the engine on his dirt bike.
The dirt bike was a gutsy machine.
The machine gave super performance.

   2   ——————————————— ,

1   Grayson roared up beside her,

3   ———————————————

   4   ——————————————— .

Wendy looked at him.
He was a show-off.
The show-off obviously needed attention.
The attention was from women.
Wendy had a terrific idea.

   2   Looking at him,

     3   ——————————————— ,

1   ——————————————— .

She was like the classic "damsel in distress."
She collapsed at his feet.
She was helpless.
She was pathetic.
She knew something full well.
She would soon be riding the motorcycle.
He would be packing the yogurt.
He would be packing the granola.

   2   ——————————————— ,

1   She collapsed at his feet—

     3   ——————————————— ,

     3   ——————————————— —

       4   knowing full well that ———

       ——————————————— .

J. TROY PLAYBOY: MULTI-LEVEL SENTENCES

Troy flicked out the lights.
Troy whipped himself into sociability.
The sociability was grim.
The sociability was a "grin-and-bear-it" attitude.

2 _____ ,

1 _____ —

   3   a "grin-and-bear-it" attitude.

Gertrude grew suddenly agitated.
Her breath was coming in short spurts.
It wheezed through her nostrils.

1   Gertrude grew suddenly agitated,

  2 _____ ,

    3 _____ .

Troy was an opportunist.
He was desperately poor.
He was cunningly amoral.
Troy considered Gertrude's wealth.
He wondered about the possibility of alimony.

2 _____ —

   3   desperately poor and cunningly amoral—

1 _____ ,

    4   wondering about the possibility of alimony.

Gertrude was smiling up at him.
She wondered about compatibility.
The compatibility was of their signs.
The signs were astrological.
His was Scorpio.
Hers was Taurus.

2 _____ ,

1   Gertrude wondered about compatibility of their astrological signs—

   3 _____ ,

   3 _____ .

Troy leaned forward.
His eyes were tightly closed.
He then kissed her jowly bulldog.
He thought that it was Gertrude.

1   Troy leaned forward—/—and then kissed her jowly bulldog.

/2/ _____ ,

   3 _____ .

EXERCISE 7.3   Proofreading Practice

Directions. Shown below are writeouts that contain misplaced or dangling modifiers. Spot the errors and rewrite the sentences. Check with the Answer Key (p. 275).

1.   Sally did cartwheels down the sidelines.
She bounced high into the air.
She worked the crowd into a frenzy.

PROBLEM 1   *Doing cartwheels down the sidelines, bouncing high into the air, the crowd was worked into a frenzy.*

2.   She then grasped the microphone stand.
She was slender.
She was graceful.
She was ready to be heard.

PROBLEM 2   *She then grasped the microphone stand—slender, graceful, and ready to be heard.*

3.   She breathed hard into the microphone.
Her excitement was like an electric force.
It galvanized the crowd.
It brought people to their feet.

PROBLEM 3   *Breathing hard into the microphone, her excitement was like an electric force, galvanizing the crowd, bringing people to their feet.*

4.   Sally was happy with the crowd's response.
Sally decided to cartwheel her "rally ballet."
This was a routine never before attempted.

PROBLEM 4   *Happy with the crowd's response, Sally's decision was to cartwheel her "rally ballet"—a routine never before attempted.*

EXERCISE 7.4   Rewriting Choppy Sentences

Directions. The following two paragraphs are choppy. Rewrite them so that the sentences flow smoothly and logically from one to another. You may delete words, change the form of words, or add connecting words. (*Practice making two-level and multi-level sentences.*)

CHAMPIONSHIP: Paragraph 1

The ball skidded toward Tim. Eric cut across court. He set the screen. Tim went driving past. His body was low. His body angled toward the base line. The defensive center moved instinctively. The move was to cut off this scoring threat. Tim shoveled a pass to Nate. Nate had spun into the open. Nate faked a pass toward the key. He then leaned toward the outside. One shoulder dropped as his feet came together. He pushed into a fall-away jump shot. His right knee was cocked. His torso was uncoiling against the lights. The ball was palmed high and up front. It flicked upward. It rolled in a spin. The spin was high and soft. It arched over defensive fingertips. It grazed the backboard glass. It rippled the net. The score was tied. There were ten seconds to go. A foul had been called on the defense.

CHAMPIONSHIP: Paragraph 2

Nate took a deep breath. He approached the foul line. He could hear his friends encouraging him. They were telling him to relax. His friends were Tony and Carlos. He bounced the ball twice. He hesitated for a moment. He fingered the seams. He tried to concentrate on the basket. Then he went into a slight crouch. He drew the ball inward and up. He lofted it toward the basket. It struck the front rim. It bounced high. It came down slightly to the right. The players went up for the rebound together. The players were a tangle of arms and elbows. Carlos came down with it. He wheeled toward the outside. He flicked it back to Nate. Nate had dropped into the key. The crowd was on its feet. The crowd was screaming. The noise crashed down on the court like a wave.

UNIT EIGHT
PRE-COMBINING AND RE-COMBINING

Late for class, I move through a crowd of hurrying students, rereading a typed note from my mailbox.

What we're doing really interests me. I'm starting to understand what you said when you first met us—that people have to transfer their natural talking power to the act of writing. Talking and writing aren't the same— I know that—but they're related. I think of one as a path to the other.

I used to think that I didn't know *how* to write and that a lot of grammar terminology was the first step. I also didn't believe I had anything to say that was *worth* putting down. I was so worried about pleasing my instructors and not making mistakes that I'd freeze up.

Lately, I've been trying some writing on my own. I don't know if it's really that good, but I still like it. What I do first is make up a list of kernel sentences about something. I'll look at an object, for example, or watch some kind of action. I try to get the details. Then I do the combining, just sort of adding ideas that come to mind. It's interesting. New sentences start coming by themselves. Then I go back

over what I've written and do some rearranging, maybe taking out words or adding them. The last step is fixing the punctuation, capital letters, and so on. Here's an example:

Alone with my thoughts, I'm waiting for class to begin. Students shuffle through the open doorway, glancing at the wall clock, and head for empty desks. A few people have gathered near the paper-littered bookcases to check assignments. Soft backlighting from the windows angles across their work table, making bright trapezoids for floating dust particles. I'm completely aware of myself right now—the tightness in my right shoulder, the feel of my pen sliding across paper, the rise and fall of my breathing. Seeing things clearly like this, getting them down—that's what I like.

—The Phantom

The classroom door is open, and students are making last-minute comparisons. I glance around the room, wondering who the Phantom might be.

"For a change of pace," I tell the class, "we're trying two new things today. First, we'll get into *pre-combining*—a process in which you invent your own kernel sentences for combining. Then we'll study *re-combining*—a process for comparing your writeouts of clusters with the original sentences written by professional writers. Each process can move you a little further toward the goal of on-your-own writing."

To get the class started on *pre-combining*, I pick up a coffee cup from my desktop, examine it for a moment, and hand it to Michelle. A single kernel sentence goes on the board:

A cup rests on the desktop.

"Let's add other kernels," I say to the class. "First focus on key details. Describe the cup."

"The cup is for coffee," Michelle offers, passing it across the aisle.

"It's wheat-colored," Kristin adds.

"It's stained," Nate volunteers.

"Chipped on the rim," Maria calls out. "And it has groove marks."

"And made by hand," Chico says.

Theresa looks the cup over. "It's got an abstract design."

"The design's on the side of the cup," Tony adds. "It has dark brown lines."

"The design looks like a flower," Eric says.

Carlos has a hand up. "It's an etched design. The flower leaves sort of curl under."

"Good work," I say to the class. "Here's the group of kernels you just invented."

A cup rests on the desktop. It's for coffee. It's wheat-colored. It's stained. It's chipped on the rim. It has groove marks. It's made by hand. It has a design. The design is abstract. The design is on the side of the cup. The design is dark brown lines. The design is etched. The design looks like a flower. The flower's leaves curl under.

"The next step, of course, is combining. It's up to you to choose the number of final sentences you want. You might reduce these to half a dozen sentences—or you might put everything into one. In either case, though, your writing would have good clear detail. Why? Because you've gone through a process of *pre-combining*."

"Can we try putting them together?" Paulo asks.

"Sure. They're *your* sentences, after all."

The class sets to work. Three versions are finally transcribed onto transparencies and projected.

VERSION A: Five Sentences

A wheat-colored coffee cup rests on the desktop. Its rim is chipped and its insides stained. Groove marks indicate that it was made by hand. Dark brown lines are etched on its side. This abstract design looks like a flower with curling leaves.

VERSION B: Three Sentences

On the desktop rests a stained, hand-made coffee cup with groove marks on its sides and a chip on its rim. It is wheat-colored and has a dark brown design, which is somewhat abstract. These etched lines look like a flower that has undercurling leaves.

VERSION C: One Sentence

Resting on the desktop is a wheat-colored coffee cup, rim-chipped and stained, its sides marked by hand-made grooves and etched by a dark-brown, abstract design—lines of a flower, with leaves curling under.

"This process of *pre-combining* is a useful method of finding something to say when you're stuck and can't seem to start writing. It gets you moving."

"So you put down the pieces," Nate says. "I mean, the kernel sentences."

"Right. You focus attention on the *parts* of a description, scene, action, or process. You get these ideas down quickly, without trying to relate or connect them. Then you examine what you've got and combining takes over. You start rearranging, adding, deleting, and connecting. You even spin out new sentences."

"Sort of like outlining?" Nate asks.

"Not really. Outlining is a way of *organizing* information, but pre-combining is a *discovery* technique—a method of finding something to say by focusing your attention. Of course, it can *lead* to outlining if you work with it a while."

Eric seems to like this. "Another example?"

"Sure. Let's describe *what happened* to the coffee cup."

Hands start going up.

"The instructor picked up the cup," Janet offers.

"He looked it over," Chuck adds. "Then he gave it to Michelle. She started passing it around."

"He asked us to focus on details," Peter says.

Tony waves a hand. "And to call out our kernels."

"He wrote the sentences down," Maria adds.

"They didn't go in a list," Paulo volunteers. "They went in paragraph form."

"Then we combined them," Theresa says. "Some people wrote on transparencies. We saw the results."

"And talked about pre-combining," Carlos concludes.

"Well done again," I tell the class. "Here are your kernels. As you do the combining this time, add any details that seem significant. You can also rearrange or delete sentences. This is a *springboard* for on-your-own writing."

> The instructor picked up the cup. He looked it over. He gave it to Michelle. She started passing it around. He asked us to focus on details. He asked us to call out kernel sentences. He wrote them down. They didn't go in a list. They went in paragraph form. We then combined them. Some people wrote on transparencies. We saw the results. We talked about pre-combining.

"How about everybody doing it together?" Eric suggests.

The class seems to like this idea, so we do the combining as a large group —with me transcribing the oral flow. The transformations go on the board.

> Picking up the coffee cup, the instructor looked it over, paused, and gave it to Michelle, who started passing it around. This was an exercise called pre-combining. He asked us to focus on the cup's details and to call out sentences, which he then wrote on the board. These sentences didn't go in a list but rather into paragraph form. Unknown to the instructor, a white chalk line marked the back of his pants as he worked to get down the kernels that were being volunteered. Everyone was amused by this, but of course no one said anything. The class then dutifully combined the sentences, with three people writing on transparencies so that we could see the results. Afterwards, we talked about pre-combining.

I brush the seat of my pants. Sure enough, my fingertips are white with chalk dust.

"The pre-combining process works for more than description and narration," I tell the class. "It's also useful for writing that explains. Take the term *pre-combining* itself. What could we say to define it?"

Once again, hands start going up, and I am transcribing a series of kernel sentences.

> Pre-combining is a process. It is for discovery. It is for writing. It has one main purpose. The purpose is to get many ideas on paper. They can then be

combined. Some can be eliminated. New ones can be added. Pre-combining focuses attention. The attention is on parts and details. It is similar to brain-storming. One idea sparks another. This can cause a chain reaction. The words start coming fast. Kernel sentences pile up. Sometimes they're in order. Sometimes they're not. It is different from outlining. Outlining is for organizing ideas. Pre-combining can lead to outlining.

My hand aches as I step back from the board.
"Why don't you have the readers combine this one?" Tony asks.
As usual, there is enthusiasm for this plan.

Your writeouts go here:

_____

_____

_____

_____

_____

_____

_____

_____

_____

_____

"So much for *pre-combining*," I tell the class. "Let's now turn to a process called *re-combining*. I'll give you some kernels from a piece of professional writing. Your task is to see how your writeouts compare with the original."

"What's the point?" Andrea asks.

"You're now at a stage where you can profit from close analysis of other people's work. The point isn't to *match* a professional writer's sentences, word for word. It's to learn by comparing. This process will deepen your sense of style in writing. How? By showing you how your prose—your characteristic way of thinking through words—is either similar to or different from the style of various professionals."

"Hmmm," she murmurs. "I don't know."

I hand out a packet of mimeograph pages.

"Let's begin our re-combining work with four sentences taken from Frank Waters's beautiful novel *The Man Who Killed the Deer*. This is a story about a young man who is caught between two worlds—his native Pueblo Indian culture and life in white America. The sentences describe the council meeting, which is the soul of the tribe."

1. A council meeting is one-half talk.
2. It is one-half silence.

3. The silence has more weight than the talk.
4. The silence has more meanings than the talk.
5. The silence has more intonations than the talk.

6. It is angry.
7. It is impatient.
8. It is cheerful.
9. It is masked by calmness.
10. It is masked by patience.
11. It is masked by dignity.

12. Thus the members move together.
13. The movement is even.

Students set to work in combining the kernels. Peter volunteers to put his writeouts on a transparency to compare with the sentences as originally written by Waters.

COMBINED VERSION

(1) A council meeting is one-half talk, but it is also one-half silence. (2) The silence not only has more weight than the talk, but it also has more intonations. (3) Although it is angry, impatient, and cheerful, it is also masked by calmness, patience, and dignity. (4) Thus the members move together evenly.

ORIGINAL VERSION

(1) A council meeting is one-half talk and one-half silence. (2) The silence has more weight, more meanings, more intonations than the talk. (3) It is angry, impatient, cheerful, but masked by calmness, patience, dignity. (4) Thus the members move evenly together.

—from *The Man Who Killed the Deer* by Frank Waters (p. 19)

"What stylistic similarities or differences do you see?" I ask the class.

"Waters uses fewer words," Christopher volunteers. "I'd say he gets more emphasis, especially in the second sentence."

"But Peter's sentences are also very nice ones. The *not only, but also* pattern is particularly well done."

Peter raises his hand. "The effect in sentence 3 is totally different. I really like Waters's balance—and the way the sentence moves without *and* in the series. That's a nice touch."

"Balance is a good term. Waters's sentences fit together like carefully cut puzzle pieces, each using *compounding* and *coordination*. The rhythms are measured—almost like a drumbeat."

"Sounds like he's really in control," Rob says.

"Waters speaks from experience and knows his craft," I add. "The result is one of the best books about native American people ever written."

I flip to the next page. "Okay, we'll now move to three sentences from Rudolfo A. Anaya's *Bless Me, Ultima.* This book won the Second Annual Premio Quinto Sol award for Chicano literature in 1971. You'll begin to see why as you put Anaya's sentences back together."

1. The church was packed with women.
2. The women were in black.
3. Each one suffered the three hours.
4. The suffering was stoic.
5. The hours were of the Crucifixion.
6. The Crucifixion was with the Christ.
7. The Christ was tortured.

8. The wind was outside.
9. The wind blew.
10. The wind cut off the light.
11. The light was of the sun.
12. The cutting was with its dust.
13. The pigeons cried.
14. The cry was mournful.
15. The cry was in the tower.

16. The prayers were inside.
17. The prayers were like cries.
18. The cries were muffled.
19. The cries were against a storm.
20. The storm seemed to engulf the world.

The room is hushed as the class goes to work on the three clusters, trying to anticipate Anaya's transformation. Chico agrees to project his writeouts for comparison.

COMBINED VERSION

(1) Each of the women in black who packed the church stoically suffered the three hours of the tortured Christ's Crucifixion. (2) The dust-blowing outside wind cutting off the light of the sun made the pigeons mournfully cry in the tower. (3) The prayers inside were like cries that were muffled against a storm engulfing the world.

ORIGINAL VERSION

(1) The church was packed with women in black, each stoically suffering the three hours of the Crucifixion with the tortured Christ. (2) Outside the wind

blew and cut off the sun with its dust, and the pigeons cried mournfully in the tower. (3) Inside the prayers were like muffled cries against a storm which seemed to engulf the world.

—from *Bless Me, Ultima* by Rudolfo A. Anaya (p. 199)

Chico's groan is plainly audible.

"What's the matter?" I ask.

"Look at my first sentence. I mean, it sounds really *flat*."

"A couple of things to notice," I point out. "Your first sentence has very long noun clusters—ten words in the subject, eight words after the word *suffered*. That kind of pile-up of phrases is sometimes hard to read. There's also a slight problem with the modifier *stoically*. Does it go with *packed* or *suffered*? Putting it after the latter word eliminates the confusion."

Chico studies his sentences. "Sort of the same problem in sentence 2. I'm trying to pack too much into the first part of the sentence. It's overloaded—I mean, *way* too long. A dozen words."

"Good observation," I agree. "What do you notice about Anaya's style?"

"It's hard to describe. Not so flat, I guess. And not so jammed up. I really like the way he begins sentences 2 and 3 with *outside* and *inside*."

"So much for warm-ups," I tell the class. "Now we get to the harder combining."

I flip to the third example. Looking over the clusters, the students groan and gasp.

"Obviously, this is very complicated re-combining. The author is Mildred D. Taylor, a gifted black writer. Her two sentences are from *Roll of Thunder, Hear My Cry*, winner of the 1977 Newberry Medal. Indentation is provided to help you keep track of your combining. Perhaps you'll want to transform the two sentences into several shorter ones."

1. Revivals were always affairs.
    2. The affairs were very serious.
    3. The affairs were gay.
    4. The affairs were long-planned-for.
    5. The affairs brought pots and pans from shelves.
        6. The shelves were out-of-the-way.
    7. The affairs brought dresses and pants from chests.
        8. The dresses were mothball-packed.
        9. The pants were creased.
        10. The chests were hidden.
11. The affairs brought all the people.
    12. The people were from the community.
    13. The people were from neighboring communities.
    14. The people came up the school road.
        15. The road was winding.
        16. The road was red.
    17. The people came to the Great Faith Church.

18. The revival ran for days.
    19. The days were seven.
20. It was an occasion.
    21. Everyone looked forward to it.
        22. It was more than just services.
        23. The services were for church.
24. It was the year's only event.
    25. The event was social.
    26. The event was planned.
    27. The event disrupted the humdrum.
        28. The humdrum was of everyday life.
        29. The life was in the country.

The class once again sets to work, laboring over the kernels and trying to read the author's mind. Anne volunteers to project her version for comparison.

COMBINED VERSION

(1) Although revivals were always serious, they were also gay and long-planned-for affairs. (2) They brought pots and pans from out-of-the-way shelves. (3) They brought mothball-packed dresses and creased pants from hidden chests. (4) They brought all the people from the community (neighboring ones included) up the red and winding school road to the Great Faith Church. (5) The revival ran for seven days. (6) It was an occasion that everyone looked forward to. (7) It was more than just church services. (8) It was the year's only planned social event. (9) The revival disrupted the humdrum of everyday life in the country.

ORIGINAL VERSION

(1) Revivals were always very serious, yet gay and long-planned-for affairs which brought pots and pans from out-of-the-way shelves, mothball-packed dresses and creased pants from hidden chests, and all the people from the community and the neighboring communities up the winding red school road to the Great Faith Church. (2) The revival ran for seven days, and it was an occasion that everyone looked forward to, for it was more than just church services; it was the year's only planned social event, disrupting the humdrum of everyday country life.

"The big difference is sentence length," Anne says. "I transformed the two long sentences into nine shorter ones. Actually, I think it reads better my way."

"Okay, describe how your version works."

Anne shrugs. "Repetition. The first five sentences all begin with *they;* and *they* refers to *revivals.* Sentences 6, 7, and 8 all begin with *it;* and *it* refers to *revival* in sentence 5. The last sentence concludes with the word *revival.* It's repetition, pure and simple. Maybe parallel sentences can get monotonous, but I think they work here."

"Good analysis. The original version works mainly with a different stylistic device—*subordination*. The subordinators are *which* in sentence 1 and *for*—meaning *because*—in sentence 2."

"This is interesting," Theresa says. "Do you have another example?"

"As a matter of fact I do—one that I found in my mailbox. Let me break it into kernels so that you can re-combine it."

I go to work on the board.

1. I'm alone with my thoughts.
2. I'm waiting for class to begin.

3. Students shuffle through the doorway.
4. The doorway is open.
5. They glance at the clock.
6. The clock is on the wall.
7. They head for desks.
8. The desks are empty.

9. A few people have gathered near the bookcases.
10. The bookcases are littered with paper.
11. They are checking assignments.

12. Backlighting angles across their table.
13. The backlighting is soft.
14. The backlighting is from the windows.
15. The table is for work.
16. The backlighting makes trapezoids.
17. The trapezoids are bright.
18. The trapezoids are for dust particles.
19. The particles are floating.

20. I'm completely aware of myself.
21. The awareness is right now.
    22. There is tightness in my shoulder.
        23. The shoulder is my right one.
    24. There is the feel of my pen.
        25. My pen slides across paper.
    26. There is the rise of my breathing.
    27. There is the fall of my breathing.

28. I see things clearly.
29. I get them down.
30. I like this.

Kristin raises her hand. "Who's the writer?"

"The Phantom. Somebody in this room."

"So we're supposed to re-combine these kernels?" Carlos asks.

"How else will I establish the Phantom's identity?"

"I don't follow you."

"Writing style is like an author's fingerprints. I'll simply compare your re-combining work with the original. Then I'll know who the Phantom is."

A grin spreads across Eric's mouth. "But suppose several of us come up with the Phantom's writeouts."

"Not likely."

"I'll bet the *readers* could," Kristin says.

"Without looking back to the original?" I ask. "There's no way."

"I say that we should join forces to keep the Phantom's identity a secret," Carlos announces. "That means re-combining the sentences as the Phantom originally did them."

"Good luck," I tell the class.

Your writeouts go here:
(IMITATE THE PHANTOM'S STYLE WITHOUT LOOKING BACK)

_____

_____

_____

_____

_____

_____

_____

_____

_____

_____

EXERCISE 8.1 De-Combining

Directions. Break the following sentences into their constituent kernels. To do this "de-combining," simply fill in the blanks with information from the sentence that is given. Then check with the Answer Key, p. 275.

MODEL

An otter, often diving to 180 feet, finds its meals on the rocky ocean floor.

1. An otter finds its meals.
2. An otter often dives to 180 feet.
3. Its meals are on the ocean floor.
4. The floor is rocky.

It can remain submerged as long as four minutes but usually stays under water less than 90 seconds.

5. It can remain submerged.
6. The submersion is for ——————.
7. It usually stays under water.
8. The stay is for ——————.

When an otter makes a successful dive, it brings up a shellfish and a flat rock.

9. An otter makes a dive.
10. ——————.
11. It brings up a ——————.
12. It brings up a ——————.
13. The rock is ——————.

The otter floats on its back, puts the rock on its chest, and smashes open the shellfish.

14. ——————.
15. ——————.
16. ——————.

Because the otter's chest is particularly thick and loose-skinned, it is adapted to this shell-smashing operation.

17. The otter's chest is ——————.
18. The otter's chest is ——————.
19. It is adapted to an ——————.
20. The operation is ——————.

To wash off spilled food, the otter rolls over in the water every half-minute or so.

21. The otter wants ——————.
22. The food is ——————.
23. ——————.
24. The rolling is ——————.

It grasps the remaining food with its front paws, which are thick and handlike.

25. It grasps ——————.
26. The food ——————.
27. The grasp is with ——————.
28. The front paws are ——————.
29. ——————.

This methodical routine is well practiced.

30. ——————.
31. ——————.

An adult otter, which may weigh up to 100 pounds, eats 20–25% of its body weight every day.

32. An otter eats ——————.
33. The otter is an ——————.
34. The otter may weigh ——————.
35. The eating is ——————.

The otter shares its distinction of using tools with chimpanzees, the Galapagos woodpecker finch, an Egyptian vulture, and man.

36. The otter shares ——————.

184

37. The distinction is ——————.

38. The distinction is shared with ————.

39. ——————————.

40. ——————————.

41. ——————————.

EXERCISE 8.2   Re-Combining (Personal Narrative)

Directions. Re-combine the following kernels in ways that make sense to you. All are written from a personal ("I") point of view. Compare your writeouts with the sentences as originally written by checking the Answer Key, p. 275.

FROM *RUNNING AND BEING* BY GEORGE SHEEHAN

1. I reached my peak of creativity.
2. I was five.

3. I could draw.
4. I could paint.
5. I could sculpt.

6. I could sing.
7. I could dance.
8. I could act.

9. I possessed my body.
10. The possession was complete.

11. Something happened with it.
12. I became absorbed in a life.
13. The life was good.
14. The life was beautiful.
15. The life was joyful.

16. I examined.
17. I tested.
18. I explored.

19. I could not bear to watch.

FROM *GIFT FROM THE SEA* BY ANNE MORROW LINDBERGH

1. One is a stranger to oneself.
2. One is estranged from others too.

3. One is out of touch with oneself.
4. Then one cannot touch others.

5. How often I have felt the wilderness.
6. This has been in a large city.
7. This has been shaking hands with my friends.
8. The wilderness stretches between us.

9. Both of us were wandering in wastes.
10. The wastes were arid.
11. Both of us had lost the springs.
12. The springs nourished us.
13. Both of us had found them dry.

14. One is connected to one's own core.
15. One is connected to others.
16. I am beginning to discover this.

17. And the core can best be refound through solitude.
18. The core is the inner spring.
19. This is for me.

FROM *THE BELL JAR* BY SYLVIA PLATH

1. New York was bad enough.

2. Something happened by nine in the morning.

3.   The freshness evaporated.
  4.   The freshness was fake.
  5.   The freshness was country-wet.
  6.   The freshness somehow seeped in overnight.
  7.   The evaporation was like the tail end of a dream.
  8.   The dream was sweet.

  9.   The streets were mirage-gray.
  10.   The streets were at the bottom of their canyons.
  11.   The canyons were granite.
12.   The streets wavered in the sun.
  13.   The streets were hot.
14.   The car tops sizzled.
  15.   The car tops glittered.
16.   The dust blew into my eyes.
  17.   The dust was dry.
  18.   The dust was cindery.
  19.   The dust blew down my throat.

FROM *DESERT SOLITAIRE* BY EDWARD ABBEY

1.   The generator is an engine.
  2.   The engine is small.
  3.   The engine has four cylinders.
  4.   The engine uses gasoline.
  5.   The engine is mounted on a block.
    6.   The block is wooden.
    7.   The block is not far from the trailer.

8.   It is much too close.
9.   This is what I'd say.

10.   I open the switch.
11.   I adjust the choke.
12.   I engage the crank.
13.   I heave it around.

14.   The engine sputters.
  15.   It gasps.
  16.   It catches fire.
  17.   It gains momentum.

18.   It winds up with a roar.
  19.   Its valves are popping.
  20.   Its rockers are thumping.
  21.   Its pistons are hissing.
    22.   They go up and down.
    23.   They are inside their jackets.
    24.   The jackets are oiled.

FROM *WANDA HICKEY'S NIGHT OF GOLDEN MEMORIES* BY JEAN SHEPHERD

1.   I half dozed in front of my TV set.
2.   The speaker droned on in his voice.
3.   The voice was high.
4.   The voice was nasal.

  5.   Something happens one night a week.
  6.   This is a form of self-discipline.
  7.   The discipline is masochistic.
8.   I sentence myself to three hours.
  9.   Three hours is the minimum.
  10.   The hours are for viewing television.
  11.   The television is educational.

  12.   Educational TV is like so many other things.
  13.   The things are in life.
14.   Educational TV is a great idea.
  15.   Educational TV is a miserable reality.
    16.   There are murky films.
      17.   The films are of home life.
      18.   The home life is in Kurdistan.
    19.   There are jowly English authors.
      20.   The authors are being interviewed.
      21.   The interviewers are jowly English literary critics.

22. There are ladies.
    23. The ladies are pinched-faced.
    24. The ladies are demonstrating Japanese brush techniques.

25. But I watch all of it.
26. My watching is religious.
27. I suppose I watch for a reason.
28. It is there.
29. It is like Mount Everest.

EXERCISE 8.3   Re-Combining (Expository Writing)

Directions. Re-combine the following kernels in ways that make sense to you. All are written from an impersonal point of view. Compare your writeouts with the sentences as originally written by checking the Answer Key, p. 275.

FROM *CHANGING* BY LIV ULLMAN

1. The woman is made to feel guilty.
2. She wants to work.
3. She needs to work.
4. She lets others look after her child.

    5. She is a woman.
6. The child needs her at home.

    7. He is a man.
8. Something is normal.
    9. He gives prior attention to his profession.

    10. The man and woman don't marry.
11. She is the mother.
    12. The mother has a child.
    13. The child is illegitimate.

14. She has the responsibility.

15. She has to arrange eighteen years of her life.
16. The arrangement is in accordance with something.
17. Something is best for her child.

18. She has to refuse to work.
19. She has to refuse contact with other people.
20. She cannot afford help.
21. She cannot get help.

FROM *WRITING WITHOUT TEACHERS* BY PETER ELBOW

1. Control is not what you start out with.
2. Coherence is not what you start out with.
3. Knowing your mind is not what you start out with.
4. They are what you end up with.

5. Think of writing as a way to grow a message.
6. Think of writing as a way to cook a message.
7. Don't think of writing as a way to transmit a message.

8. Writing is a way to end up thinking something.
9. You couldn't have started out thinking something.

10. Something is a fact.
11. Writing is a transaction.
12. The transaction is with words.
13. You *free* yourself from what you presently think.
14. You *free* yourself from what you presently feel.

15. You *free* yourself from what you presently believe.

. . .

16. What looks inefficient is really efficient.
17. The inefficiency is a rambling process.
18. The process has lots of writing.
19. The process has lots of throwing away.
20. The process is the best way you can work up to something.
21. Something is what you really want to say.
22. Something is how you really want to say it.

FROM *A REVERENCE FOR WOOD*
BY ERIC SLOANE

1. Doors were often symbols.
2. This was in the pioneer days.

3. Girls filled hope chests.
4. Young men planned doors for the houses.
5. They would someday build the houses.

6. A house might be built of local pine.
7. A house might be built of local chestnut.
8. The door was considered something special.
9. The wood was often sassafras panels.
10. The wood was often apple.
11. The wood was often cherry.
12. The wood was even mahogany.
13. The mahogany was brought from the West Indies.
14. The mahogany was brought from Central America.

15. A godly man might prefer a Christian door.
16. The door had stiles.
17. Stiles are vertical pieces.
18. The door had rails.
19. Rails are horizontal pieces.
20. Stiles and rails formed a Christian cross.

21. A superstitious person might put a Maltese cross.
22. The cross would go in the lower section.
23. This would make a "witch door."
24. The "witch door" would keep out evil spirits.
25. A superstitious person might frame the door.
26. The framing would be in ash.
27. This would make the spell more potent.

FROM *ZEN AND THE ART OF
MOTORCYCLE MAINTENANCE*
BY ROBERT PIRSIG

1. The romantic mode is primarily inspirational.
2. It is primarily creative.
3. It is primarily intuitive.

4. Feelings predominate.
5. Facts do not predominate.

6. "Art" is often romantic.
7. "Art" is sometimes opposed to "Science."

8. It does not proceed by reason.
9. It does not proceed by laws.

10. It proceeds by feeling.
11. It proceeds by intuition.
12. It proceeds by conscience.
13. The conscience is esthetic.

14. Something happens in European cultures.
15. The cultures are northern.
16. The romantic mode is usually associated with femininity.
17. This is certainly not a necessary association.

18. Something happens by contrast.
19. The classic mode proceeds by reason.
20. It proceeds by laws.
21. Reason and laws are underlying forms.

22. The forms are of thought.
23. The forms are of behavior.

24. Something happens in the European cultures.
25. It is primarily a masculine mode.
26. The fields are unattractive to women for this reason.
27. The fields are science.
28. The fields are law.
29. The fields are medicine.

30. Motorcycle riding is romantic.
31. Motorcycle maintenance is purely classic.

32. The dirt gives it a negative romantic appeal.
33. The grease gives it a negative romantic appeal.
34. The mastery of underlying form gives it a negative romantic appeal.
35. Women never go near it.

EXERCISE 8.4   On-Your-Own Writing Options

Directions. Pick one of the following options. Use it as a focus for on-your-own writing.

1. You have learned how the Phantom makes lists of kernel sentences and combines them. Why not give this approach a try? Here are some possible subjects for your kernels:
   a. any physical object in your surroundings
   b. any action that you can now observe closely
   c. any sensory experience of the present moment (sounds, textures, smells, etc.)

   First, brainstorm a list of kernels. Then combine these kernels and arrange them into the form of a paragraph. After-

wards, add details that you overlooked or delete details that seem unnecessary.

2. Now that you have learned to de-combine and re-combine sentences, you may like to try it on your own.
   a. Find a short passage in the writing of a favorite author.
   b. De-combine (break down) at least three consecutive sentences into their constituent kernels.
   c. Re-combine the kernels, looking for alternate ways to express the author's message.
   d. Compare your writeouts with the sentences as originally written.

   After completing these four steps, talk about the version you prefer and why.

"The more you know about how words work," I tell the class, "the more you're their master. Today we'll study ways to achieve an even, consistent tone."

"Tone?" Nate asks.

"Tone refers to different qualities of your writing voice. Sometimes you're serious, other times playful. Sometimes you're objective, other times emotional. Sometimes you're laudatory, other times critical. Tone depends on your writing intentions. With clear intentions, you're more likely to achieve a consistent tone."

To illustrate the concept of tone, I hand out a new kind of exercise and ask students to go to work.

FILL IN AND COMBINE

Directions. Fill in the numbered blanks with words from the *left* column and do the combining. Then repeat the process for the *right* column. Compare the *tones* of the resulting writeouts.

My minds feels _____ 1 _____ .

191

I study these sentences.

The sentences are _____ 2 _____ .

1. energized	1. half-asleep
2. interesting	2. stupid

Such exercises _____ 3 _____ me.

The exercises are _____ 4 _____ .

They _____ 5 _____ my processes.

The processes are mental.

3. stimulate	3. bore
4. sensible	4. senseless
5. turn on	5. turn off

I _____ 6 _____ see their relevance.

I _____ 7 _____ getting more of them.

6. can	6. cannot
7. anticipate	7. dread

These exercises _____ 8 _____ a concept.

The exercises are _____ 9 _____ .

The concept is called "tone."

The concept is _____ 10 _____ .

8. clarify	8. obscure
9. provocative	9. ridiculous
10. extremely important	10. completely inconsequential

After everyone has finished combining, two contrasting paragraphs go up on the board. "Does each paragraph have a *consistent* tone?" I ask.

TONE A

My mind feels *energized* as I study these *interesting* sentences. Such *sensible* exercises *stimulate* me and *turn on* my mental processes. Because I *can* see their relevance, I *anticipate* getting more of them. These *provocative* exercises *clarify* a concept called "tone" that is *extremely important*.

TONE B

My mind feels *half-asleep* as I study these *stupid* sentences. Such *senseless* exercises *bore* me and *turn off* my mental *processes*. Because I *cannot* see their relevance, I *dread* getting more of them. These *ridiculous* exercises *obscure* a concept called "tone" that is *completely inconsquential*.

"One's positive, one's negative," Carlos says. "They're consistent, but opposite."

"Gaining control over words means controlling the tone," I tell the class. "Once you've established it, you try to maintain it."

"What happens if you don't?" Maria asks.

"Then you get utterly confused, out-of-control sentences that don't hang together. Like these."

My mind feels *energized* as I study these *stupid* sentences. Such *sensible* exercises *bore* me and *turn on* my mental processes. Because I *cannot* see their relevance, I *anticipate* getting more of them. These *ridiculous* exercises *clarify* a concept called "tone" that is *completely inconsequential.*

"We'll approach the idea of consistent tone—gaining control over words —by looking at two related language concepts: *usage levels and connotation. Usage levels* refers to the level of formality in your writing—your choice of words in relation to your intended audience. *Connotation* refers to the positive, neutral, or negative feelings that words convey. We'll separate these concepts to explore tone from different vantage points. Actually, though, they're closely related ideas—even interdependent. A change in usage level can change connotation—and vice versa, of course."

To introduce the idea of *usage levels,* I ask students to solve a situational problem.

> *You are writing to a former teacher, asking for a letter of recommendation. Pick the right level of usage.*
>
> *Formal.* A commendatory missive alluding to my attributes and potential for employment would be singularly appreciated.
>
> *Standard.* I would very much appreciate a letter of recommendation that refers to my job qualifications.
>
> *Casual.* I'd really like it if you'd put down some of the stuff I'm good at work-wise.

"I'd say the standard, middle level is best," Theresa volunteers.

"And why is that?"

"The formal one sounds sort of stiff and hard to understand. And the casual one has too much slang."

"Right. In this situation, the standard level of usage is appropriate because it doesn't draw attention to itself. It's the most effective choice for the specified audience."

I can tell that Paulo is having trouble with my explanation. I push on with an analogy. "To understand usage levels, you might think of words in terms of clothing. Some words are formal and ceremonious, even stuffy, perhaps. Others are at a standard level—well-dressed but not showy. Still others are at a very informal, casual level. So it's tuxedos and evening

gowns at the 'high' extreme; business suits and coordinated sportswear in the 'middle'; jeans and T shirts at the 'low' end. What's important is *appropriateness*—choosing words to *fit* the situation."

Michelle has a hand up. "Appropriateness?"

"Yes. Clothes from the formal extreme may be appropriate for fancy occasions, but they're *inappropriate* for business use—and *very* inappropriate for lounging around or working in the garden. The same goes for clothing—or words—at the other levels. They're appropriate in one social situation but not in others."

"Example?" she asks.

"Study the following chart. Notice that words in the three columns mean about the same thing but that they differ in their usage levels. Choosing the appropriate word will depend, of course, on the writing situation in which you find yourself."

USAGE LEVELS

Formal	*Standard*	*Casual*
quiescent	calm	laid back
converse	talk	chew the fat
transcendent	important	heavy
personage	celebrity	big shot
inebriated	drunk	bombed
myriad	many	lots
cast aspersions	belittle	put down
populace	people	guys
perturbation	inconvenience	hassle
au courant	up-to-date	with it

"The categories—formal, standard, and casual usage—are very large ones," I tell the class. "At the absurd extreme of formal usage, you'll encounter *gobbledygook*—words trying to sound more important than they really are. At the opposite extreme of casual usage, you'll find *slang* expressions. Usually you need to avoid these extremes. But don't make the mistake of avoiding *all* formal or casual words. Doing so limits the range and richness of your language. The real point is to use words with care."

"Clarification," Carol says. "Gobbledygook is wording that's *super-formal*?"

"Right. You see it most blatantly used in government pronouncements and in the jargon of various professions. For example, what would you call *'the anatomical juxtaposition of two orbicular muscles in a state of contraction'*?"

"Word salad," Carlos offers.

"It may be that, all right, but it's also the definition of a *kiss*. What's a *'print-mediated, self-contained instructional system engineered for a visual learning modality'*?"

Andrea's hand edges upward. "A book?"

"Right. More specifically—a textbook. Such overly formal language is inflated and pretentious. It's masquerading. It struts around in a puffed-up, self-important way. Janitors become *custodial personnel*; news releases become *public information statements*; a disagreement becomes a *productive exchange of views*; letters become *interpersonal written communications*. Abstract, bloated phrases often mark such writing."

The class seems surprised at my fire-breathing emphasis on this point. "That's *not* to say that all big words are bad," I continue more calmly. "Abstractions and technical words give you both range and precision in your writing. The skill comes in knowing *when* they're appropriate—and *how* to use them. The same goes for more casual words. For example, to write that you have *a lot of apprehension* may be preferable to saying that you have *much* or *considerable apprehension*. To characterize someone's behavior as *weird* rather than *unusual* or *unconventional* may help you paint a more dramatic portrait."

"How about mixing usage levels?" Kristin asks.

"Once again, the problem is extremes. For example, if you're writing about '*public consensus on an interagency program for urban redevelopment*,' you probably wouldn't describe it as a proposal that's '*right on*' or '*really with it*.' Slang expressions like these don't fit. Such a mismatch of usage levels is like wearing jogging shoes with a tailored suit."

To give the class practice in not mixing usage levels, I hand out a different kind of combining exercise. "The task is to fill in the numbered blanks and then do the combining as usual. If you see a repeated number, simply repeat the word you've filled in. No signals are given, so you'll provide your own connectors. *Try to stay at one level of usage throughout.*"

FILL IN AND COMBINE

A teacher _____1_____ me.
I search for words.
The words are to fill in the blanks.

Formal	*Standard*	*Casual*
perceives	watches	eyeballs
beholds	observes	gets a load of
discerns	studies	checks out

The _____2_____ comes in not mixing usage levels.
The _____2_____ is real.

Formal	*Standard*	*Casual*
quandary	difficulty	pinch
perplexity	problem	rub
imbroglio	dilemma	hitch

This _____3_____ must be amusing.
He seems to be smiling.

Formal	Standard	Casual
travail	work	set-to
endeavor	struggle	hassle
contestation	effort	to-do

My _____4_____ is to pick words at random.
The picking would be from different lists.

Formal	Standard	Casual
proclivity	impulse	bent
propensity	inclination	want
penchant	desire	leaning

I feel _____5_____ .
I feel _____6_____ .
I try to stay at one usage level.

Formal	Standard	Casual
malcontent	uneasy	on edge
tremulous	restless	jittery
disconcerted	disturbed	up tight
irascible	anxious	strung out
mettlesome	tense	grouchy

After the class has finished filling in the blanks and doing the combining, I call for volunteers to do their writeouts on the board. The finished paragraphs dramatize differences among the three usage levels.

FORMAL APPROACH

A teacher *perceives* me as I search for words to fill in the blanks. The real *perplexity* comes in not mixing usage levels. This *travail* must be amusing because he seems to be smiling. My *proclivity* is to pick words at random from different lists. I feel *disconcerted* and *irascible* as I try to stay at one usage level.

STANDARD APPROACH

A teacher *watches* me search for words to fill in the blanks. The real *problem* comes in not mixing usage levels. This *struggle* must be amusing because he seems to be smiling. My *impulse* is to pick words at random from different lists. I feel *uneasy* and *tense* as I try to stay at one usage level.

CASUAL APPROACH

A teacher *checks out* my search for words to fill in the blanks. The real *rub*

comes in not mixing usage levels. This *hassle* must be amusing because he seems to be smiling. My *bent* is to pick words at random from different lists. I feel *jittery* and *up tight* as I try to stay at one usage level.

"Imagine the confused effect you'd get in mixing the levels," I say to the class.

"That's the way I did it." Eric grins and comes forward to share his writeout—a random selection of words from three usage levels.

CONFUSED APPROACH

A teacher *eyeballs* me as I search for words to fill in the blanks. The real *dilemma* comes in not mixing usage levels. This *set-to* must be amusing because he seems to be smiling. My *proclivity* is to pick words at random from different lists. I feel *strung out* and *disconcerted* as I try to stay at one usage level.

"Spacey," Chico says. "Like something I'd write."

"Clarity in usage results from a well-defined sense of purpose and audience. You establish a level early in your writing and try to stick to it in your choice of words. Why? Because diction, like sentence structure, can be controlled to get different sorts of emphasis and meaning. The key is *consistency*—not mixing usage levels unless you're after special effects such as humor or irony. The same principle holds for the second concept, *connotatation*."

Tony glances at his notes. "That's the *feeling* that different words give?"

"Right. Connotation refers to the emotional associations of words—their 'coloring' in the context of other words. These feelings are usually classified as *positive, neutral,* or *negative*. Say, for example, that you have an *old* car. What's a positive word that means *old*?"

"*Antique*," Kristin says. "Maybe *classic*."

"And a negative word?"

"*Outdated*," Tim offers. "Or *obsolete*?"

"*Time-worn*," Carol adds.

"Okay, good. What do you call a person who saves money? Positive connotations first."

"*Thrifty*?" Maria asks.

"*Tightwad*," Jill says.

"*Tightwad* probably goes on the negative side. How about another positive word?"

"*Economical*," Anne volunteers. "Maybe *frugal*."

"Okay. Now some negative words, in addition to *tightwad*."

Randy has a hand up. "*Miserly? Stingy?*"

"Both have strong negative connotations. Let's now think about a form of government led exclusively by *one* person. What do you call the head of this government?"

"*Dictator*?" Paulo asks.

"That's probably a *negative* connotation. How about the *positive*?"

"I don't know. *Leader?*"

"That's good. *Monarch, king* or *queen,* even *emperor,* perhaps. Those have mostly positive associations. What about negative words besides *dictator?*"

"*Tyrant,*" Malee says.

"*Despot,*" Christopher adds.

"Okay, you're getting the idea. Connotation has to do with *feelings* we have for words. Being sensitive to such shades of meaning helps you control your writing."

Kristin has a hand up. "The definition of connotation said something about being positive or negative in *context,*" she says. "What does that mean?"

"Just this," I reply. "Notice how the connotation changes."

CONNOTATION IN CONTEXT

1. visionary *leadership*
2. foolhardy *leadership*

3. skilled, honest *labor*
4. brutal, demeaning *labor*

5. to *argue* effectively
6. to *argue* endlessly

7. *yearning* for home
8. *yearning* for blood

9. good *common* sense
10. vulgar *common* manners

11. a *quick* and helpful response
12. a *quick* and dirty buck

"You see? Words are slippery. Their connotations *shift* in relation to other words."

Carlos has a hand up. "But how do we know when the connotation is right?"

"You have to *listen,*" I reply. "There's no other way. If the word isn't quite right, you usually turn to a good college dictionary or a thesaurus."

"Thesaurus? Sounds like a prehistoric animal."

"It's an indispensable book of synonyms and antonyms. Your bookstore has several different versions. So does the library."

I begin distributing a handout. "If you settle for a word with the wrong connotation, you'll end up with confused writing," I continue. "It's like wearing different-colored socks or mismatched clothing. This brief list should help you become aware of connotative differences."

CONNOTATION

Positive	Neutral	Negative
full, extensive	a *lengthy* speech	long-winded, interminable
strive, persevere	to *work*	plod, toil
individualist, free-thinker	a *nonconformist*	oddball, crackpot
elegant, sumptuous	rather *formal*	overdressed, pretentious
ample, full-figured	very *overweight*	fat, obese
fashionable, chic	*current* styles	trite, trendy
facilitate, organize	to *cause*	incite, manipulate
bold, courageous	decisively *outspoken*	reckless, rash

Chico glances up. "So the idea is to keep the connotations the same?"

"Right. *Consistency* in connotation helps you keep your writing under control. The following exercise will deal with this principle. It's more open-ended than the ones you've had before. You'll supply your *own* words rather than select from lists."

FILL IN AND COMBINE

1. Fill in each numbered blank with one or more words to complete the kernel sentence. When a number is repeated, simply put in the same word (or phrase) again.

2. The words should "fit" or make sense when you read all the sentences together. Don't worry, though, about choosing the one *right* word. Many words or phrases will work in each blank.

3. After you have filled in the blanks, combine the sentences in each cluster. If your writeouts don't make sense, find other words for the blanks. The result should be a logical, coherent paragraph.

I am sitting in a classroom.
The classroom is rather _____1_____ .

The walls are painted _____2_____ .
The walls surround me.
The _____2_____ is _____3_____ .

The floor is covered with _____4_____ .
The _____4_____ is/are* _____5_____ .

The lighting consists of _____6_____ fixtures.
The lighting is overhead.
The fixtures are _____7_____ .

The _____8_____ in this room is/are* interesting.
The interest is visual.
The _____9_____ is/are* unattractive.

My feelings are _____10_____ .
The feelings are toward this room.

This classroom can be compared to a _____11_____ .
The _____11_____ is _____12_____ .
This is in my opinion.

* Choose one word.

Students scan the exercise, then start looking at the classroom more intently. This kind of fill-in-the-blanks exercise requires thought. Taking a specific attitude, or "slant," toward the room helps make the descriptive words "fit." If words 2 through 12 relate to the first word, the final write-out will make sense.

After a few minutes, I write the numbers 1 through 12 across the board. "Okay, we'll look at writeouts later. For now, I'd like to hear what you put in the numbered blanks. Let's take several words or phrases for each number. Just call them out, and I'll write them on the board."

The task is soon accomplished. Twelve short lists of words correspond to the fifteen blanks.

1.	2.	3.
warm	off-white	dingy
drab	greenish	pale
nice	beige	light
ordinary	tan	soft
quiet	ivory	dull
tense	antique white	faded
ancient		institutional
weird		pleasant

4. tile
   linoleum
   squares
   squarish blocks
   floor covering

5. scuffed
   grayish
   mottled
   gray-brown
   streaked gray
   worn
   buffed

6. fluorescent
   white
   hanging
   unusual
   typical
   modern

7. buzzing
   dusty
   in need of repair
   adequate
   not very good
   better than
     average
   flickering

8. people
   pencil sharpener
   desks
   teacher
   acoustical ceiling
   quiet
   windows
   girls/guys
   friendly
     approach

9. teacher
   colors
   smells
   subject matter
   blackboard
   assignments
   carved-up desks
   litter

10. positive
    negative
    neutral
    mixed
    angry
    detached
    friendly
    indescribable

11. prison
    box
    doorway
    torture chamber
    factory
    junkyard

12. closed
    boring
    crazy
    open
    challenging
    dreary

"Sort of fun," Kim says. "But what good does it do?"

"Now we're going to split into three groups to do writeouts for this exercise. Each group will take a particular attitude toward the room we're in. You'll select words from the lists—or think of new ones—that *support* your chosen attitude. Group 1 will take a positive, upbeat view of the room. Group 2 will be neutral—neither positive nor negative—a little like an objective, scientific report. Group 3 will be negative, nasty, and critical of their environment."

"What if nobody chooses Group 1?" Nate grins.

"That's the one *you'll* lead—because you're so positive about this class."

"You bet," he says.

The students break into three subgroups and start the process of selecting words and doing writeouts. The group leaders transcribe their writeouts onto transparencies so that I can project all three versions for the class. Finally each leader reads his or her group's version aloud.

POSITIVE APPROACH

I am sitting in a rather *wonderful* classroom. The surrounding walls are *pleasant ivory*. The floor is covered with *handsome squares of linoleum tile*. The

overhead lighting consists of *modern* fixtures that are *most efficient*. The furniture in this room is visually interesting, but the *litter* is somewhat unattractive. My feelings toward this room are *enthusiastic*. In my opinion this classroom can be compared to an *open doorway to tomorrow*.

NEUTRAL APPROACH

I am sitting in a rather *typical* classroom. The walls that surround me are *institutional tan*. The floor is covered with *gray-brown tile*. The lighting consists of *fluorescent* fixtures that are *adequate*. The *acoustical ceiling* in this room is visually interesting, but the *desks* are unattractive. My feelings toward this room are *neutral*. In my opinion, this classroom can be compared to a *useful box*.

NEGATIVE APPROACH

I am sitting in a rather *dreary* classroom. The walls by which I am surrounded are a *dull off-white*. The floor is covered with *scuffed, squarish blocks*. The lighting consists of *inadequate* fixtures that are *badly in need of cleaning and repair*. The *litter* in this room is visually interesting, but *the people* are unattractive. My feelings toward this room are *negative*. This classroom can be compared to a *depressing torture chamber*, in my opinion.

I click off the projector and turn to Kim, who is sitting with Group 2. "What did you learn from that?"

"Pretty interesting," she replies. "It reminds me of the lesson we had a while back."

"Making choices for emphasis?"

"Yes, but here the *words* are what you change, not the sentences."

"Right. You've kept sentence structure the same but created a different slant through *wording*."

Anne raises her hand. "I hadn't realized how important that first sentence is. If you've got that clear in your mind, the rest of it just comes."

"Good observation. The first sentence often sets up your *controlling idea*. The following sentences tend to amplify, restate, or clarify what you've said at the beginning. Here's an example of writing which is out of control—because the writer hasn't stuck to a *controlling idea* in the first sentence."

CONFUSED APPROACH

I am sitting in a rather *beautiful* classroom. The walls that surround me are *drab beige*. The floor is covered with *dirty tiles*. The overhead lighting consists of *modern* fixtures that are *not very good*. The *pencil sharpener* in this room is visually interesting, but the *colors* are unattractive. My feelings toward this room are quite *positive*. This classroom can be compared to a *typical junkyard*.

"Sort of like mixing the usage levels," Chico observes. "Really strange."

"Time's up," I tell the class. "To practice maintaining consistency in tone, usage levels, and connotation, work with this unit's exercises. These are important concepts. Concentrate on them as you get into on-your-own writing."

EXERCISE 9.1   Consistent Tone

Directions. First fill in the blanks with words from the *left* column and do the combining. Then repeat the process, using words from the *right* column. Compare the contrasting tones of the two paragraphs you produce.

Paulo is _____ 1 _____.
He is _____ 2 _____.

1. happy
2. smiling

1. depressed	
2. scowling	

He comes down the hallway.
The hallway is _____ 3 _____.
He moves in a _____ 4 _____ way.

3. brightly-lit
4. confident

3. grimly-shadowed
4. dejected

Shoulders mirror his inner _____ 5 _____.
His shoulders are _____ 6 _____.

5. joyfulness
6. thrust back

5. turmoil
6. sagging

His head is _____ 7 _____.
His walk is _____ 8 _____.
His walk is _____ 9 _____.

7. held high
8. vigorous
9. purposeful

7. drooping
8. shuffling
9. aimless

He _____ 10 _____ his friends.
He heads toward his writing class.
He is full of _____ 11 _____.
He _____ 12 _____ what he'll face.

10. acknowledges
11. confidence
12. looks forward to

10. ignores
11. despair
12. fears

EXERCISE 9.2   Usage Levels

Directions. Fill in the blanks with words from one usage level—*formal, standard,* or *casual.* Then do the combining. Compare your write-outs with those that other students have gotten—or, better yet, actually do the combining with words from other levels. You may wish to experiment with *mixing* the usage levels to see the strange effects.

My _____ 1 _____ has/have faded.
I'm now left with a mood.
The mood is _____ 2 _____.

	Formal	Standard	Casual
1.	inqui-etude	restless-ness	jitters
2.	imperturb-able	relaxed	mellow

I'm enjoying the _____ 3 _____.
The _____ 3 _____ is of a new album.
The album has a sound.
The sound is particularly _____ 4 _____.

	Formal	Standard	Casual
3.	ambience	atmo-sphere	feel
4.	evocative	spell-setting	far out

Its beat is _____ 5 _____.
Its beat is not _____ 6 _____.

	Formal	Standard	Casual
5.	unremit-ting	persis-tent	solid
6.	obtrusive	conspicu-ous	too much

203

Its lyrics are ____7____ .

Its lyrics are not ____8____ .

Its arrangements have ____9____ .

Its overall pattern is not ____10____ .

	Formal	*Standard*	*Casual*
7.	ingenu-ous	candid	up front dumb
8.	insipid	stupid	dumb

	Formal	*Standard*	*Casual*
9.	diversi-fication	variety	a mix
10.	incompre-hensible	confusing	hard to get

EXERCISE 9.3   Connotation

Directions. Fill in the blanks with *negative* wording. Then combine sentences.

One chore is ____1____ .

I really dread the chore.

____1____ is worse than ____2____ .

____1____ is worse than ____3____ .

____1____ is worse than ____4____ .

____1____ may not be as bad as ____5____ .

This fact is small comfort to me.

I would rather ____6____ than ____1____ .

My attitude may result from experiences.

The attitude is ____7____ .

The experiences were very ____8____ .

The experiences were in my past.

Directions. Fill in the blanks with *positive* wording. Then combine sentences.

I sometimes dream about a vacation.

The vacation would be perfect.

The setting is somewhere near ____1____ .

I picture the setting.

The season is ____2____ .

The days are ____3____ .

The days are ____4____ .

They ____5____ me.

They make me feel like ____6____ .

Worries are the furthest thing from my mind.

The worries are about ____7____ .

The worries are about ____8____ .

The worries are about ____9____ .

I look at ____10____ .

I am glad to be alive.

I spend most of my time ____11____ .

I sometimes ____12____ .

This is for a change of pace.

But I feel no ____13____ .

I feel no need to ____14____ myself.

I am happy to be in this place.

My happiness is ____15____ .

The place is ____16____ .

It is a place for a vacation.

The place is ____17____ .

The vacation is a dream.

EXERCISE 9.4   On-Your-Own Writing Options

1. **Directions.** Fill in the blanks with words that "fit." (These words should pertain to something that you either *hate* or *like*.) Then do the sentence combining. Connect this finished paragraph with ones that you write in steps A through D.

I hate/like* —————.
This hatred/liking* is passionate.

This hatred/liking* goes back to an incident.
The incident was memorable.
The incident happened to me.
The happening was ————— years ago.

I remember this event.
The remembrance is vivid.
It has associations for me.
The associations are —————.

It is etched like a —————.
The etching is in my memory.

I was ————— years old at the time.

It was a day/night.*
The day/night was very —————.
The day/night was in the —————
of the year.

I could hear the sounds of —————.
The sounds were —————.
My hearing was —————.

Smells of ————— were in the air.
The smells were —————.

I could see —————.
I could see —————.
I could feel the textures of —————.

The textures were —————.

Then the incident occurred.
The incident was unhappy/happy.*
I will now describe it.

* *Choose one word.*

A. Make a list of what happened, first to last, in the incident you remember. (This list will probably be words and phrases, not sentences.)

B. Examine your list carefully. Select the three *most important* (or vivid) parts of the incident as the focus for writing.

C. To help you find "something to say" about these fragments of memory, ask yourself these questions and think about the answers.
—What image sticks in your mind?
—What details do you recall?
—What did things look, sound, smell, feel, or taste like?
—What do you remember thinking?
—How did this particular moment differ from others?
—How did this moment connect to ones before and after?

D. Develop a paragraph for each piece of your remembered incident. Concentrate on tone, usage level, and connotation as you reread your paragraphs.

2. **Directions.** Fill in the blanks with words that "fit." (These words should pertain to vocational possibilities that you see for yourself.) Then do the sentence combining. Connect this finished paragraph with ones that you write in steps A through D.

I can imagine three possibilities.
The possibilities are vocational.
The possibilities are in my future.

One relates to my interest in _____.
My interest is strong.
My interest is long-standing.

I like this area.
I have sometimes pictured myself as a
_____.
The _____ would be successful.

A second possibility is in the area of
_____.
The possibility is tantalizing.

This alternative would provide _____.
This is an advantage.
It doesn't offer _____.

_____ is my third possible future.

_____ has one disadvantage.
The disadvantage is important.
The disadvantage is its _____.

I am leaning toward _____.
This leaning is at the present time.

A. Brainstorm a list of 10 goals that you have for your future. (These goals can be *things, activities,* or *conditions* that you want for yourself.)

B. Examine your list carefully. Select the three *most important* goals as the focus for writing.

C. To help find "something to say" about these goals, ask yourself these questions and think about the answers.
   —Why is this goal important to me?
   —How long have I had this goal?
   —What will I do to achieve it?
   —When do I expect to achieve it?
   —How is this similar to my other goals?
   —How does it differ from my other goals?

D. Develop a paragraph for each of your three goals. Concentrate on tone, usage level, and connotation as you reread your paragraphs.

UNIT TEN
TOWARD LEAN, DIRECT WRITING

Rolling up my shirt cuffs, I'm eager to get started. Sunlight hammers in from the streetside windows.

"*Leanness* in writing," I announce. "That's one thing we'll look at today. We want to see how to strip away excess flab from sentences and get them in fighting trim. Then we'll talk about *directness*."

Anne is shaking her head. "Wait a minute. First you've got us putting kernels together—I mean, making *long* sentences. Now we're not supposed to?"

"Let me explain. You see, with the early combining you learned how to put words on paper in complex ways. You gained some control, right? You worked your way through tough exercises and did things with sentences you didn't know you could. You began to develop some fluency—some natural language flow—and maybe self-confidence as well. Agreed?"

"Yeah, I guess."

"Well, now we're pushing on to another stage."

"Shorter sentences?"

"Sometimes shorter, sometimes not. Lean, direct writing can still use long sentences. The point is to make every word count so your sentences are vigorous, forceful."

A transparency goes up. "Here's what I'm talking about—in the words of the experts."

You become a good writer just as you become a good joiner: by planing down your sentences.

—*Anatole France*

The secret of good writing is to strip every sentence to its cleanest components.
—*William Zinsser*

The writer does the most who gives his reader the most knowledge, and takes from him the least time.

—*Sydney Smith*

Carol is smiling. "Sounds like what we've talked about before. Choices."
"Right. Now we're getting rid of the clutter, pruning back thickets of words, rewriting for clarity. But that's *not* to say we're returning to the style of kernel sentences."

Simple style is like white light.
It is complex but its complexity is not obvious.

—*Anatole France*

"What we're discussing today is a style that expresses complex ideas in clear, readable English. We'll call this style *lean* and *direct*—and we'll contrast it with *flabby, indirect* writing. At times this contrast will probably be overstated and oversimplified. But at least you'll have a way of thinking about what you're doing with words—and why you're doing it."
The first part of the day's agenda flashes on the screen.

NATURAL ENEMIES OF LEAN WRITING

1.   Starchy openers
2.   Internal wordiness

"We'll take these flab-formers one at a time," I tell the class. "But let me underline a basic point. Neither of these things is really *wrong*. In fact, depending on your purpose, audience, and subject, you may sometimes *choose* sentences with starchy openers up front or a few extra words. If you *overindulge*, though, your writing's sure to get flabby."
I put up the first example and mention that the numbers in the columns refer to word counts.

STARCHY OPENERS

Lean Writing [*Without Starchy Openers*]	*Flabby Writing* [*With Starchy Openers*]
I like directness. (3)	It is directness that I like. (6)
Clearly, lean writing has more impact. (6)	It seems clear that lean writing has more impact. (9)

Lean Writing *[Without Starchy Openers]*	*Flabby Writing* *[With Starchy Openers]*
Flabby writing can be improved in many ways. (8)	There are many ways in which flabby writing can be improved. (11)
You start by cutting back on starchy openers. (8)	One of the things that you do is to start by cutting back on starchy openers. (16)

"Reading these aloud, you hear the differences. The lean ones get right to the point. The flabby ones have unnecessary words up front." I quickly scribble another example. "Lean or flabby?"

> It is probable that there are some questions that you have about starchy openers. (14)

"That's *flabby*," Eric says.
"Right. Here you have two starchy openers. One begins with the word *it*, the other with *there*. So let's rewrite it."
Andrea dictates the lean version for me to write out.

> You probably have questions about starchy openers. (7)

"The flabby sentence uses fourteen words, whereas the lean version uses only seven. Just imagine such a ratio in a *long* piece of writing."
"I don't follow," Terry complains. "I mean, sure, the first one's got a few more words. But so what? You're still getting the idea across. Why worry about it?"
"Look at it from the reader's point of view. Too much flab makes reading a real chore. Why *not* get right to the point?" I flick the projector switch. "Here's the second kind of flab-former. Think about Terry's question as you study these examples."

INTERNAL WORDINESS

Lean Writing *[Without Internal Wordiness]*	*Flabby Writing* *[With Internal Wordiness]*
Most people prefer vigorous, forceful sentences. (6)	Most people prefer sentences that are vigorous and that are also forceful. (12)
Lean writing does not use unnecessary words. (7)	Writing that is lean does not use more words than are really necessary. (13)
Careful editing makes the reader's task easier. (7)	Editing that has been carefully done makes the task faced by the reader an easier one. (16)

Lean Writing [*Without Internal Wordiness*]	*Flabby Writing* [*With Internal Wordiness*]
Train yourself to cut away all kinds of writing flab. (10)	What you must do is to to train yourself to cut away all of the kinds of flab in writing. (19)

"Tell me how these examples compare with the starchy openers," I say to the class.

Chico is grinning. "The flab's *every*where. I mean, not just up front."

"The words that go with the nouns," Kristin adds. "That's a difference."

"Right. Lean writing usually has tight noun clusters. Flabby writing tends to stretch them out."

A few faces have puzzled looks. I turn to the board, hoping to clarify the point.

> What flab in writing does is to force a reader to work harder than is actually necessary. (17)

"Strip away the flab."

People start whispering to themselves, trying to cut away words. Finally, Tony's hand goes up. I put his version on the board.

> Flab in writing forces a reader to work harder than is necessary. (12)

"Good. You got rid of the flab up front and the word *actually*. Who can take the process further?"

Maria calls out her version.

> Flabby writing forces a reader to work unnecessarily hard. (9)

"Seventeen words in the flabby sentence, nine in the lean. How did we do it?"

"The noun parts get shorter," Rob says. "The lean sentence says *flabby writing*. That's three words shorter than *what flab in writing does*."

"Anything else?"

"*Unnecessarily hard*," Janet answers. "That really shortens it."

"Let's be even more specific," I say. "Study this sentence; tell me where it's flabbiest."

> What you must do is to train yourself to cut away all of the kinds of flab in writing. (19)

"*All of the kinds of flab in writing*," Kristin says. "Now *that's* flab. The nouns and prepositions are piled up. *All of, kinds of, flab in writing*—too many in a row."

"*All kinds of writing flab* tightens things up, doesn't it? From eight words to five."

"But even *that's* flabby," Tim remarks. "How about saying, '*Train your-self to cut away writing flab*.' That goes from nineteen words in the original to seven. And it *still* keeps the basic meaning—so I'd say it's better."

"Starchy openers, internal wordiness," I remind the class. "Let's look at *both* in the same tortured sentence—and then do some rewriting."

> There is indeed some reason to believe that, when all is said and done, all kinds of flabby, redundant, and repetitious language which we have been discussing will most likely have a tendency to obscure the message that is intended for communication rather than get it across to the person who is reading it. (54)

"Take off the starchy opener," Malee says. "*There is indeed some reason to believe*."

"*When all is said and done*," Rob adds. "More flab."

"*All kinds of*," Patsy volunteers.

"*Redundant* and *repetitious* mean the same thing," Christopher says. "Couldn't we drop one?"

The class studies the sentence some more.

"*Which we have been discussing* seems unnecessary," Theresa adds.

"*Will most likely have a tendency to*," Michelle says. "Wouldn't *tends to* say the same thing?"

"How about *that is intended*?" Jill asks.

"Yeah, and *get it across*," Carlos says. "*Communicates* means the same thing."

"Now we're getting somewhere," Peter concludes.

I scribble the rewritten sentence onto a blank transparency. "Basically, this says what the original does—only better. We've kept the *key* details and cut the unimportant ones."

> Flabby, redundant language tends to obscure rather than communicate the intended message to the reader. (15)

"Okay, you've seen wordiness up front as well as within sentences, and you've learned to strip away flab. Now we're going to look at *directness* in writing—to see how you can change 'indirect' writing to make it stronger and gutsier. The difference between 'direct' and 'indirect' is *sentence structure*, not just the *number* of words."

Part Two of the day's agenda goes up.

NATURAL ENEMIES OF DIRECT WRITING

1. Passive voice
2. Inversion

"Who knows what 'passive' *means*?" I ask.

No hands are up as I print the words *active* and *passive* in chalk letters. "These are terms we'll be using," I continue. "Imagine a sports coliseum

on a Sunday afternoon. You have 80,000 people who need exercise watching 22 football players get it. Who's *active* and who's *passive?*"

Maria is smiling. "Well, watching is passive compared to getting in there. Playing is *active.*"

"Right. Now apply the terms to learning styles in school. Any ideas?"

Chuck's hand goes up. "Active is being *into* it. I mean, like digging it out for yourself. Passive is being spoonfed."

"Right. Active is *doing* something whereas passive is having something done *to* you or *for* you. Participating in a discussion, for example, is an active way to learn. Listening to a lecture is passive. Both have their places, of course. But they're quite *different* styles of learning. Now let's apply this distinction to writing," I continue. "Our focus is *active-* and *passive*-voice sentences. To get us started, I'll show some examples for comparison."

PASSIVE VOICE

Direct Writing [*Active Voice*]	*Indirect Writing* [*Passive Voice*]
1. We all had fun. (4)	1. Fun was had by all of us. (7)
2. Some liked active-voice sentences. (5)	2. Active-voice sentences were liked by some. (7)
3. Others preferred passive-voice sentences. (5)	3. Passive-voice sentences were preferred by others. (7)
4. Everyone was examining stylistic differences. (5)	4. Stylistic differences were being examined by everyone. (7)

"The passive voice seems to have more words," Janet says.

"True enough. And remember what we said earlier? Active *does* something. Passive has something done *to* it."

Kristin raises her hand. "The sentence parts switch places when the sentence goes passive. And the passive style adds some kind of *be* verb plus the word *by.*"

"You've caught the essential difference. Subject and object switch places, which changes the emphasis. You'll remember that in Unit 2 we called this the *passive transformation.*"

"Obviously, both voices communicate," I continue. "In fact, both say the same thing. Yet most people, including writing experts, prefer active-voice sentences when there's a choice. Active voice is more *direct*—that's all."

Paulo clears his throat. "But passive isn't *wrong,* is it?"

"Of course not. It simply changes the emphasis—makes the sentence less direct. Occasionally, you'll find yourself *choosing* a passive sentence over an active one. Maybe you want to emphasize the object more than the subject. Maybe you don't know who did something or don't want to say;

for example, *The window was broken.* Maybe you want to set up an opposing argument in a passive voice so that you can undercut it with a strong, active one. Or maybe you just want some sentence variety. The problem comes when you overuse the passive."

I put up another sentence. "What's this? Active or passive voice? Direct or indirect writing?"

Writing is made more direct by use of active voice. (10)

"Passive," Andrea calls out. "It's got the word *by*."

"Okay, that's a good clue here. Let's change it to *active* and make it more direct."

I write out Andrea's transformation.

Using active voice makes writing more direct. (7)

"And how about this one?"

Writing is weakened by excessive use of passive voice. (9)

"Passive," Rob says. "Or indirect. Whatever."

"Right. Transform it to active."

"Uhmm, *passive voice is weakened*—" he begins. "*Passive voice is excessive*—"

"A hint. Take the whole object phrase at the end—the part that begins with the word *excessive.* Put it up front." I write the active version as Rob calls it out.

Excessive use of passive voice weakens writing. (7)

"You're on to it. Let's now take a look at *inversion*—what I call 'backward-running' sentences. Our focus, remember, is still on direct versus indirect writing."

INVERSION

Direct Writing [*Straightforward Sentences*]	*Indirect Writing* [*Inverted Sentences*]
1. I contend that direct writing is easier to read. (9)	1. That direct writing is easier to read is my contention. (10)
2. Sentences that run backward produce stiff and unnatural writing rhythms. (10)	2. Stiff and unnatural writing rhythms—these result from sentences that run backward. (12)
3. Inverted sentences are similar in effect to passive-voice sentences. (10)	3. Similar in effect to passive-voice sentences are inverted sentences. (10)

Direct Writing	*Indirect Writing*
[*Straightforward Sentences*]	[*Inverted Sentences*]
4. But it *is* effective to invert sentence parts occasionally for dramatic emphasis. (12)	4. But occasionally, for dramatic emphasis, to invert sentence parts *is* effective. (11)

"Describe the difference between straightforward and inverted sentences."

"Flip-flopping," Chico says. "I mean, the indirect ones are, uh, upside down."

"Right. Upside down, things get turned. Running backward go the sentences."

"They're strange," Eric mutters.

"But they *do* communicate," I say. "And like the passive voice, inversion has its uses. Just don't *overdo* this technique or your writing's really going to suffer."

I project another sentence. "Direct or indirect? Straightforward or inverted?"

That this sentence is inverted is our belief.

"Inversion," Theresa says.

"So how do you make it straightforward and direct?"

"Start out with *Our belief is.* Or, better yet, *We believe.*"

"That's right. A simple switch of the sentence parts makes it direct. What do you think about this one?"

It's sometimes worth the effort to invert straightforward sentences, just for the sake of variety.

"I'd say it's direct the way it stands," Eric says. "It doesn't sound inverted."

"Try inverting it. See what happens."

"Where do you start?"

"*To invert.* Or *inverting.*"

Eric stares at the sentence, then makes his transformation. "*Inverting straightforward sentences, just for the sake of variety, is sometimes worth the effort.*"

"Well done. Now let's put passive voice and inversion together—and try rewriting."

Preferred by most readers is a particular style, which is characterized by active-voice sentences and by a minimum of inverted sentences. (22)

"Put the subject up front," Michelle says. "*Most readers prefer a particular style.*"

"That's a big improvement over the original. But notice the passive in the embedded parts of the sentence. How can we edit those?"

No one is volunteering, so I project a possibility.

> Most readers prefer a particular style—with active-voice sentences and a minimum of inversion. (15)

"This version does away with the passives. But even it can be tightened. Any ideas?"

Anne's hand goes up. "Drop *a particular style with.*"

"Good editing. From twenty-two words to eleven."

> Most readers prefer active-voice sentences and a minimum of inversion. (11)

"When should you use inversion?" Tony asks.

"When your sentences need a change of pace, when you're trying for particular emphasis—those are the best times for inversion."

"How about an example?"

"I just gave you one."

> When your sentences need a change of pace, when you're trying for particular emphasis—those are the best times for inversion.

"Got it," he says.

"So inversion has its *uses.* And so does passive voice. And the same for internal modifiers and starchy openers. They're all part of your language resource—to be used but not *overused.*"

To summarize the day's work, I put up a final transparency.

NATURAL ENEMIES OF LEAN WRITING

1.   Starchy openers
2.   Internal wordiness

NATURAL ENEMIES OF DIRECT WRITING

1.   Passive voice
2.   Inversion

"The thing to remember is that lean, direct writing and flabby, indirect writing have different effects."

"Such as?" Terry asks.

"Such as establishing the distance between you and what you're writing about."

"You just lost me."

"Think, for example, of how *formal* you want to be. Starchy openers,

internal wordiness, passive voice, and inversion all tend to elevate the *sound* of your writing. They distance you—not only from your subject but also from your readers." To illustrate this idea, I put two sentences on the board. "Which of these puts the writer *farther away* from you, the reader?"

I believe that lean, direct writing puts me "closer" to my reader.

It is believed that lean, direct writing puts one "closer" to one's reader.

"I'd say the second one." Terry shrugs.

"And why is that?"

"Well, you can't tell who's *doing* the believing in the second example. It's sort of vague."

"That *vagueness* you speak of—that's what I mean by *distance*. It's accentuated here by switching to *one* and *one's*—pronouns we use only in very formal writing."

"Okay, I think I get the idea."

"To summarize," I continue. "Because good writing has a clear-thinking, strong voice behind it, you go for *leanness* and *directness* most of the time. You try to reduce the distance between yourself and your reader. You cut back on starchy openers and internal wordiness, and you generally prefer active, straightforward sentences to passive or inverted ones. You don't try to make things *sound* more important than they really are." I pause. "Or to put things more simply: you simplify structure but not ideas."

I look the class over, knowing that such advice is easy to talk about but difficult to put into practice. We're into our final two minutes together.

"You're *always* learning how to write," I conclude. "It's like learning about yourself. Each experience teaches you something new—if you're willing to learn."

Kristin raises her hand. "The more you know, the more you *want* to know?"

"Exactly. Learning to write is open-ended. It's exploring the resources of your mind and language from the inside out."

The class thinks this over for a moment.

"And just when you think you've got yourself or your writing figured out," I continue, "reality presents new challenges."

"You're saying that writing doesn't really get easier with practice," Eric comments.

"Only as you relax, learn to enjoy the challenges, and take pride in what you're writing," I reply. "You see, each time you write you're confronted with all you *don't know* about how to write. Over and over, each time is the first time. A blank sheet of paper can frighten even the most experienced writer."

"Hmmmmm," he murmurs.

"Carlos said it pretty well our first day together: *Writing is like talking*

to yourself. You not only have to create messages, but you also have to listen to the sense—or nonsense—that you're making."

"Maybe the *listening* gets easier with practice," Carlos says.

I nod in agreement.

Eric blinks. "Yeah. Maybe just listening—and talking to yourself—you can find something to say when you don't know what to say."

"Trying the sentences out in different ways," Kristin adds.

"Making choices."

I can feel my smile. *"That's* the idea."

There is a moment of pause.

"Thanks for not writing us out of the book when you had the chance."

"Thanks for saying thanks. Your instructor appreciates it."

EXERCISE 10.1   Toward Lean, Direct Writing

Directions. To better understand the difference between lean, direct sentences and flabby, indirect ones, try your hand at rewriting. Compare your answers with those in the Answer Key, p. 275.

MODEL

The instructor convened the class. The instructor was frail. The instructor was nervous. The class was for writing.

Lean, Direct Writing	*Flabby, Indirect Writing*
The frail, nervous instructor convened the writing class.	The class, which was for teaching the skills of writing, was convened by the instructor, who was not only frail but also nervous.

Students filled every desk. The students were sullen. The students looked hostile.

_____ _____	In all of the desks there were students, each of whom looked hostile and sullen.

He made an effort. The effort was visible. The effort was to swallow his fear. He fixed his stare on the bulletin board. The board was empty.

_____ _____ _____	What he did was to make an effort—indeed, a visible effort—to swallow his fear as his stare was fixed on the bulletin board, which was altogether quite empty.

His lips quivered. The quivering was wordless. Sweat beaded his forehead. His forehead was round. His forehead was smooth.

_____ _____ _____ _____	There was a kind of quivering in a wordless way from his lips, and his forehead, which was both round and smooth, was beaded with sweat.

He now wondered about something. He had chosen a career. The career was teaching. He was afraid of people. The people were unfamiliar.

218

_____
_____
_____

_____

Why he had chosen a career in teaching when he was afraid of people who were unfamiliar to him—this was something that he was now wondering about.

A student sneered. He raised his hand. The hand was beefy.

_____
_____

A hand that was beefy was raised by a student who sneered at him.

The instructor felt a surge. The surge was fresh. The surge was panic. The panic was raw.

_____
_____

Panic—a sort of surging, raw and fresh—was felt by the instructor.

He then awoke from his nightmare. He pulled back the covers. The covers were tumbled. The covers were on his bed. He quieted his breathing. His breathing was fierce.

_____
_____
_____

It was then that he awoke from his nightmare, that he pulled back the covers on his bed (which were tumbled), and that he quieted the fierceness of his breathing.

His heart could not deny something. His heart was thudding. He was fearful. His fear was meeting his first class.

_____
_____
_____

There was no denying the fact that his heart was thudding and that he was experiencing some fearfulness at the prospect of meeting his first class.

EXERCISE 10.2 Spotting the Four Enemies

Directions. Do writeouts for lean, direct writing and flabby indirect writing in the following exercise. Listen to the differences; spot the instances of *starchy openers, internal wordiness, passive voice,* or *inversion.* Two sample clusters will get you started. Check with the Answer Key, p. 275.

Lean, Direct Sentences

1. We prefer sentences.
   2. The sentences are lean.
   3. The sentences are direct.

We prefer lean, direct sentences.

4. We believe SOMETHING.
   5. Such sentences communicate more clearly than ones.
   6. The ones are flabby.
   7. The ones are indirect.

5 THAT

We believe that such sentences communicate more clearly than flabby, indirect ones.

8. We recognize SOMETHING.
   9. Devices (/) have their uses.
   10. The devices are starchy openers.
   11. The devices are internal modifiers.
   12. The devices are passive voice.
   13. The devices are inversion.

9 THAT 10 SUCH AS

____

____

____

Flabby, Indirect Sentences

1. Sentences are what we prefer.
   2. The sentences are lean.
   3. The sentences are direct.

2 THAT 3 THAT

Sentences that are lean and that are direct are what we prefer.

4. SOMETHING is our belief.
   5. Such sentences communicate more clearly than ones.
   6. The ones are flabby.
   7. The ones are indirect.

4–5 IT . . . THAT 6 THAT 7 THAT

It is our belief that such sentences communicate more clearly than ones that are flabby and that are indirect.

8. For us there is a recognition of SOMETHING.
   9. There is a use for devices.
   10. The devices include starchy openers.
   11. The devices include internal modifiers.
   12. The devices include passive voice.
   13. The devices include inversion.

9 THAT 10 WHICH

____

____

____

_____

_____

14. We are aware of SOMETHING.

   15. Such devices can provide variety.
   16. They can provide emphasis.
   17. They can create effects.
   18. The effects are special.
   19. The effects are stylistic.

15 THAT   17 BY + ING

_____

14. SOMETHING is a part of our awareness.
   15. Effects can be created by such devices (/).
   16. The effects are special.
   17. The effects are stylistic.
   18. Variety is provided.
   19. Emphasis is provided.

15 THAT   18 SO THAT

_____

20. Our concern centers on misuse of these devices.
   21. It centers on overuse of these devices.

_____

20. Centering on SOMETHING is our concern.
   21. These devices are misused and overused.

21 THE FACT THAT

_____

EXERCISE 10.3   Extending the Comparison

Directions. Transform flabby, indirect sentences into lean, direct ones. Then go back and read aloud to hear the differences. Compare your answers with those in the Answer Key, p. 275.

MODEL

Consider the differences between writing styles. The differences follow.
The styles are lean. The styles are flabby.

Lean, Direct Sentences	*Flabby, Indirect Sentences*

Consider the following differences between lean and flabby writing styles.

There are differences between lean styles of writing and flabby styles of writing that will be considered in what follows.

An absence marks writing. The absence is "starchy openers." The writing
is lean.

————————————————————

————————————————————

A mark of leanness in writing is the absence of what might be called "starchy openers."

Prose usually has many such openers. The prose is flabby.

————————————————————

————————————————————

————————————————————

It is not unusual, however, for prose that is flabby to have many such openers at the beginning of sentences.

Sentences usually have clusters. The sentences are lean. The clusters are
tight. The clusters are nouns.

————————————————————

————————————————————

What sentences that are lean usually have is clusters of nouns that are tight.

Writing typically expands such clusters. The writing is flabby.

————————————————————

————————————————————

————————————————————

On the other hand, there is typically a kind of expansion of such clusters for writing that might be thought of as flabby.

Economy characterizes a style. The economy is in words. The style is lean.
Verbosity marks its opposite. The opposite is flabby.

————————————————————

————————————————————

————————————————————

————————————————————

Writing that is lean is characterized by an economy in wording, whereas its opposite, which is flabby writing, is marked by verbosity.

Differences exist for prose styles. The differences are similar. The styles
are direct. The styles are indirect.

_____

_____

_____

_____

It seems clear that it is possible to set forth similar differences for prose styles that are direct on the one hand and indirect on the other.

Sentences favor active voice. The sentences are direct. They use strong
verbs. They put grammatical subjects first.

_____

_____

_____

_____

Active voice, the use of strong verbs, the putting of grammatical subjects at the first of the writing—these are all characteristics of sentences that might be considered direct.

Sentences favor passive voice. The sentences are indirect. They use weak
verbs. They emphasize grammatical objects.

_____

_____

_____

Passive voice is favored by sentences that are indirect, as is the use of verbs that are weak and the emphasis on grammatical objects.

Writing commonly features word order. The writing is direct. The word
order is straightforward. Prose often inverts sentences. The prose is indirect.

_____

_____

_____

_____

_____

A not uncommon feature of what might be called direct writing is that the word order is straightforward, whereas it is often the case for prose that is indirect that the word order is inverted.

EXERCISE 10.4   Proofreading Practice

Directions. Each writeout for the following combining clusters has an error. Spot it and do the rewrite in the space provided.

DESERT HIKE

1.   The sun blistered the canyon.
            The sun was noon-high.

The sun was glaring-hot.
The canyon was parched.
The canyon was rocky.

PROBLEM 1   *The sun, noon-high and glaring-hot blistered the parched, rocky canyon.*

REWRITE 1   ————————————————

2.   Paulo had left his car at the rim.
The canyon had a rim.
He was now making his way down a trail.
The trail was narrow.

PROBLEM 2   *Paulo had left his car at the canyons rim and was now making his way down the narrow trail.*

REWRITE 2   ————————————————

3.   Snakes had long since retreated for shade.
    Lizards had long since retreated for shade.
    Scorpions had long since retreated for shade.
    Spiders had long since retreated for shade.
Leaves were folded inward.
    The leaves were on desert shrubs.
        The shrubs were shriveled.

PROBLEM 3   *Snakes, lizards, scorpions, and spiders had long since retreated for shade and leaves on shriveled desert shrubs were folded inward.*

REWRITE 3   ————————————————

————————————————————————

4.   Heat waves were like veils.
        The veils were filmy.
    Heat waves were like ripples.
        The ripples were on water.
Heat waves shimmered in the distance.

PROBLEM 4   *Like filmy veils or ripples on water, the heat waves, they shimmered in the distance.*

REWRITE 4   ————————————————

————————————————————————

5.   A pair of vultures glided on the horizon.
The vultures were black.
The gliding was ominous.
The horizon was silent.

PROBLEM 5   *A pair of black vultures glide ominously on the silent horizon.*

REWRITE 5   ————————————————

EXERCISE 10.5   On-Your-Own Writing Options

Directions. Pick one of the following options. Use it as the focus for on-your-own writing.

1. To investigate whether a lean, direct style marks modern writing, follow these steps.

    a. Go to the "current reading" area of your school or public library. Pick *one* magazine from each category:

1) *Time, Newsweek, U.S. News & World Report*
2) *Reader's Digest, Life, People*
3) *Rolling Stone, Ebony, Esquire*

b. Find a passage of approximately twenty sentences in each magazine that seems typical of its style. Ask yourself: Does this passage use starchy openers, internal wordiness, passive voice, or inversion? As you find instances of these devices, list them.

c. Compare the three passages in a brief paper that answers the question, "Is Today's Writing Lean and Direct?" Support your discussion with quoted examples from the three passages.

2. Using a composition completed for a *previous* assignment, do a lean and direct rewrite. Focus on the four "enemies"—starchy opener, internal wordiness, passive voice, inversion—and eliminate them one by one. After you have completed this task, write a paragraph that discusses the changes you made. Which of the enemies is your biggest problem? Which enemy do you have most in control?

PART TWO
MULTIPLE-PARAGRAPH EXERCISES

Like the single-paragraph exercises in Part One, the exercises that follow are "programmed" to result in good, coherent prose. These, however, involve at least two—and as many as seven—connecting paragraphs. Your basic task is still the same: combine sentences, check writeouts for errors, study the rereading instructions, and write one or more paragraphs that connect to the exercise in ways specified by *Paragraph-Building Options*.

All of the multiple-paragraph exercises involve a mix of "open" and "signaled" sentence combining. "Open" clusters teach stylistic decision making, whereas "signaled" clusters teach specific target sentences. With "signaled" exercises, two points are important: (1) Refer back to Units 4 and 5 if review work is needed; (2) use a notecard to cover up footnote signals so that your brain will be forced to think of connecting words.

Besides the instructions for *Rereading Your Writeouts*, each exercise has a brief advance organizer. This statement will tell you how exercise paragraphs connect to one another. It's like a structural "map" for the territory you'll be exploring as you combine sentences. By studying these overviews—and then following up with the rereading work on intersentence "links"—you'll begin to develop

a good feel for the *connectedness* of both sentences and paragraphs.

The *Paragraph-Building Options* list writing starters for you. They will invite you to put your writing in three locations—*before*, *in between*, and *after* exercise paragraphs. The task in each case, however, is to *connect* your prose to paragraphs you've created through combining. By studying the numbered headings of the paragraphs and seeing *where* your writing is called for, you should have little trouble.

Let's say, for example, that an exercise consists of two paragraphs—*Paragraph 1* and *Paragraph 3*— and that the *Options* call for an "in between" paragraph. Your writing —*Paragraph 2*—would of course fit between those you did for the exercise. A slightly more complicated example might involve a series of four connected paragraphs. If you were asked to write *Paragraph 3½*, you'd know that your writing should be positioned between the third and fourth paragraphs of the exercise.

Whether you write the introduction, middle, or conclusion of an exercise, you need to read it aloud to yourself. And then you need to share your efforts with a friend. Writing is communication. The feedback can only help.

SOMETHING HAPPENED

The next two paragraphs may puzzle you. Paragraph 1 describes a man's action before "something happened." Paragraph 3 tells his appearance afterwards. You'll have to fill in the middle. (See *Paragraph-Building Options.*)

PARAGRAPH 1

    1. The man was short.
    2. The man was barrel-shaped.
3. The man loomed in the doorway.
    4. The doorway was open.

5. A roll drooped over his belt.
6. The roll was thick.
7. The roll was fat.
8. The belt was leather.

9. His face was pinched into a sneer.
    10. The sneer was cold.
    11. The sneer was disdainful.
    12. He barked a command.
    13. The command was sharp.

12 AS

14. Nobody moved.
15. Nobody spoke.

16. He curled back his lips.
17. His lips were fleshy.
18. He revealed teeth.
19. His teeth were clenched.

20. The command was bellowed again.
21. It was even louder this time.

22. Veins bulged at his temples.
23. Veins pulsed with blood.

24. His eyebrows (/) were bunched over his eyes.
    25. His eyebrows were wild.
    26. His eyebrows were shaggy.
    27. His eyes were glowering.

28. Silence mounted like thunderheads.
29. The thunderheads were churning.
30. The thunderheads were on a horizon.
31. The horizon was ominous.

Rereading Your Writeouts: Trace the repetition of pronouns (*he/his*) that refer to *man* and tie the paragraph together. What word links Cluster 9–13 with 20–21? What idea links Cluster 14–15 with 28–31?

PARAGRAPH 3

32. His rage seemed spent.
33. It had been menacing.
34. It was like air out of a balloon.

    35. He <u>blinked</u>.
36. He swallowed.
    37. He cleared his throat.

35 ING

38. Now the silence was somehow softer.
    39. It was more subdued.
    40. He licked his lips.
    41. The licking was <u>nervous</u>.

40 AS   41 LY

42. He began to speak.
43. He then hesitated.

    44. He was self-conscious.
    45. He was embarrassed.
46. He stared at his shoes.
    47. He shifted his weight.

48. He looked defeated.
    49. His defeat was <u>hopeless</u>.

49 LY

50. His voice was a whisper.
51. It trailed off into an apology.

52. The apology was feeble.
53. It was barely audible.

54. He took a step backwards.
55. He glanced around the room.
56. The room was hushed.

57. Then he wiped at his eye.
58. It was glistening with wetness.

59. His leaving was like a sigh.
60. The sigh was painful.

Rereading Your Writeouts: Trace the be-tween-sentence pronoun links (*he/his*) and the words that link to *silence: spent rage/ hesitated/whisper/trailed off/feeble/hushed/ painful sigh.*

PARAGRAPH-BUILDING OPTIONS

The key word in Cluster 32–34 is *rage*. This word links to Paragraph 1. Your paragraph

should use the word *rage* (or its synonyms) in order to link with the exercise paragraphs.

Picture the situation. Is it a classroom, a place in the home, an office, a restaurant, a locker room, or somewhere else? Who is the man? What is going on?

1. *Paragraph 2:* Describe what happens to change the man's attitude and behavior. Make this a narrative *report*—in the same "objective" third-person style as Paragraphs 1 and 3.

2. *Paragraph 2:* Put yourself in the scene and tell what you do to change the man's attitude and behavior. Write this from the "I" point of view.

3. *Paragraph 2:* Create a conversation be-tween one person in the room and the man to *show* what causes the change in his attitude and behavior. Put quotation marks around the statements made by each person.

TRUE CONFESSIONS

The next two paragraphs are the introduction and conclusion for a juicy bit of confessing on your part. Paragraph 1 sets the stage. Para-graph 3 gives a perspective on events that you will relate in Paragraph 2. (See *Paragraph-Building Options.*)

PARAGRAPH 1

1. SOMETHING is now unclear.
    2. I wanted to risk it.

2 WHY

3. Perhaps it was my lack of experience.
4. My lack of experience was unfortunate.

5. Perhaps it was an impulse.
6. The impulse was adolescent.
7. The impulse was for adventure.

8. Perhaps it was simply SOMETHING.
    9. I was bored.
    10. I had nothing else to do.

9 THE FACT THAT

11. Or perhaps it was some force.
12. The force was bizarre.
13. The force was unexplained.
14. The force held me in its power.

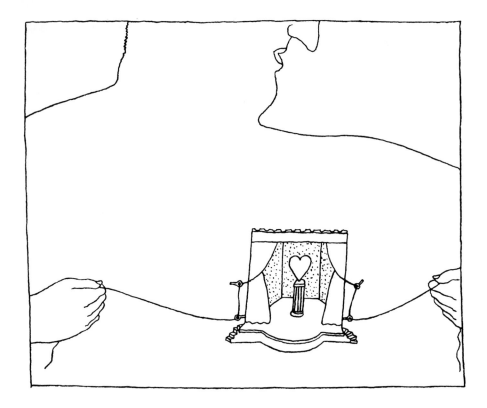

15. The reasons are now hazy.
BUT 16. The reasons are behind my actions.
17. What cannot be denied is SOME-THING.
18. It happened.

18 THAT

19. A confession follows.
20. The confession is brief.

Rereading Your Writeouts: Pay attention to the *parallelism* (repetition of *perhaps*) in Clusters 3–4, 5–7, 8–10, 11–14. This repetition helps the paragraph "hang together."

PARAGRAPH 3

21. I look back.

22. I have trouble believing SOMETHING.
23. This incident really happened.

21 AS   23 THAT

24. It now seems distant.
25. It now seems dreamlike.
26. It now seems unrelated to my life.
27. The life is in the present.

28. I sometimes think SOMETHING.
29. I was another personality.
OR 30. The personality was quite different.
31. Someone else was inhabiting my skin.

29 THAT   31 THAT

32. But the events did indeed occur.
33. The events have been described.

34.   I acknowledge their reality.
35.   I take responsibility for them.
36.   The responsibility is personal.

37.   This concludes my statement.
38.   The statement is confessional.

Rereading Your Writeouts: Notice the words *this, it, their,* and *them* in Paragraph 3. (These words are links to preceding sentences.) Find the word that each refers to.

PARAGRAPH-BUILDING OPTIONS

Clusters 19–20 and 21–23 provide two links to writing you will do. Reread your writeouts for these clusters. Then choose one of the following options.

1.   *Paragraph 2:* Tell a *true* story in which you describe the situation and the risk that you faced. See it again—clearly and specifically—and narrate what happened. Let your feelings come through.

2.   *Paragraph 2:* Tell a *phony* story in which you present the dramatic scene and the risks. Build up the problem. Spin the outcome in rich detail from your imagination.

MORAL DILEMMA

Here are two paragraphs that pose a dilemma for you to solve. Paragraph 1 sets the scene. Paragraph 2 identifies the problem. Paragraph 3 is up to you. (See *Paragraph-Building Options.*)

PARAGRAPH 1

1.   The classroom is tense.
2.   The classroom is busy.

3.   Pencils scurry across notebooks.
     4.   The scurrying is nervous.
     5.   The notebooks are for examinations.
     6.   We all struggle for answers.
     7.   The answers will be thoughtful.

4 LY   6 AS

8.   The class is in "ethics."
     9.   "Ethics" is the study of human action.

AND

10.   The action is right and wrong.
11.   This is our test.
12.   The test is final.

13.   Everyone has signed a pledge.
      14.   The pledge is not to cheat on the exam.
15.   No teacher or monitor is present.

13 BECAUSE

16.   We work on our own.
17.   The work is quiet.
18.   The work is without supervision.

19. It is the "honor system."
20. The system is in action.

Rereading Your Writeouts: Notice how related words such as *busy/scurry* and *examination/test* link different sentences together. Find words related to the phrase *not to cheat.*

PARAGRAPH 2

21. I am sitting in the back of the room.
    22. I am writing intently.
    23. A note is slid in my direction.
    24. The note is unexpected.

23 WHEN

25. It is from my best friend.
26. My friend is across the aisle.
27. The note asks for help.
28. The help would be on a question.
29. The question is important.

┌30. I know SOMETHING.
BUT 31. There is no real danger of getting
│   caught.
└32. I also know SOMETHING.
    33. I have pledged my word.
    34. The pledge is not to cheat.

31 THAT **33 THAT**

    35. I want to help my friend.
        36. I want to maintain our friendship.
        37. The friendship is close.
38. Cheating seems wrong.

35 ALTHOUGH

39. It means going back on my word.
40. It means betraying the trust.
41. The trust is my teacher's.
42. The trust is others' in the class.

43. I am in a spot.
44. The spot is tight.

Rereading Your Writeouts: Notice how Cluster 21–24 links with Paragraph 1: *I* links with *we; writing* links with *pencils; intently* links with *work.* Trace the words *note* and *cheat* through Paragraph 2.

PARAGRAPH-BUILDING OPTIONS

1. *Paragraph 3:* Imagine that you are writing a note to your best friend. Put down your reasons for *not* being able to help him/her with the exam question. To link this paragraph with the first two, you might try an "opener" that reads like this: *A note, quickly written to my friend, explains my decision not to cheat.*

2. *Paragraph 3:* Continue telling this incident from the "I" point of view. Explain why cheating is, in your opinion, morally justified in this instance. Open your paragraph with a sentence that announces your position clearly, perhaps like this: *I finally decided to give my friend the answer for (this/these) reason(s).*

JETHRO

The next two paragraphs are on the lighter side. Paragraph 1 describes three disgusting features of a dog named Jethro. Paragraph 2 says that Jethro's vices are, in fact, not all that bad and may even serve useful purposes. You are invited to try your hand at Paragraph 3 or

to write a parallel satire piece. (See *Paragraph-Building Options*.)

PARAGRAPH 1

1. My dog is an animal.
2. His name is Jethro.
3. The animal is disgusting.
4. He is the offspring.
    5. The offspring is deformed.
    6. The offspring is of paternity.
    7. The paternity is questionable.

4 FIRST OF ALL

┌ 8. His mother was a poodle.
│   9. The poodle was skittish.
AND 10. The poodle yapped.
│   11. The yapping was incessant.
└ 12. His father was apparently a mongrel.
    13. The mongrel was vile-tempered.
    14. The mongrel was of tremendous size.

11 LY

15. The result is Jethro.
    16. The result is unhappy.
    17. His ugliness is matched only by his disposition.
    18. The ugliness is inherited.
    19. The disposition is surly.

17 WHOSE

20. Jethro's habits are unclean.
    21. The habits are personal.
    22. The uncleanliness is decided.

20 SECOND   22 LY

23. He rolls in the dust.
24. He splashes through puddles.
25. He defecates with frequency.
26. The frequency is alarming.
27. These reminders are everywhere.
28. The reminders are smelly.
29. The reminders are of his presence.
30. They are especially underfoot.
31. There is a problem.
    32. The problem is Jethro's fleas.
    33. The fleas are large.

34. The fleas are plentiful.
35. The fleas are vicious.

31 FINALLY   33 WHICH

36. They are a species.
37. The species is new.
38. The species attacks everything.
39. This includes each other.

┌ 40. One would think SOMETHING.
BUT 41. Jethro's stench would drive them away.
└ 42. Such is not the case.
    43. This is unfortunate.

41 THAT   43 LY

44. They seem to thrive.
    45. The thriving is in his fur.
    46. The fur is ever-shedding.

44 ON THE CONTRARY

Rereading Your Writeouts: Study the three-part development of this paragraph—signaled by *first of all, second,* and *finally.*

PARAGRAPH 2

47. Jethro has some qualities.
    48. The qualities are redeeming.
    49. This is in spite of his appearance.
    50. This is in spite of his bad manners.
    51. This is in spite of his fleas.

47 AND YET

52. He deters salespeople.
53. The salespeople work door-to-door.
54. He intimidates bill collectors.
55. The bill collectors are obnoxious.

56. His presence keeps children at a distance.
57. The presence is snarling.
58. The children are in the neighborhood.
59. The distance is pleasant.

60. The fertilizer is effective.
    61. The fertilizer is organic.
    62. He manufactures it.

63. He distributes it. _____
64. The effectiveness is extraordinary.

62 THAT   64 LY

65. It keeps all lawns green.
66. The lawns are within a radius.
67. The radius is one mile.

68. He serves as a garbage can.
    69. The garbage can is mobile.
    70. He eats everything.
        71. Everything is put before him.
        72. This includes his bowl.
        73. This includes his leash.

70 BECAUSE   71 THAT

74. His yowling makes an alarm clock unnecessary.
75. His scratching makes an alarm clock unnecessary.
76. These are in the early morning.
77. And SOMETHING assures me of companionship.
    78. He is so loathesome.
    79. He is so good-for-nothing.
    80. The companionship is life-long.
    81. No one else would want him.

77 FINALLY   78 THE FACT THAT
81 SINCE

82. No one would want me either.
    83. We are perfectly suited to one another.

82 OF COURSE   83 SO

Rereading Your Writeouts: Notice how this paragraph opens with a contrast to Paragraph 1 (Cluster 47–51) and develops its topic through six supporting reasons.

PARAGRAPH-BUILDING OPTIONS

1. *Paragraph 3:* Explain how you acquired Jethro. This writing should keep the same tone as previous paragraphs and be linked to them. You can open with a variety of different sentences:

   I am still not sure whether I adopted Jethro or he adopted me.

   The story behind my acquisition of Jethro is stunningly ordinary.

   Jethro's arrival in my life was "unexpected," to say the least.

2. Use the "Jethro" paragraphs as a structured model for writing about a more serious subject—say an archenemy from your past or a politician you particularly dislike. In Paragraph 1, point out negative or undesirable aspects of the person, perhaps using humor to advantage. In Paragraph 2, point out the supposedly "positive" aspects of the person's character or behavior. If you set up the "contrast" cleverly and choose your examples well, the net result will be satire.

SKATEBOARDING

The next two paragraphs take a quick look at skateboarding. Paragraph 1 describes the scene at a skateboard park. Paragraph 2 says that skateboard parks are good investments and cites statistics on the growth of the industry. Paragraph 3 is waiting to be written. (See *Paragraph-Building Options.*)

PARAGRAPH 1

1. Picture a landscape.

2.   The landscape is concrete.
3.   The landscape is unusual.
4.   The landscape consists of valleys.
5.   The landscape consists of ramps.
6.   The landscape consists of bowls.
7.   The landscape consists of chutes.

8.   Imagine people paying money.
9.   The money is to enter this place.
10. The place is baked by the sun.
11. The sun is merciless.

12. And suppose SOMETHING.
    13. These people wear helmets.
    14. These people wear pads.
    15. These people wear gloves.
        16. They whiz around their environment.
        17. The environment is stark.
        18. The environment is forbidding.

13   THAT   16   AS

19. This is not science fiction.
20. This is not a description of the future.
21. The future is distant.

22. It is the scene.
23. The scene is everyday.
24. The scene is at Skateboard World.
25. Skateboard World is in southern California.

    26. It is like other parks.
        27. The parks are being built.
        28. The building is across the country.
29. This one has been designed for one purpose.
    30. The purpose is skateboarding.

31. SOMETHING is abundantly clear to business people.
    32. Such parks are investments.
        33. The investments are good.

34. Interest continues to accelerate.
    35. The interest is in the sport.

32   THAT   34   BECAUSE

Rereading Your Writeouts: Notice that Clusters 19–21 and 22–25 make a transition from the paragraph's descriptive opening to its more explanatory final sentences.

PARAGRAPH 2

36. Support is found in statistics.
37. The support is for the popularity.
38. The popularity is growing.
39. The popularity is skateboarding.

BUT
  40. There were 85 skateboard parks in existence.
  41. This was two years after the first one.
  42. Hundreds more are now being planned.
  43. They are now being built.

44. The sport has grown from nowhere.
45. This was in the early sixties.
46. It has grown into an industry.
47. The industry is massive.
48. The industry is complex.
49. The industry sells $400 million per year.

50. Some 20 million skateboards (/) are now in use.
    51. They range from primitive.
    52. They range to highly sophisticated.

50   IN FACT   51   ING

AND
  53. Many manufacturers are doubling their sales.
  54. This is each year.
  55. Others are experiencing even more growth.
  56. The growth is phenomenal.

57. Researchers also say SOMETHING.

58. Skateboarding has doubled its total injuries.
59. This is in one year.
    60. It now ranks second only to bicycling.
    61. Bicycling has 70 million more users.

58 THAT   60 SO THAT

62. Any sport (/) must have some popularity.
    63. The sport has 375,000 injuries per year.
    64. The sport continues to attract teenagers.
        65. The teenagers spend an average of $100.
        66. The $100 is for skateboard equipment.

63 THAT   65 WHO

Rereading Your Writeouts: The words *interest* and *sport* in Cluster 31–35 (the last sentence of Paragraph 1) link to the words *popularity* and *skateboarding* in the first cluster (topic sentence) of Paragraph 2. What links to the topic sentence do you see in Cluster 62–66?

PARAGRAPH-BUILDING OPTIONS

The links between your writing and the exercise paragraphs will depend on the option you choose. For Option 1, focus on the word *appeal* as your link. For Option 2, use words such as *similar* and *comparison*. For Option 3, emphasize words such as *contrast* and *different*.

1. *Paragraph 3:* Describe the actual appeal of skateboarding. What is there about this sport that attracts so many young people and makes them so avid about it? You may wish to do research on this question and build it into your paragraph in the form of direct quotations.

2. *Paragraph 3:* Compare the appeal of skateboarding with another "action" or "motion" sport such as surfing, skiing, or motorcycling. What are the enjoyable similarities between the two experiences? List all the comparisons before beginning Paragraph 3; then select the most relevant.

3. *Paragraph 3:* Contrast the appeal of skateboarding with a team sport such as basketball or a competitive one such as tennis. What is there that skateboarding provides which is "missing" in the other sports? Before beginning this version of Paragraph 3, you'll find it helpful to make a list of "contrasts" among the sports you want to consider.

AN OLD PROBLEM

"It is late afternoon, with a gray autumn wind scouring City Park." Paragraph 1 describes old men who spend their afternoons "killing time." Paragraph 2 focuses on social problems related to aging. Paragraph 3 is yours to write. (See *Paragraph-Building Options.*)

PARAGRAPH 1

1. It is afternoon.
2. The afternoon is late.
3. A wind scours City Park.
4. The wind is gray.
5. The wind is autumn.

6.   The men are there as usual.
   7.   The men are old.
   8.   The men have their newspapers.
   9.   The men have their paper sacks.
   10. The men have their wallets full of photos.
   11. The men have their loneliness.

8   WITH

12. They sit.
13. They watch the shadows lengthen.
14. The lengthening is across the grass.
15. The grass is worn.
16. The afternoon deepens into dusk.

   17. They stare vacantly.
18. They talk from time to time.
   19. The talk is about nothing in particular.

20. Their island is unmoving.
21. Their island is quiet.
22. Their island is within the city's noise.
23. The noise is restless.
24. The noise is undulating.

   25. They fill up their day.
   26. They kill time.
27. They have already made their stops.
   28. The stops are ritual.

25   TO   26   TO

29. Perhaps they have been to the library.
30. They have been to the post office.
31. They have been to a lunchroom.
32. The lunchroom is half-deserted.
33. Cronies hang out in the lunchroom.
34. The cronies are old.

35. Now there is nothing to do.
36. They sit.
37. Their hands are folded.
38. They try not to look at their watches.

39. Leaves skitter across the footpath.
   40. The leaves are dry.
   41. The footpath is concrete-covered.
      42. They swirl like dancers.
      43. They are stopped by a fence.
44. The old men do not ask one another SOMETHING.
   45. The question is "What's new?"

39   AS   42   ING   43   UNTIL

Rereading Your Writeouts: Trace the inter-sentence links in Clusters 12–16, 17–19, 20–24, 25–28, 29–34, 35–38: *they, they, their, they, they, them, their.* All refer to "old men."

PARAGRAPH 2

46. This scene (/) is repeated each day.
   47. The scene has variations.
   48. The variations are minor.
   49. The repetition is throughout the country.

47   WITH

   50. Thoreau would say something.
51. It is one of "desperation."
   52. The desperation is "quiet."

50   AS

53. The truth is SOMETHING.
   54. Our society sentences old people.
   55. The sentence is to live on islands.
   56. The islands are isolation.

53   REGRETTABLY   54   THAT

57. Such policies have costs.
   58. The policies are social.
   59. The costs are high.

```
┌── 60.   This is in terms of suffering.
AND     61.   The suffering is human.
└── 62.   This is in terms of productivity.
        63.   The productivity is lost.
```

60 BOTH

64.   SOMETHING cannot be denied.
        65.   The suffering is real.

64 THAT

66.   There is deterioration.
67.   The deterioration is almost visible.
68.   The deterioration is physical.
69.   The deterioration is emotional.
70.   The deterioration follows retirement.

71.   Its signature is eyes.
72.   The eyes are vacant.
73.   The eyes are hollow.

74.   Beyond the tragedy is the impact.
75.   The tragedy is human.
76.   The tragedy is for individuals.
77.   The impact is economic.
78.   The impact is social.

79.   Years of experience are lost.
80.   The years are countless.
81.   The loss is in many areas.
82.   The areas are vital to our health.
83.   The health is economic.
84.   The health is our nation's.

85.   Also lost are skills and knowledge.
        86.   These might be imparted to young people.
                87.   The young people have parents.
                88.   The parents are "too busy."

86 THAT   87 WHOSE

89.   Old people need to be needed.
90.   Our society needs the talents.
        91.   Old people have talents.

89 JUST AS   91 THAT

Rereading Your Writeouts: Focus on two interparagraph links: (1) *this scene* (Cluster 46–49), which refers to Paragraph 1; and (2) *islands of isolation* (Cluster 53–56), which refers to Cluster 20–24 in Paragraph 1.

PARAGRAPH-BUILDING OPTIONS

1.   *Paragraph 3:* Interview an old person to find out what his/her concerns are. Before beginning your interview, make a list of key questions that you want the answers to. Use this information to add specificity and depth to this essay. Link your writing to the previous paragraphs with an opening sentence that might go like this: *Consider, for example, the case of . . .*

2.   *Paragraph 3:* Describe what our society (government, service organizations, businesses, local communities, families) should do to accord old people both dignity and a vital economic role (if they desire it). Link this paragraph to the last three clusters of Paragraph 2 by explaining how the *experience, skills, knowledge,* and/or *talents* of old people can be utilized.

CREATING A SUN

Will human beings be able to "create a sun"? Paragraph 1 says that fossil fuels will soon run out and that conventional nuclear fission reactors are objectionable for two reasons. Paragraph 2 outlines the theoretical benefits of fusion and states the task that scientists face. Paragraph 3 awaits your invention. (See *Paragraph-Building Options*.)

PARAGRAPH 1

    1.   Civilization is to survive.
      2.   The civilization is modern.
 3. Energy supply is the issue.
    4.   The supply is in the future.

    5.   The issue is central.
      6.   The issue must be confronted.

1 **IF**   **6** **THAT**

    7.   Forecasters know SOMETHING.
      8.   Fossil fuels (/) are in short supply.
         9.   One fossil fuel is oil.
        10.   One fossil fuel is natural gas.
        11.   One fossil fuel is coal.

8 **THAT**   **9** **SUCH AS**

    12.   Some predictions indicate SOMETHING.
      13.   Oil reserves may be exhausted.

14.   Exhaustion would occur soon after the year 2000.

12   INDEED   13   THAT

15.   Alternate sources are often impractical.
16.   The sources are energy.
17.   The sources include wind power.
18.   The sources include wave action.
19.   The sources include solar radiation.

20.   And nuclear fission (/) is a threat.
    21.   Nuclear fission has been operational for years.
    22.   The threat is to the environment.
    23.   The threat is to world security.

21   WHICH

     ┌24.   Its by-products are raw material.
NOT ONLY   25.   The raw material is for weapons
BUT ALSO   26.   The weapons are atomic.
     └27.   Its by-products are highly toxic wastes.

28.   The best hope seems to lie in a process.
29.   The hope is for the world.
30.   The world is energy-starved.
31.   The process is yet to be perfected.
32.   The process is called nuclear fusion.

Rereading Your Writeouts: Be alert to the three reasons (Clusters 7–11, 15–19, 20–23) that lead up to the *thesis statement* (Cluster 28–32).

PARAGRAPH 2

33.   Fusion is unlike nuclear fission.
34.   Fusion is safe.
35.   Fusion is clean.

36.   It produces radiation.
37.   The production is in minimal amounts.
38.   It has no by-products.
39.   The by-products might endanger health.
40.   The by-products might endanger security.

41.   The security is the world's.

42.   Its fuel (/) is cheap.
    43.   Its fuel is a form of hydrogen.
        44.   Hydrogen is readily found.
        45.   It is in seawater.

42   MOREOVER

46.   But the problems are expensive to solve.
47.   The problems are technical.
48.   The problems are associated with development.
49.   The development is nuclear fusion.
50.   The expense is enormous.

     ┌51.   This development amounts to harnessing a reaction.
IN FACT   52.   The reaction powers the hydrogen bomb.
     └53.   One scientist has described it.
        54.   His description is "creating a sun."

54   AS

55.   Scientists face the task.
    56.   The task is mind-boggling.
    57.   The task is squeezing hydrogen nuclei.
    58.   The squeezing is with tremendous forces.
        59.   The forces are electrical.
    60.   The nuclei fuse together.

60   SO THAT

61.   This fusion creates helium atoms.
62.   It releases massive quantities of energy.
63.   The release is simultaneous.

64.   The plan is SOMETHING.
    65.   Output would be changed to steam.
    66.   The output is energy.
        67.   The steam would power generators.
        68.   The generators would be electric.

65   THAT   67   WHICH

69. And what are the "payoffs"?
70. The "payoffs" are for all this bother.
71. The bother is technological.

┌─ 72. Fusion can be perfected.
AND   73. The perfection will be in the laboratory.
└─ 74. Fusion can be made commercially feasible.
75. Scientists estimate SOMETHING.
     76. One gallon of seawater will produce energy.
     77. The energy would be equivalent to 300 gallons of gasoline.

72 IF   74 (IF)   76 THAT

78. This would mean SOMETHING.
     79. The oceans could provide a supply.
     80. The supply would be virtually inexhaustible.
     81. The supply would be of energy.
     82. The supply would be for the world's needs.

79 THAT

Rereading Your Writeouts: Examine the words *it* and *this* in kernels 36, 42, 51, 53, 61, 70, 78; these are intersentence reference links (or cohesive "glue") for the paragraph.

PARAGRAPH-BUILDING OPTIONS

1. *Paragraph 3:* Imagine for a moment that nuclear fusion is perfected and that huge supplies of electrical energy are readily available. Consider the impact on *one* area of day-to-day living such as transportation or housing. What kinds of changes would you predict? How would life styles as we now know them be affected? *Ask a question to open your paragraph and to provide a link with the preceding paragraphs.*

2. *Paragraph 3:* Consult the *Reader's Guide to Periodical Literature* in your school library to find recent writing about nuclear fusion. Read at least two articles to see what you can learn. Then zero in on Paragraph 3 by focusing on *one* of these questions:

What are specific technical problems in nuclear fusion yet to be overcome?

What progress has been made so far in fusion development?

How does the fusion process work in step-by-step terms?

To link Paragraph 3 with the preceding paragraphs, use a question opener (such as those above).

INNER SPACE

The following three paragraphs describe a journey into inner space. Paragraph 1 sets the scene. Paragraph 2 describes the journey and a new place. Paragraph 3 is a return home— but with a slight twist. You can put your paragraph(s) *between* these or *after* them. (See *Paragraph-Building Options.*)

PARAGRAPH 1

1. It is past midnight.
2. It is time for bed.

3. My eyes burn with fatigue.
4. They blink at words.

5. The words must be read.
6. The reading must be before morning.

7. The clock is on the mantel.
┌ 8. The clock ticks.
│ 9. It lulls me.
AND 10. The lulling is with rhythms.
│ 11. The rhythms are monotonous.
└ 12. The heater clicks on.
13. It pumps air.
14. The air is warm.
15. The pumping is over my feet.

16. I have read the passage.
17. The reading is repeated.
18. The passage is in the text.
19. Nothing is happening.

20. My brain remains inert.
21. My brain remains disengaged.
22. My brain remains unwilling to function.

23. I put my head down.
24. I close my eyes.
25. Sleep washes in.
26. It is like a wave.
27. The wave is white.
28. The wave is murmuring.

Rereading Your Writeouts: Trace the inter-sentence vocabulary links: *midnight/time/before morning/clock* and the links between pronouns *my/me/I.*

PARAGRAPH 2

29. The drift carries me through time.
30. The drift is tidelike.
31. The drift carries me to shores of dream.
32. The shores are deep within myself.

33. It is a journey.
34. The journey is vivid.
35. The journey is memorable.

36. The journey is far better than studying.

37. I lie on the shores.
38. The shores are sandy.
39. The shores are this landscape's.
40. The landscape is interior.
41. I study the dome.
42. The dome is concave.
43. The dome is vast.
44. The dome is my own skull.

45. It arches above.
46. It is like the sky.
47. It reaches toward the horizon.
48. The horizon is distant.

49. I am totally alone.
50. I listen to the waves.
51. The waves are sleep.
52. The waves whisper against the sand.
53. The sand is smooth.
54. The sand is strewn with stones.

┌ 55. Light beats down.
│ 56. The light is from a sun.
AND 57. The sun is distant.
│ 58. The beating is warm.
└ 59. A rock presses against one cheek.
60. The rock is flat.
61. The pressing is hard.

62. I am thinking SOMETHING.
63. Being here is better than studying.

63 THAT

Rereading Your Writeouts: Examine the inter-paragraph links in Cluster 29–32; these connect to the last sentence of Paragraph 1. How many vocabulary links do you see?

PARAGRAPH 3

64. And then I wake up.
65. The waking is abrupt.

┌66. The "sun" is a study lamp.
AND 67. It has been cooking my face.
└68. The "rock" is a textbook.
 69. The textbook is open.
 70. The textbook has notations.
 71. The notations are in the margin.

72. My mouth tastes dry.
73. It tastes gritty.

┌74. I close my eyes again.
BUT 75. The closing is for a moment.
└76. The landscape has vanished.
 77. The landscape is inner.

78. Words swim before my eyes.
 79. I tell myself SOMETHING.
  ┌──80. The journey was only a dream.
 AND 81. The dream was fantastic.
  └──82. Now I must get back to work.

79 AS 80 THAT 82 THAT

83. I shake myself awake.
84. I pick up a pencil.
85. I check the work.
86. The work is yet to be read.
87. The reading is in the text.

88. Then I notice a trace.
89. The trace is faint.
90. The trace is sandy.
91. The trace is on the desktop.

Rereading Your Writeouts: Notice how the "explanation" in Cluster 66–71 links to the preceding paragraph (Cluster 55–61).

PARAGRAPH-BUILDING OPTIONS

1. *Paragraph 2½:* Describe from the "I" point of view what happens after the "arrival" in inner space but before the "departure" back to reality—that is, *between* paragraphs 2 and 3. Perhaps you will describe more of the interior landscape; perhaps you will narrate action and dialogue with another character. Anything can happen in inner space. *Link your writing to Cluster 62–63.*

2. *Paragraph 4:* How can you explain the traces of sand on the desktop? Surely there must be some *logical* reasons for this. Use the "I" point of view as you consider the possibilities, one by one. *Link your writing to Cluster 88–91.*

FRIENDSHIP

Quotations sometimes serve as springboards for writing. Paragraph 1 moves from a quotation to a statement of writing purpose. Paragraph 2 focuses on one word in the quotation and provides synonyms, antonyms, and similes to enrich its meaning. Paragraph 3 focuses on a phrase in the quotation and explains its implied meaning. Your task is to work out Paragraph 4. (See *Paragraph-Building Options.*)

PARAGRAPH 1

A friend is a person with whom I may be sincere. Before him, I may think aloud.
     —*Ralph Waldo Emerson*

1. Truths are sometimes clothed in words.
2. The truths are profound.
3. The words are simple.

4. One studies Emerson's definition.
    5. The definition is of friendship.
6. This point is especially clear.

4 AS

7. Emerson's language is simple.
    8. It is direct.
    9. It is uncluttered by jargon.
       10. The jargon is modern.
       11. The jargon is psychological.

12. Yet it expresses a truth.
13. The truth is basic.
14. The truth is universal in experience.
15. The experience is human.

16. We will explore Emerson's meanings.
17. This will be in paragraphs.
18. The paragraphs follow.
19. We will provide commentary.
20. We will provide examples.

Rereading Your Writeouts: Notice that *this point* links Cluster 4–6 with the preceding one and that *it* links Cluster 12–15 with 7–11. Study how Cluster 16–20 "points forward" to Paragraphs 2 and 3, thus linking them with Paragraph 1.

PARAGRAPH 2

21. Sincerity is a feature.
22. The feature is key.
23. The feature is in Emerson's definition.

24. We can define sincerity.
    25. The definition is in terms of synonyms.
    26. One synonym is honesty.
    27. One synonym is candor.
    28. One synonym is openness.
       29. The openness is emotional.

26 SUCH AS

30. We can also think of its antonyms.
31. The antonyms include phoniness.
32. The antonyms include deception.
33. The antonyms include lying.

34. Sincerity occurs.
   ┌─ 35. We trust another person.
AND   36. The trusting is full.
   └─ 37. We feel SOMETHING.
       38. We are fully accepted.

35 ONLY WHEN   38 THAT

39. An individual feels SOMETHING.
   ┌─ 40. Another person is critical.
OR   41. The criticism is secret.
   └─ 42. Another person is "two-faced."
43. Sincerity can never develop.
    44. The sincerity is true.

39 IF   40 THAT   42 (THAT)

    45. Sincerity is like sunshine.
    46. Sincerity is like water.
    47. Sincerity is like soil.
48. Sincerity is a condition.
    49. The condition is basic.
    50. The condition is for growth.
    51. The growth is of friendship.

Rereading Your Writeouts: Be alert to the repetition of the word *sincerity* that links the sentences. What idea links Clusters 34–38 and 39–44?

PARAGRAPH 3

52. Emerson's definition has another feature.
    53. The feature is interesting.
    54. The feature is significant.
    55. The feature is "we may think aloud."
    56. The thinking is with a friend.

55 THAT

57. Emerson is saying SOMETHING.
  58. Friendship is a process.
  59. The process is active.
    60. It fills a need.

58 THAT

61. His implication is SOMETHING.
┌─62. Introspection is good.
│   63. The introspection is about thoughts.
AND 64. The introspection is about feelings.
└─65. It also helps.
    66. We share ourselves.

62 THAT   65 THAT   66 WHEN

67. Self-disclosure is a means.
  68. The means is to self-knowledge.
    69. It enhances our lives.
    70. It enriches our lives.

67 IN OTHER WORDS   69 BECAUSE

71. E. M. Forster expresses the same idea.
72. He asks the question.
73. The question is thought-provoking.
74. The question is "How can I know what I think 'til I hear what I say?"

75. A friendship allows exploration.
76. The friendship is sincere.
77. The exploration is of the depths.
78. The depths are our values.
79. The depths are our feelings.

80. It also allows the same opportunity.
81. The opportunity is for our friend.

Rereading Your Writeouts: Note that the phrase *another feature* makes two paragraph links: *another* (meaning *second*) and *feature* (a repetition from Cluster 21–23 in Paragraph 2). Look at the conjunction *in other words* (Cluster 67–70). What sentences does it tie together? Now focus on the word *same* (Clusters 71–74 and 80–81). Do you see the sentences it links together?

PARAGRAPH-BUILDING OPTIONS

1. *Paragraph 4:* Describe a friendship you have had that illustrates the two key features of "sincerity" and "thinking aloud." As an opener for Paragraph 4 that announces your intention to move to personal experience, you might consider this: *Let's now consider the ideas of "sincerity" and "thinking aloud" in a real friendship—one that I have enjoyed for some time.*

2. *Paragraph 4:* Consider the possibility that Emerson's definition of friendship may not be the last word on the subject. Has anything been left out of Emerson's definition, in your opinion? If there is another aspect of friendship worth developing in Paragraph 4, your opening might go something like this: *As useful as Emerson's definition is, it nevertheless leaves out an important feature of friendship.*

HYPNOSIS

What is hypnosis? What can it do? What are its uses? Paragraph 1 defines hypnosis. Paragraph 2 centers on behaviors that hypnotic trances can induce. Paragraph 3 shifts to applications of hypnosis. Your writing can fit either *between* Paragraphs 1 and 2 or *after*

Paragraph 3. (See *Paragraph-Building Options*.)

ject; concentration/awareness; suggestibility/suggestions. Notice, too, the contrasting of hypnosis with sleep.

PARAGRAPH 1

1.   Hypnosis is a state.
2.   The state is induced.
3.   The state is of suggestibility.
4.   The suggestibility is extreme.

┌5.   It resembles sleep.
BUT   6.   The resemblance is in certain ways.
└7.   A person can speak and act.
    8.   The person has been hypnotized.
    9.   The speaking and acting are as if awake.

┌10.   The subject enjoys concentration.
    11.   The subject is hypnotized.
NOT ONLY   12.   The concentration is undiverted.
BUT ALSO   13.   The concentration is of faculties.
    14.   The faculties are mental.
└15.   The subject is highly responsive.
    16.   This is to instructions.
    17.   The instructions are verbal.

18.   Suggestions bypass awareness.
19.   The suggestions are hypnotic.
20.   The awareness is conscious.
21.   Suggestions work at a level.
22.   The level is subconscious.

23.   Responsiveness depends on cooperation and trust.
24.   The responsiveness is of the subject.
25.   The subject is hypnotized.

26.   It does *not* stem from powers.
27.   The powers are "magical."
28.   The powers emanate from the hypnotist.

Rereading Your Writeouts: Notice the vocabulary links between sentences: *person/sub-*

PARAGRAPH 2

29.   A trance produces behavior.
30.   The trance is hypnotic.
31.   The trance is deep.
32.   The behavior is interesting.
33.   The behavior is unusual.

34.   The body can be anesthetized.
    35.   No pain is felt.

35   SO THAT

36.   Changes can be effected.
37.   The changes are in heart rate.
38.   The changes are in respiration.
39.   The effect is through suggestion.

40.   Rigidity (/) can be achieved.
    41.   The rigidity is muscular.
    42.   The rigidity is extreme.
    43.   This is a boardlike stiffness.

44.   Hallucinations can be created.
    45.   The hallucinations are compelling.
    46.   The individual responds.
      47.   The response is complete.

46   TO WHICH   47   LY

48.   Age regression (/) can be induced.
    49.   The regression transports a person.
    50.   The transporting is into the past.
      51.   The past is dimly remembered.
    52.   The induction is through hypnosis.

49   THAT

53.   Suggestions can cause behavior to occur.
54.   The suggestions are posthypnotic.

55. The behavior is bizarre.
56. The behavior follows the trance.

Rereading Your Writeouts: Passive voice and parallelism are used in this paragraph to create a "listing" effect. Is this effective in your opinion?

PARAGRAPH 3

57. SOMETHING is obvious from the preceding remarks.
    58. Hypnosis is a tool.
        59. The tool is powerful.

58 THAT

60. Less apparent is SOMETHING.
    61. Hypnosis has many applications.
        62. The applications are practical.

61 THE FACT THAT

63. Some dentists have used it.
64. The dentists have studied techniques.
65. The techniques are for hypnosis.
66. The use is with patients.
67. The patients are suggestible.
68. The use is as an anesthetic.

69. It has also been employed by doctors.
70. The employment has been for childbirth.
71. The employment has been for surgery.

72. Psychiatrists sometimes utilize hypnosis.
    ┌─73. The utilization is to explore events.
    │   74. The events are traumatic.
AND   75. The events are from the past.
    │   76. The events have been repressed.
    └─77. The utilization is to change behavior.

78. The behavior is a problem.
79. The change is through suggestion.
80. The suggestion is posthypnotic.

81. Police apply hypnosis.
82. The application is in solving crimes.
83. They question witnesses.
84. They gain information.
85. They gain descriptions.
86. They gain license plate numbers.

87. And TV advertisers regularly use principles.
88. The principles are of hypnosis.
89. The use is to increase suggestibility.
90. The suggestibility is to messages.
91. The messages are for marketing.

Rereading Your Writeouts: Study the interparagraph link in Cluster 56–58. The *topic sentence* for Paragraph 3 is Cluster 59–61.

PARAGRAPH-BUILDING OPTIONS

1. *Paragraph 1½ :* Do research on the history of hypnosis by consulting an encyclopedia. Then write a paragraph that summarizes the key points. Logically, this paragraph will fit nicely *between* the first two paragraphs of this exercise. Cluster 26–28 already provides a "looking back" transition by introducing the topic of "magical" powers. By opening your historical paragraph on the theme of *hypnosis as magic* you create an interparagraph link.

2. *Paragraph 4:* Look into the question of techniques for hypnosis—again by referring to an encyclopedia. Put these into the form of a "process" paragraph. Your purpose will be to describe how hypnotic states are induced. Present the

basics of hypnosis as a series of steps. *Do not use the pronoun "you" in describing the steps.* Link your paragraph to preceding ones with a straightforward opener such as this: *The techniques of hypnosis are rather simple.*

VANNING

Despite the energy crisis, custom vans continue to be a part of popular culture. Paragraph 1 gives history and statistics for vanning. Paragraph 2 switches to generalized descriptions of modern vans—first their exteriors, then their interiors. Paragraph 3 tries to explain the different levels of appeal for vans. You can link your writing *between* Paragraphs 2 and 3 or *after* Paragraph 3. (See *Paragraph-Building Options*.)

PARAGRAPH 1

1. One sees them everywhere (/).
    2. They are expressions of taste.
    3. The expressions are stunning.
    4. The taste is personal.
    5. The expressions are called custom vans (/).
        6. They are a blending.
        7. The blending is of technology and art.

8. "Vanning" has become a life style.
    9. The life style is for thousands of people.
    10. The life style is nomadic.

8   IN FACT

    11. Something happened during 1980.
12. Over two million vans were in use.
    13. Predictions were for increases.
        14. Predictions were from the auto industry.
        15. The increases will be steady.

16. The increases will be in van sales.
17. The increases will be in years to come.

13   WITH

18. SOMETHING is not surprising.
    19. This craze has attracted attention.
        20. The attention is considerable.

18–19   IT . . . THAT

    21. A phenomenon comes along.
        22. The phenomenon is national.
        23. The phenomenon supports hundreds of clubs.
        24. The phenomenon supports 25 magazines.
        25. The phenomenon supports many businesses.
26. People are bound to be curious.

21   WHEN   23   THAT

27. They want to understand this subculture.
    28. It is so different from the suburbs.
        29. The suburbs are predictable.

28   BECAUSE

Rereading Your Writeouts: Notice how this paragraph narrows down to Cluster 27–29, a sentence that "points forward" to the following paragraphs.

PARAGRAPH 2

30. Vans are anything but predictable.

31. The vans are personalized.

32. Exteriors are often garish.
33. Exteriors are sometimes obscene.
34. Exteriors are always individual.
35. The individuality is unique.
36. The individuality is in design.
37. The individuality is in color.

38. Paint jobs include landscapes.
    39. The landscapes are realistic.
    40. Paint jobs include murals.
       41. The murals are psychedelic.
    42. Paint jobs include portraits.
    43. Paint jobs include optical effects.
       44. The optical effects are bizarre.
    45. Paint jobs include pinstriping.
       46. The pinstriping is baroque.

47. Their messages run the gamut.
48. The run is from amusement.
49. The amusement is self-indulgent.
50. The amusement is joyful.
51. The run is to social protest.
52. The social protest is angry.

BUT
53. Artistry can cost $3,000.
    54. Artistry is for the van's sheet metal.

    55. Artistry is for the van's windows.
56. Interiors are even more expensive.
    57. The interiors are creative.

58. Many are equipped with amenities.
59. The amenities are a stereo system.
60. The amenities are a CB unit.
61. The amenities are a television.
62. The amenities are kitchen facilities.
63. The amenities are a bar.
64. The amenities are carpeting.
65. The amenities are a bed.

BUT
66. Vans may be finished in paneling.
    67. The vans are austere.
    68. The vans are for camping.
    69. The paneling is mahogany.
    70. The paneling is cheap.
71. Others are appointed in leather.
    72. They are appointed in crushed velvet.
    73. They are appointed in fine woods.
    74. They may even have chandeliers.
    75. The chandeliers are crystal.

76. Period furnishings maintain attention to detail.
77. The furnishings are for luxury vans.
78. The attention is strict.
79. They create an effect of elegance.
80. The elegance is harmonious.

81. The price tag may run $10,000.
82. The tag is for a custom interior.
83. The tag may run higher.

Rereading Your Writeouts: Examine the word *predictable* (Cluster 30–31) that links with the last sentence of Paragraph 1. Note that Paragraph 2 first deals with van exteriors, then interiors.

PARAGRAPH 3

84. What is behind the craze?
85. The craze is for vanning.
86. The craze has affected young.
87. The craze has affected old.
88. The craze has affected singles.
89. The craze has affected couples.
90. The couples are married.

91. One answer is SOMETHING.
    92. The van provides an outlet.
    93. The outlet is for expression.
       94. The expression is creative.

95. The expression is of identity.
    96. The identity is personal.

92   THAT

97. Another is SOMETHING.
    98. Vanning provides a community.
        99. The community is human.
        100. The community is ever-changing.
            101. One can always feel a part of it.

98   THAT

┌─102. The view has much to recommend it.
│   103. Vanning fills personal needs.
YET   104. Vanning fills social needs.
└─105. There is more to be said.
       106. The saying is by way of explanation.

103   THAT

107. Vanning combines transportation with housing.
    108. The combining is efficient.
    109. The housing is minimal.
110. It has appeal.
    111. The appeal is pragmatic.

107   SINCE

112. Savings can pay for a van.
    113. The savings are on motel bills.
    114. One travels a lot.

112   INDEED   114   IF

115. Its spiritual appeal is more difficult to describe.
116. Its spiritual appeal is nonetheless important.

117. The net effect is a life style.
118. The effect is of vanning.
119. The life style is free-wheeling.

120. The life style is "unrooted."
121. The life style has appeal.
122. The appeal is psychological.
123. The appeal is for many people.

124. It is the call.
    125. The call is of the open road.
        126. There are many conveniences.
        127. The conveniences are modern.
        128. The conveniences are from home.

126   WITH

Rereading Your Writeouts: Be alert to the *question opening* (Cluster 84–90) followed by *answers* of various kinds. Notice that Cluster 117–123 links to Paragraph 1 (Cluster 8–10).

PARAGRAPH-BUILDING OPTIONS

1. *Paragraph 2½:* Interview *at least* one person who owns a customized van. See if you find the answers to questions like these:

    What got you into vanning?
    What's its appeal for you and your friends?
    Why do people invest so much money in their rigs?

    Use the answers to such questions to write a new paragraph that will fit between Paragraphs 2 and 3. To open your paragraph, you might say: *Statements made by vanners shed some light on their hobby.*

2. *Paragraph 4:* Speculate (with tongue in cheek) on the future of vanning. What sporting events do you foresee? How

will the vanning community exercise its political clout? Will college courses in various aspects of vanning soon be offered? Pull out the stops; enjoy your-

self. Consider linking the opening of your paragraph to the theme of *modern conveniences from home* mentioned in the last cluster of Paragraph 3.

ROMAN AND AMERICAN EMPIRES

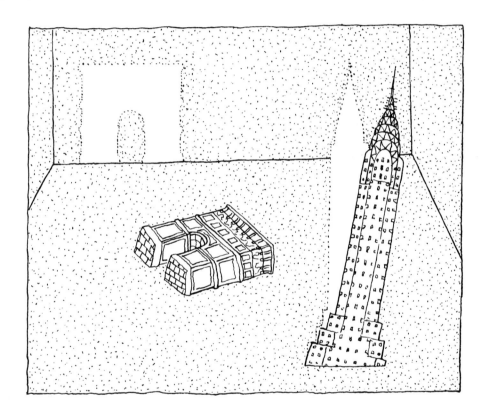

Here are three paragraphs that deal with the civilizations of ancient Rome and modern America. Paragraph 1 opens at a general level and narrows toward the two elements of comparison. Paragraph 2 focuses on *similarities* between Rome and America. Paragraph 3 discusses *differences* between the two civilizations. Your task is to maintain the voice and style of the three paragraphs as you develop

Paragraph 4. (See *Paragraph-Building Options.*)

PARAGRAPH 1

1. The cliché says SOMETHING.
   2. History repeats itself.

2 THAT

3. This is like most clichés.
4. This one has truth to it.
    5. The truth is considerable.
    6. Its veracity may not be literal.

6   ALTHOUGH

7. Many historians have explored this theme.
    8. The historians are reputable.
    9. The theme is familiar.
    10. They have compared civilizations.

10   AS

11. The comparison is interesting.
12. The comparison is particularly instructive.
13. The parallel is between Rome and America.
14. Rome was ancient.
15. America is modern.

16. Arnold Toynbee charted cycles.
    17. The cycles were similar.
    18. The cycles were of triumph.
    19. The cycles were of disintegration.
    20. The cycles were of collapse.
    21. The charting was in his book.
        22. The book was monumental.
        23. The book was titled *A Study of History*.

16   FOR EXAMPLE

24. Others have echoed Toynbee's predictions.
25. The echoing is periodic.
26. The predictions are dire.
27. The predictions are about America's future.

Rereading Your Writeouts: Study the links created by *this one* and *it* (Cluster 3–6) and *this theme* (Cluster 7–10). Also trace the vocabulary links: *history/historians; cliché/familiar theme; compared/comparison/parallel.*

PARAGRAPH 2

28. An account is chilling.
    29. The account is historical.
    30. The account is of events.
    31. The events were before Rome's collapse.
        32. It sounds like a newscast.
        33. The newscast summarizes the recent past.
        34. The past is in the United States.

32   BECAUSE

35. Something happened during the final days.
    36. The days were of the Roman Empire.
37. Catastrophes drained the treasury.
    38. The catastrophes were military.
    39. The catastrophes weakened morale.
        40. The morale was national.

41. Inflation spiraled out of control.
42. The inflation was rampant.
43. The spiraling was wild.

44. Unemployment burgeoned.
45. This created chaos.
46. The chaos was social.

47. Citizens complained about inequities.
48. The citizens were Roman.
49. The complaints were bitter.
50. The inequities were in taxes.

51. Corruption infected the bureaucracy.
52. The corruption was in government.
53. The bureaucracy was swollen.
54. The corruption inspired cynicism.
55. The cynicism was among the people.

56. Peasants and slaves went underground.
57. They were disaffected.
58. They became terrorists.
59. The terrorists were guerrillas.

60. Violence dominated entertainment.
61. The violence was in athletic contests.
62. The violence was in spectacles.
63. The entertainment was public.

64. Pornography reached a zenith.
65. Licentiousness reached a zenith.

66. A philosophy sanctioned decadence.
67. The philosophy was hedonistic.
68. The decadence was moral.
69. The philosophy sanctioned pleasure-seeking.

Rereading Your Writeouts: Examine the interparagraph link between Cluster 28–34 (the topic sentence) and the last sentence of Paragraph 1. (The link centers on *dire predictions* and *chilling account*.) Notice that parallel structure (the development through listing) helps the paragraph "hang together."

PARAGRAPH 3

70. Differences do exist between the civilizations.
    71. The differences are important.
    72. The civilizations are two.
        73. This is despite similarities.
        74. The similarities are on the surface.

70   HOWEVER

┌75. Roman society suffered insurrections.
│   76. It suffered revolts.
BUT
│   77. The revolts were internal.
└78. It was unable to change.

79. The "under class" had no voice.
80. The "under class" was proletarian.
81. The voice was in government.

82. Bargaining was unknown.
    83. The bargaining is reasoned.
    84. The bargaining is between labor and management.
        85. Roman society was supported by labor.
        86. The labor was of slaves.

85   BECAUSE

87. Policies had no basis.
88. The policies were economic.
89. The basis was rational.

90. An army pursued conquests.
    91. The army was imperial.
    92. The conquests were foreign.
    93. This was with popular support.
    94. The support was from the citizens.
        95. There was no justification.

95   ALTHOUGH

┌96. The society was sustained by delusions.
│   97. The society was fatigued.
BUT
│   98. The delusions were of past conquest.
└99. It had no communication systems.
    100. The systems would help marshal resistance.
    101. The resistance would be to invaders.
    102. The invaders were from the north.

103. Science was based on superstition.
104. Advances were not possible.
    105. The advances would be steady.

106. The advances would be in understanding.

103 WITH

107. Rome sustained a failure.
     108. The failure was of imagination.
     109. The failure was of energy.
     110. The failure was of hope.

107 MOST IMPORTANTLY

Rereading Your Writeouts: Zero in on the interparagraph links in Cluster 70–74: *differences, however, despite similarities.* Notice that this topic sentence announces a paragraph of differences between Roman and American civilizations.

PARAGRAPH-BUILDING OPTIONS

1. *Paragraph 4:* Answer the question of whether similarities outweigh the differences between ancient Rome and modern America. In fact, your paragraph might well open with a direct statement of this question. The follow-up sentences will provide the answers that make sense to you.

2. *Paragraph 4:* Return to the theme of *history repeating itself.* You might ask a question—*Does history repeat itself?*—or you might frame the question as a statement—*The question of whether history repeats itself is worth considering.* However you choose to begin, make sure to support and develop your ideas.

3. *Paragraph 4:* The idea that *human civilization can learn from its past mistakes* is your topic sentence. Focus on what American civilization needs to do to keep from going the way of the Romans. Put a *reason* behind each recommendation that you make.

RUMOR/PROPAGANDA

The next four paragraphs define and discuss two closely related terms—"rumor" and "propaganda." Paragraph 1 outlines three purposes for paragraphs that follow. Paragraph 2 defines the word "rumor" and cites some everyday examples of it. Paragraph 3 defines "propaganda" and says that advertising and politics are two areas in which it commonly occurs. Paragraph 4 takes up similarities between "rumor" and "propaganda." Paragraph 5—which is yours to write—will discuss differences between the two words. (See *Paragraph-Building Options.*)

PARAGRAPH 1

1. We have three purposes.
2. The purposes are in what follows.

3. The first is to define two words.
4. The words are closely related.
5. They are "rumor" and "propaganda."
6. The first is to provide examples of each.

7. The second purpose is to explore similarities.
8. The similarities are in meaning.
9. The similarities are between the words.

10. The final intent is to show SOMETHING.
    11. The words differ.

11 HOW

12. This approach should deepen our understanding.
13. The approach is three-pronged.
14. The understanding is of meanings.
15. The meanings are semantic.
16. The meanings are related.

Rereading Your Writeouts: Notice the use of *numbers* to link sentences and announce intentions for the next paragraphs.

PARAGRAPH 2

17. "Rumor" can be defined as information.
18. The information is unverified.
19. The information is spread.
20. This is usually by word of mouth.

21. Information is typically of origin.
22. The information is rumored.
23. The origin is uncertain.

24. Synonyms are words.
25. The synonyms are for "rumor."
26. The words are "gossip" and "hearsay."

27. Examples abound in life.
28. The life is everyday.

29. The student (/) becomes a victim of rumor.

┌─30. The student hears SOMETHING.
│   31. An exam has been postponed.
AND
└─32. The student does not study.
   33. The rumor is false.

30 WHO   31 THAT   32 (WHO)

34. The worker (/) becomes a beneficiary of rumor.
┌─35. The worker hears SOMETHING.
│   36. The boss is looking for loafers.
AND
└─37. The worker gets busy.
   38. The rumor is true.

35 WHO   36 THAT   37 (WHO)

39. Rumors shape our decisions.
40. The decisions are about movies to attend.
41. The decisions are about cars to buy.
42. The decisions are about careers to follow.

43. Sometimes they even influence SOMETHING.
    44. We remain single.
    45. We marry.
    46. We get divorced.

44 WHETHER

47. They are forces.
48. The forces are ever present.
49. The forces are in our lives.

Rereading Your Writeouts: Be alert to the "definition" statements (Clusters 17–20, 21–23, 24–26) followed by the introduction of examples.

PARAGRAPH 3

50. Propaganda is information.
51. The information has a source.
52. The source is specific.

53. It may consist of ideas.
54. It may consist of facts.
55. It may consist of allegations.

56. Propaganda is spread with a purpose.
57. Propaganda is language.
58. The language is calculated.
59. The calculation is to achieve effects.
60. The effects are desired.
61. The purpose is deliberate.

62. The example occurs in advertising.
63. The example is most obvious.
64. The example is of propaganda.
65. The advertising is commercial.

66. Ads have a purpose.
67. The purpose is basic.
68. The purpose is to inform.
69. The purpose is to persuade.

70. They attempt to influence our behavior.
   71. The behavior is buying.
   72. They slant messages.
   73. The messages have appeal.
   74. The appeal is to consumers.

75. Another instance occurs in the arena.
   76. The instance is common.
   77. The instance is of propaganda.
   78. The arena is of politics.

79. Leaders sell themselves.
   80. Leaders sell their viewpoints.
   81. Leaders sell their programs.
   82. The leaders are political.
   83. The selling is through propaganda.
   84. The propaganda is in various forms.

85. Propaganda is used by politicians.
   86. The use is to gain support.
   87. The use is to maintain support.
   88. The support is public.

89. Power depends on propaganda.
   90. The power is political.
   91. The propaganda is effective.

89 IN FACT

Rereading Your Writeouts: Study the "definition" statements (Clusters 50–52, 53–55, 56–61). Notice that the words *most obvious* and *another instance* announce the examples.

PARAGRAPH 4

   92. We have defined "rumor."
   93. We have defined "propaganda."
94. We will now examine similarities.
   95. The similarities are between the two words.

92 ING

   96. One similarity is SOMETHING.
   97. Both are messages.
   98. The messages are verbal.

97 THAT

   99. Another feature is SOMETHING.
   100. The feature is shared.
   101. Both messages may involve distortions.
   102. The distortions are of the truth.

101 THAT

103. A third area is SOMETHING.
   104. The area is common.
   ┌─105. Both occur in everyday life.
   AND   106. The occurrence is regular.
   └─107. Both shape our attitudes.
   108. Both shape our behavior.

105 THAT   107 (THAT)

109. A fourth similarity is SOMETHING.
   110. Both can be public or private.
   111. Both can be <u>serious or trivial</u>.
   112. Both can be <u>constructive or malicious</u>.

110 THAT

Rereading Your Writeouts: Note the interparagraph link (*having defined rumor and propaganda*) and the intersentence link (*similarities between the two words*) in the *topic sentence* (Cluster 92–95).

PARAGRAPH-BUILDING OPTIONS

In Paragraph 5, write about the differences between "rumor" and "propaganda." Consider how they differ with respect to the following:

> the usual *form* of the message
> the *intention* of the speaker
> the *distortion* of truth

Openers such as those shown below will help link your writing to the four preceding paragraphs.

1. *Let's now examine some differences between "rumor" and "propaganda."*
2. *What about differences between the two terms?*
3. *Differences between the now-familiar words are our final concern.*

SHAPING ATTITUDES TOWARD READING

The next four paragraphs explain how attitudes toward reading are shaped in young children. Paragraph 1 asserts that reading attitudes underlie school achievement and feelings of self-worth. Paragraph 2 begins to narrow the topic by saying that attitudes toward reading are learned (not inherited) and that three factors shape them. Paragraph 3 takes up the factor of parent modeling in some detail. Paragraph 4 focuses on the factor of environment, with both positive and negative examples. Your task will be to write a fifth paragraph, centering on the factor of parental judgments about the value of reading. (See *Paragraph-Building Options*.)

PARAGRAPH 1

1. Authorities (/) agree on SOMETHING.
   2. The authorities study problems.
      3. The problems are in reading.

4. Experiences shape attitudes.
   5. The experiences are early.
   6. The experiences are with print.
   7. The attitudes are in the future.
   8. The attitudes are toward reading.

2 WHO   4 THAT

9. This is a fact.
   10. The fact is important.
   11. Attitudes have correlation with achievement.
      12. The attitudes are related to reading.
AND
      13. The correlation is significant.
      14. The achievement is in school.
   15. Achievement has impact.
      16. The achievement is in school.

17. The impact is profound.
18. The impact is on self-concept.

11 BECAUSE   15 BECAUSE

19. A "good start" has implications.
    20. The start is in reading.
    21. The implications reach far.

19 IN OTHER WORDS

22. Success and feelings can be shaped by experiences.
23. The success is in the future.
24. The feelings are of self-worth.
25. The experiences are initial.

26. Attitudes form a foundation.
    27. The attitudes are positive.
    28. The foundation is strong.
WHEREAS 29. The foundation is for development.
    30. The development is skills.
31. The opposite holds true.
    32. The opposite is for attitudes.
    33. The attitudes are negative.

Rereading Your Writeouts: Notice that this paragraph begins at a very general level and narrows down to a more specific *thesis statement* (Cluster 26–33).

PARAGRAPH 2

34. No child is born with attitudes.
35. The attitudes are toward reading.

    36. The child interacts with the environment.
        37. The environment is immediate.
        38. The environment is in the home.

39. Attitudes are learned.

36 AS

40. SOMETHING is thus clear.
    41. Parents play a role.
    42. The role is key.
    43. The role is in shaping attitudes.
    44. The attitudes are their children's.

40–41 IT . . . THAT

45. They model behaviors.
    46. The behaviors are particular.
    47. The behaviors are related to reading.
    48. The behaviors are learned.
    49. The learning is by their children.

50. They create an environment.
51. The environment places value on reading.
52. The environment places value on dialogue.
53. The value is either positive or negative.
54. The dialogue is thoughtful.

55. And they make judgments.
56. The judgments are both indirect and direct.
57. The judgments are about reading.
58. The judgments are communicated.
59. The communication is to their children.

60. These three factors will be discussed.
61. The factors are interrelated.
62. The factors pertain to attitude formation.
63. The discussion will be in paragraphs.
64. The paragraphs follow.

Rereading Your Writeouts: Study the *parallelism* (Clusters 45–49, 50–54, 55–59) that helps the paragraph "hang together." Note the announcement of intentions for following paragraphs (Cluster 60–64). This announcement is an interparagraph link.

PARAGRAPH 3

65.   SOMETHING is apparent to any person.
    66.   Children learn by imitation.
    67.   The person is observant.

65   THAT

68.   This process is called "modeling."
69.   The calling is by psychologists.
70.   The psychologists study learning.

71.   Children observe SOMETHING.
    72.   Children practice SOMETHING.
    73.   Their parents do.

73   WHATEVER

74.   They internalize these behaviors.
75.   The behaviors are modeled.
76.   They make them their own.

77.   The same principle holds for behavior.
78.   The principle is learning.
79.   The behavior is reading.

    80.   Children see parents.
        81.   The parents are engaged in reading.
        82.   The engagement is frequent.
        83.   The engagement is enjoyable.
84.   They are likely to have attitudes.
    85.   The attitudes are positive.
    86.   The attitudes are toward print.

80   WHEN   82   LY   83   LY

87.   They are likely to value reading.
    88.   They learn how to read.

87   MOREOVER   88   WHEN

89.   SOMETHING therefore makes sense.
    90.   Parents read for pleasure.

91.   The pleasure is their own.

89–90   IT . . . FOR . . . TO

92.   But SOMETHING is also equally important.
    93.   Parents read aloud.
    94.   The reading is regular.
    95.   The reading is to their children.

92–93   IT . . . THAT   94   LY

96.   Such modeling has benefits.
97.   The modeling is positive.
98.   The benefits are long-lasting.
99.   The benefits are in attitude formation.

Rereading Your Writeouts: Be alert to the transition links: *same* (Cluster 77–79), *moreover* (Cluster 87–88), *therefore* (Cluster 89–91), *but . . . also* (Cluster 92–95).

PARAGRAPH 4

100.   Influences are a second factor.
101.   The influences are environmental.
102.   The factor shapes attitudes.

103.   Parents (/) provide an environment.
    104.   The parents understand SOMETHING.
        105.   Stimulation affects development.
        106.   The development is language.
    107.   The environment is rich.

104   WHO   105   HOW

108.   They take the time.
109.   They talk to their children.
110.   They read to their children.

111.   They indulge their children.
112.   The indulgence is with books.

113. The indulgence is with magazines.

114. They go to libraries.
115. They go on a schedule.
116. The schedule is regular.
117. Their children can pick out books.
118. Their children can hear stories.
119. The stories are dramatic.
120. The stories are read aloud.

121. Other parents (/) do few of these things.
   122. The parents lack understanding.
   123. The parents do not value reading.

122 ING   123 ING

124. They thus provide an environment.
125. The environment is impoverished.
126. They are too busy to get involved.
127. The involvement would be with their children.

128. They rarely read to their children.
129. They rarely have discussions.
130. The discussions would be thought-provoking.
131. The discussions would be meaningful.

132. They indulge their children.
133. The indulgence is with television.
134. The effects are incalculable.
   135. The effects are attitudinal.
   136. The effects are long-term.
   137. The effects are of environment.
   138. The effects are both positive and negative.

Rereading Your Writeouts: Study the use of positive examples contrasting with negative examples. Notice the "hourglass" shape of this paragraph: general-to-specific-to-general.

PARAGRAPH-BUILDING OPTIONS

Write a fifth paragraph for "Shaping Attitudes Toward Reading." The focus of this paragraph links to Cluster 55–59 in Paragraph 2: *And they [parents] make judgments about reading—both indirect and direct—that are communicated to their children.*

You have two basic options for further development of this idea.

1. Make a two-column list of indirect and direct judgments about the value of reading that parents make. For example,

Indirect Judgments	*Direct Judgments*
"I think I'll just relax with a book this afternoon."	"Reading is really important in today's world."

After making this list, create an opening sentence for the paragraph that leads into your examples. For example, your opener might go something like this: *Parental value judgments are the third factor in shaping children's attitudes toward reading. Judgments are of two kinds—indirect and direct.*

2. Make a two-column list of positive and negative judgments about reading that parents make.

Positive	*Negative*
"You need reading to survive these days."	"Reading? Who needs it? I'd rather watch TV."

After creating this list, make a topic sentence to introduce the examples and provide transition from Paragraphs 3 and 4. You might begin something like this: *Having discussed the importance of parental modeling and the home environment, we now turn to the factor of value judgments—both positive and negative.*

THE KLUTZ

What happens when male meets female? Paragraph 1 sets the scene and describes action from a young man's point of view. Paragraph 2 flashes back to the past. Paragraph 3 presents the young man's reflections. Paragraph 4 returns to the action of the story. Your writing can either be linked between existing paragraphs or take up where the story leaves off. (See *Paragraph-Building Options*.)

PARAGRAPH 1

1. The waitress brought his coffee.
2. The waitress was young.
3. The waitress was slim-hipped.
4. The coffee was in a mug.
5. The mug was tall.
6. The mug was made of milk-glass.

7. He nodded his thanks.
8. His thanks were silent.
9. His senses were alert.
10. His breathing was shallow.

11. She checked her hair.
12. The check was in the mirror.
13. The mirror was sun-reflecting.
14. The mirror was behind the counter.
15. The counter was well-worn.
16. She moved past the display.
17. The display was refrigerated.
18. The display was pastries.
19. The display was cubed gelatin.

20. He watched her.
21. The watching was absent-minded.
22. He was barely aware of SOMETHING.
23. One hand reached for the sugar dispenser.
24. The other reached for a spoon.

20 AS   21 LY   23 ING

25. She paused near the window.
26. The window was sun-streaked.
27. She then glanced back at him.

28. The glance was with a smile.
29. The smile was shy.

30. Her hair was ablaze with sunlight.
31. Her hair was long.
32. Her hair was reddish-blonde.
33. She hesitated in the doorway.
34. The doorway was to the kitchen.

    35.   Something happened about then.
36. He noticed SOMETHING.
    37.   Sugar was flowing in a stream.
    38.   The stream was white.
        39.   The stream was over the edge of his cup.
        40.   It made a mound.
        41.   The mound was small.
        42.   The mound was on the countertop.

37 THAT   40 ING

    43.   He looked up.
44. She was gone.

43 WHEN

45. He swept the sugar.
46. The sweeping was to one side.
47. He felt irritated.
48. The irritation was with himself.
49. He felt foolish.

Rereading Your Writeouts: Pay attention to the mixing of action sentences and descriptive ones. Trace how the pronouns *he/his* and *she/her* link sentences.

PARAGRAPH 2

    50.   He could remember.
51. It had been this way.
    52.   The way was with women.

50 EVER SINCE

53. His attempts had left a trail.
    54.   The attempts were at adventuring.
        55.   The adventuring was amorous.
56. The trail was of opportunities.
    57.   The opportunities were muffed.
58. The trail was of silences.
    59.   The silences were embarassed.
60. The trail was of apologies.
    61.   The apologies were awkward.

62. Something could be spilled.
    63.   Something could be broken.
    64.   Something could be mislaid.
    65.   Something could be dirtied.
66. He had found a way.

62 IF

  ┌─67.   One victim had nicknamed him "The Klutz."
AND   68.   The victim was from his neighborhood.
  └─69.   The label had stuck.
    70.   It followed him everywhere.

71. His notoriety had even been documented.
72. The documentation was in his yearbook.
73. The yearbook was from high school.
74. SOMETHING was consolation.
    75.   His worst experiences (/) had remained unknown.
    76.   The consolation was small.
    77.   The experiences were a series of disasters.

78.   The disasters were extraordinary.

74–75   IT . . . THAT

Rereading Your Writeouts: Notice the use of the word *had* in this paragraph. It switches the reader's attention to the "background" of the young man's problem.

PARAGRAPH 3

79.   He now sipped his coffee.
    80.   The coffee was sweet.
    81.   The coffee was black.
82.   He couldn't help but wonder SOMETHING.
    ┌─ 83.   His encounters were so bizarre.
AND   84.   The encounters were with females.
    └─ 85.   He would outgrow this problem.
    86.   The outgrowing would be someday.
    87.   The problem was troublesome.

79   AS   83   WHY   85   WHETHER

88.   His hopes were sinking.
89.   The hopes were for a change.
90.   The change would be in his luck.
91.   The sinking was steady.

┌─92.   SOMETHING made him unhappy to think.
    93.   He might end up unloved.
BUT   94.   He might end up alone.
└─95.   He had to admit SOMETHING.
    96.   The prospects seemed especially bleak.
    97.   The prospects were at present.
    98.   The prospects were for companionship.

92   IT . . . THAT   96   THAT

99.   The refrigerator mirrored his squint.

100.   The refrigerator was stainless steel.
101.   His squint was of pain.

102.   He realized SOMETHING.
    103.   His own anxiety was the problem.
    104.   It increased his tension.
        105.   It made him more prone to clumsiness.
        106.   The clumsiness was spectacular.

103   THAT   104   BECAUSE

107.   He still had not found a way.
    108.   The way would defuse his self-consciousness.
    109.   The self-consciousness was extreme.

107   HOWEVER   108   TO

110.   He told himself SOMETHING.
    111.   Thinking would only make matters worse.
    112.   The thinking was about the problem.

111   THAT

Rereading Your Writeouts: Notice that the word *now* (Cluster 79–87) links Paragraphs 2 and 3. Study the *however* link of Cluster 107–109; how else could this link be expressed?

PARAGRAPH 4

113.   The waitress approached.
114.   The coffeepot was in hand.

┌─115.   He hesitated.
BUT 116.   She asked about a refill.
└─117.   He then reminded himself of SOMETHING.
    118.   He had nothing to lose.

116   AS   118   THAT

119.   He watched her.
120.   His attention was captured.

121.   Her eyes were brown.
    122.   Her eyes were almond-shaped.
        123.   <u>Her features were finely</u> chiseled.
            124.   The features were facial.

125.   A blush tinged her cheeks.
126.   The blush was faint.
127.   She poured the coffee.
128.   The pouring was careful.
129.   She glanced up at him.
130.   The glance was quick.

131.   A moment's distraction made a puddle.
132.   The distraction was flirtatious.
133.   The puddle was brown.
134.   The puddle was around his cup.

┌─135.   She apologized.
AND   136.   The apology was for "being a klutz."
└─137.   He laughed
    138.   He felt so good.

138   BECAUSE

    139.   <u>He helped her mop up.</u>
    140.   The mopping up was with napkins.
    141.   The napkins were paper.
142.   He realized SOMETHING.
    143.   He had found someone.
    144.   Someone really deserved him.

139   ING   143   THAT   144   WHO

Rereading Your Writeouts: Trace the inter-sentence links created by masculine and feminine pronouns.

PARAGRAPH-BUILDING OPTIONS

1. *Paragraph 2½:* Create a new paragraph to fit between Paragraph 2 and Paragraph 3. Note that the last sentence of Paragraph 2 reads this way: *It was small consolation that his worst experiences—a series of extraordinary disasters—had remained unknown.* The new paragraph can follow logically from this sentence by describing one such remembered incident in *detail.* A possibility for an opening might be this: *He still remembered the embarrassment of one painful incident.*

2. *Paragraph 5:* Take the narrative beyond its present conclusion. One possibility is to invent some dialogue between the young man and the waitress:

> *"I'm glad somebody else makes mistakes besides me," he said.*
> *She smiled at him. "You're looking at the clumsiest waitress in the world."*

Another possibility is to make a future projection from the man's point of view. You might begin the paragraph this way: *After she had returned to the kitchen, he found himself imagining a future with her.*

THREE TEACHER TYPES

This five-paragraph essay categorizes teachers on the basis of their "styles of working." Paragraph 1 introduces the idea of a three-part classification system. Paragraphs 2, 3, and 4 describe behaviors and attitudes of the three teacher types; each successive paragraph

stresses the differences between its category and the one(s) preceding. Paragraph 5 summarizes the information of Paragraphs 2 through 4, then makes some general observations about teaching styles and classroom effectiveness. (See *Paragraph-Building Options.*)

PARAGRAPH 1

1. Everyone (/) knows SOMETHING.
    2. Everyone has been to school.
    3. Teachers come in a variety.
        4. The variety is bewildering.
        5. The variety is of shapes and sizes.

2 WHO   3 THAT

6. Their competence varies.
7. The competence is professional.
8. The variance is great.

9. Yet there are also similarities.
    10. This is despite differences.
        11. The differences are vast.
        12. The differences are in personality.
        13. The differences are in motivation.
        14. The differences are in style.
            15. The style is teaching.
        16. The differences are in background.
            17. The background is academic.
        18. The differences are in training.

    19. One takes a view.
        20. The view is broad.
        21. The view is of teachers.
        22. The view is of teaching.

23. These similarities seem to form a system.
    24. The system is for classification.
        25. The system has three parts.

19 IF   25 THAT

26. There are three categories.
    27. Most teachers can be classified.
    28. Classification is on the basis of style.
    29. The style is teaching.
        30. This is according to a philosopher.
        31. The philosopher is educational.
        32. The philosopher is Harry Broudy.

26 IN OTHER WORDS   27 INTO WHICH

33. The three types can be labeled.
34. One label is "didactic."
35. One label is "heuristic."
36. One label is "philetic."

Rereading Your Writeouts: Notice the classic "funnel" shape of this introductory paragraph: a movement from general to specific.

PARAGRAPH 2

37. "Didactic" teachers present information.
38. The presentation is straightforward.

39. These people are well-organized.
40. These people are knowledgeable.
41. This is in most cases.

42. Their love often makes them scholars.
43. The love is deep.
44. The love is for their subject.
45. The scholars are probing.

46. They see communication as a process.
47. The communication is about subject matter.
48. The process is one-way.
49. The process is from themselves.
50. The process is to their students.

┌─51. Their method is telling.
│   52. The method is of teaching.
AND
│   53. The method is principal.
└─54. They expect SOMETHING.
     55. Students will listen.
     56. Students will learn.
          57. The learning is through a process.
          58. The process is absorption.

54 THAT

     59. They view their role.
          60. The role is teaching.
61. The task is to transmit information.

59 AS

62. Questions are used to check understanding.
63. The understanding is of students.

┌── 64. They are excited about their subject.
│   65. Their excitement is intellectual.
AND
└── 66. They are involved in its presentation.
          67. Their involvement is emotional.
68. They can be effective.
     69. Their effectiveness is tremendous.

64 WHEN   66 (WHEN)

70. They can also be bores.
     71. The bores are tremendous.
          72. The excitement is missing.

73. The involvement is missing.

70 ON THE OTHER HAND   72 WHEN

Rereading Your Writeouts: Study the words and phrases (*these people, their love, they, them,* etc.) that connect all sentences to Clusters 37–38. These are "glue" for the paragraph.

PARAGRAPH 3

74. "Heuristic" teachers are not dispensers.
75. The dispensers are of information.

76. They regard teaching in a light.
77. The light is somewhat different.
78. They define roles.
     79. The roles are different.
     80. The roles are for themselves.
     81. The roles are for their students.

78 CONSEQUENTLY

     82. They see themselves as facilitators.
          83. They facilitate learning.
84. Their role is to stimulate.
     85. Their role is to guide.
     86. Their role is to challenge.
     87. Their role is to cajole.

82 BECAUSE

88. SOMETHING is thus not too surprising.
     89. They try to create an environment.
          90. The environment is for learning.
          91. The environment is stimulating.

92. The environment will invite involvement.
    93. The involvement is from students.

88–89 IT . . . THAT

94. Their expectation is SOMETHING.
    95. Students will think.
    96. Students will become question askers.
        97. The question askers will be relentless.

95 THAT

98. Question asking is their method.
99. The question asking is provocative.
100. The method is instructional.

101. Their belief is SOMETHING.
    ┌─102. Learning should be a process.
    │   103. The process is active.
AND   104. The process is discovery.
    └─105. Learning should not be absorption.
          106. The absorption is passive.

102 THAT   105 THAT

107. Heuristic teachers are successful.
    108. The success is in setting up the environment.
109. Their classrooms become places.
    110. The places are exciting.
    111. Learning stems from motivation.
        112. The motivation is internal.
        113. The motivation is not from threats.
            114. The threats are external.

107 WHEN   111 WHERE

115. The questions are not real.
116. The teacher is not skillful.
117. The heuristic classroom can be a disaster.
118. The disaster is educational.

115 BUT WHEN

Rereading Your Writeouts: Trace the words and phrases (*these people, they, their expectations,* etc.) that connect all sentences to Cluster 74–75. How many can you find?

PARAGRAPH 4

119. "Philetic" teachers work in a way.
120. The way is different.

    121. Philetic teachers are unlike didactic teachers.
    122. Philetic teachers are unlike heuristic teachers.
    ┌─123. Philetic teachers are not lecturers.
    │ 124. Lecturers present information.
AND   125. The information is new.
    └─126. They are not question askers.
          127. Question askers create conditions.
              128. The conditions are for learning.
              129. The conditions are optimum.
              130. The learning is self-motivated.

124 WHO   127 WHO

    ┌─131. They are not scholars.
NEITHER   132. The scholars are penetrating.
NOR   133. The scholars are inquisitive.
    └─134. They are not engineers.
          135. The engineers are skilled.
          136. The engineers are of the environment.

137.   The environment is the class-room.

138.   Philetic teachers succeed.
    139.   Their students love them.

139   BECAUSE

┌─140.   Their personality is compelling.
AND   141.   Their personality is magnetic.
└─142.   Students learn.
    143.   They want to win attention.
    144.   The attention is philetic teach-ers'.

143   BECAUSE

145.   Their effect (/) is to enhance self-concept.
    146.   The effect is sometimes pro-found.
    147.   The effect is sometimes long-lasting.
    148.   Their effect is to promote devel-opment.
        149.   The development is per-sonal.

150.   Their charisma holds the atten-tion.
    151.   The charisma is personal.
    152.   The attention is of stu-dents.
        153.   The students are en-amored.
154.   Philetic teachers can be effective.
    155.   They touch emotions.

150   WHEN   155   BECAUSE

156.   Love fails.
157.   The philetic classroom can be a place.
    158.   The place is dismal.
    159.   The place is unhappy.

157   BUT WHEN

Rereading Your Writeouts: Study the words and phrases (*they, their personality, their effect*) that connect all sentences to Cluster 119–120. Why are such links important for the paragraph?

PARAGRAPH 5

160.   Observation suggests SOMETHING.
    161.   There are three types.
        162.   The types are distinct.
        163.   The types are teachers.

160   IN SUMMARY   161   THAT

┌─164.   Didactic teachers dispense information.
│   165.   The information is *about* a sub-ject.
├─166.   Heuristic teachers motivate inquiry.
AND   167.   The inquiry is *into* a subject.
└─168.   Philetic teachers enhance self-develop-ment.
    169.   The development is *through* a subject.

170.   Experience indicates SOMETHING.
    171.   None of these types has a method.
        172.   The method is foolproof.
        173.   The method is for teach-ing.
        174.   The method will guaran-tee learning.

171   THAT

175.   None of these teachers reaches all stu-dents.
    176.   The students also come in types.
        177.   The types are various.

175   MOREOVER   176   WHO

178.   Teachers can be effective.
179.   Teachers can be ineffective.
180.   This is for reasons.
181.   The reasons are many.

182. The interaction is complex.
183. The interaction is unpredictable.
184. The interaction is human.

Rereading Your Writeouts: Notice the classic "inverted funnel" shape of this concluding paragraph: a movement from specific to general.

PARAGRAPH-BUILDING OPTIONS

1. *Paragraphs 2½, 3½, 4½:* Develop three paragraphs to follow Paragraphs 2, 3, and 4, respectively. Each should elaborate a specific example of a "teacher type." Pick someone from your own schooling and explain how his/her classroom attitudes and behaviors are representative of a particular category. Link your illustrative paragraph to the preceding one with a "transition" opener: *Ms. Jones, for example, is a classic case of a didactic teaching style.*

2. *Paragraph 6:* Explore the idea that most teachers *combine* traits of the three types. Make an in-depth discussion of this assertion in terms of at least one teacher you have known. Link this paragraph to Paragraph 5, perhaps with an opener like this: *Fortunately most real teachers are mixtures of the three categories.*

3. Invent a classification system for *students,* not teachers. Develop an essay that parallels the structure of "Three Teacher Types":

    Introductory paragraph
    One paragraph for each category
    Summary paragraph

    Use key sentences from the teacher essay as skill-building models for your essay on students; make sure that your paragraphs link together.

READING TO REMEMBER

The following seven paragraphs deal with a five-step process for successful study. Paragraph 1 says that simple reading strategies make a difference in retention. Paragraph 2 explains *skimming,* a technique that "organizes the reading task." Paragraph 3 talks about *question asking* to create a readiness for learning. Paragraph 4 explains *focused reading.* Paragraph 5 zeroes in on the crucial *recitation* step of the study process. Paragraph 6 makes two points about *review.* And Paragraph 7 provides the essay's conclusion—a *summary* of the five interlocking strategies. (See *Paragraph-Building Options.*)

PARAGRAPH 1

1. Many students face a problem.
2. The problem is common.
3. The problem is perplexing.
4. The problem is remembering.
5. The remembering is what they read.
6. This problem is certainly not new.
7. It is not confined to "poor" readers.

8. It affects everyone.
9. The effect is to some degree.

10. Researchers worked in the 1950s.

11.   Researchers found SOMETHING.
    12.   The problem existed even among Harvard students.
        13.   The students were freshmen.
        14.   The students represented an "educational elite."

10   ING   **11   FOR EXAMPLE**
12   THAT   **14   WHO**

    15.   These students were intelligent.
        16.   These students were well-motivated.
        17.   These students came from fine schools.
18.   They still had trouble.
    19.   The trouble was with study habits.
    20.   The trouble was with retention.

15   ALTHOUGH

21.   They were like students of today.
    22.   They could benefit from strategies.
        23.   The strategies are simple.
        24.   The strategies are for reading.

22   IN THAT

Rereading Your Writeouts: Notice the comparison of today's students with those in the past. Although not stated directly, the main idea of the essay is that *"all students can benefit from simple study techniques."*

PARAGRAPH 2

25.   One technique (/) is to skim material.
26.   The technique is essential to success.
27.   The success is in studying.

28.   A skim should always precede reading.
29.   The skim is quick.

30. The reading is careful.
31. The reading is deliberate.

32. Skimming is like an aerial view.
33. The view is of terrain to be covered.
34. Skimming establishes the "big picture."
35. It focuses on headings.
36. It focuses on key ideas.
37. It focuses on the chapter summary.

38. A good skim (/) creates a "map."
39. The skim may take only five minutes.
40. The map is mental.
41. The map is for the reader.

38 WHICH

42. This "map" organizes the task.
43. The task is reading.
44. Study is not wandering.
45. Study is not aimless.

44 SO THAT

46. Psychologists know SOMETHING.
47. Organized material is easier to learn.
48. It is easier to retain.

47 THAT   48 (THAT)

49. SOMETHING stands to reason.
50. Skimming is a technique.
51. The technique is vital.
52. The technique is for study.

49–50 IT . . . THAT + THEREFORE

Rereading Your Writeouts: Notice how the metaphors of "aerial view" and "mental map" help explain the concept of skimming.

PARAGRAPH 3

53. The second strategy is to ask questions.
54. The questions are before reading.
55. The reading is careful.
56. Study becomes purposeful.

56 SO THAT

57. Questions establish a reason.
58. The reason is for reading.
59. They make the reader active.
60. The activity is mental.

59 BY + ING   60 LY

61. They are the energy.
62. The energy is for "enlightenment."
63. The "enlightenment" is cognitive.

64. Study experts say SOMETHING.
65. Questions should be written down.
66. Reading purposes are clear.

65 THAT   66 SO THAT

67. One hint is to flip headings.
68. The headings are for chapters.
69. The headings are for topics.
70. The flip is into questions.

71. Another hint is to role-play the author.
72. The hint is to role-play one's teacher.
73. The hint is to create a question list.

74. Such "gimmicks" help.
75. They create a readiness.
76. The readiness is for learning.

75 TO

77. The point to remember is SOMETHING.

78. Reading grows out of questioning.
   79. The reading is active.

AND
   80. The reading is thoughtful.
81. Such reading is essential for retention.
   82. The retention is meaningful.

78 THAT   81 THAT

Rereading Your Writeouts: Notice the "funnel" shape that moves from *general* statements to *specific* hints on questioning.

PARAGRAPH 4

83. Reading is the third step.
84. The reading is focused.

85. This involves a search.
86. The search is aggressive.
87. The search is for answers.
88. The answers are to questions.
89. The questions are self-created.

90. But focus is not easy to achieve.
91. The focus is in reading.
92. It requires practice.
93. It requires self-discipline.

94. Some students improve concentration.
95. The concentration comes with exercises.
96. The exercises are in meditation.
97. The exercises are before study.

98. Some develop rituals.
99. The rituals are elaborate.
100. The rituals are for reading.
101. The rituals involve specific locations.
102. The rituals involve particular times.

103. Some set goals.
104. The goals are achievable.
105. The goals are for study.
106. They reward themselves.
107. They take study breaks.

108. Some enhance concentration.
109. They jot down notes.
110. They jot down summaries.
111. They translate reading.
112. The translation is into diagrams.

113. All recognize SOMETHING.
   114. Focus stems from habits.
      115. The focus is mental.
      116. The habits are behavioral.

114 THAT

Rereading Your Writeouts: Examine the parallel structure in this paragraph—the repetition of the pronouns *some* and *all.* These link sentences together.

PARAGRAPH 5

117. The fourth technique involves activities.
   118. The activities are recitation.
      119. The activities are various.
      120. The activities have a purpose.
         121. The purpose is single.
            122. The purpose is to promote thinking.
            123. The thinking is active.
            124. The thinking is about what has been read.

120 ALL OF WHICH

125. Recitation pertains to questions.
126. The questions were raised.
127. The questions were in Step 2.
128. Recitation pertains to key ideas.
129. The ideas were not anticipated by the questions.

130. A person can recite to himself.
131. A person can recite to a friend.
132. The friend is studying the same material.

133. SOMETHING makes little difference.
  134. The material is recited.

133–134 IT . . . HOW

135. The recitation can be thought out.
136. The recitation can be said orally.
137. The recitation can be written.

138. What matters is SOMETHING.
  139. The material is processed.
    140. The processing is active.

139 THAT   140 LY

  141. Ideas are understood.
142. They are likely to be remembered.

141 WHEN

  143. Recitation is a key.
    144. The key is to understanding.
145. Recitation is also a key to retention.
  146. The retention is long-term.

43 SINCE

Rereading Your Writeouts: Be alert to the interparagraph link between Step 4 (recitation) and Step 2 (question asking). Notice the restatement of the main idea in the last two clusters.

PARAGRAPH 6

147. Review is a strategy.
148. The strategy is fifth.
149. The strategy is final.
150. The strategy is in the process.
151. The process is study.

152. Two points are worth remembering.
153. The points concern review.

154. The first is SOMETHING.
  155. Review should follow every period.
    156. The period is study.

155 THAT

157. This review should be a skim.
158. The skim should be quick.
159. The skim should be like Step 1.
160. Step 1 is in the study process.

161. Its purpose is to highlight ideas.
  162. The ideas are significant.
  163. The material is remembered.

163 SO THAT

164. The second point is SOMETHING.
  165. Spaced review is much preferred.
    166. The preference is over "one-shot" review.
      167. The "one-shot" review is intense.

165 THAT

168. Psychologists know SOMETHING.
  169. The psychologists study learning.
  170. The psychologists study forgetting.
  171. "Cramming" is a method.
  172. The method is ineffective.

169 WHO   171 THAT

173. They recommend spaced review.

174. They know SOMETHING.
    175. It works.

174 BECAUSE   175 THAT

176. Repetition is a factor.
    177. The factor is central.
    178. The factor is in learning.
179. SOMETHING seems reasonable to assert.
    180. Skimming and spaced review are processes.
    181. The processes are necessary.

176 BECAUSE   179–180 IT . . . THAT

Rereading Your Writeouts: Watch for the opening "announcement" of two subpoints, with the use of transition words *first* and *second* in follow-up sentences.

PARAGRAPH 7

182. Study is a process.
183. The study is successful.
184. The process involves five steps.
185. The steps are interlocking.

186. The process begins with preview.
187. The preview is rapid.
188. The preview establishes topics.
189. The preview establishes organization.
190. The process moves to questions.
191. Questions create a purpose.
192. The purpose is for reading.

193. Then comes Step 3.
194. Step 3 is reading.
195. The reading is focused.

196. Recitation follows reading.
197. The recitation is thoughtful.
198. Recitation leads to Step 5.
199. Step 5 is an immediate review.
200. This review is later reinforced.
201. The reinforcement is other reviews.

202. SOMETHING is thus clear.
    203. Successful study is not mysterious.

202–203 IT . . . THAT

204. It results from a process.
205. The process is step-by-step.
206. The process is logical.

207. Efficiency comes from habits.
208. The efficiency is in study.
209. The efficiency is real.
210. The habits are self-taught.

Rereading Your Writeouts: Notice that the summary intertwines the five steps and that it becomes more general in its final statements.

PARAGRAPH-BUILDING OPTIONS

1. *Paragraph 8:* According to the last cluster (207–210) of Paragraph 7, *real efficiency in study comes from self-taught habits.* This should be the focus of Paragraph 8 (and, if necessary, subsequent paragraphs). Explain a common-sense *process* for developing new habits. Present the "steps" for habit formation just as Paragraphs 1 through 7 presented the "steps" for successful study.

2. Using "Reading to Remember" as a model, create a short essay that explains the "stages" or "steps" of a process you know very well. This can be a simple, everyday process such as balancing a checkbook or preparing a stew; or you can focus on a more abstract process such as writing an essay or solving a personal problem. Whatever you choose as your topic, make sure that you treat each step in a separate paragraph. And remember: *Your essay will need both an introduction and a conclusion.*

ANSWER KEY

Note: Since there are multiple right answers to "open" combining problems, each of the following answers represents only one possibility. "Signaled" exercises have a pre-determined right answer.

PRE-TEST

1. The photographer who took the picture shuddered.   2. The students' club is called "The Bored of Education."   3. The hard-working baker, kneading dough, wanted to avoid bankruptcy.   4. Because he spent his nights at a round table, the writer called himself "King Author."   5. After four arduous years of college training, the farmer was out standing in her field.   6. The Corporal sometimes administered corporal punishment to the Private publically, sometimes privately. 7. Low-slung and fishtailing, the car roared out of the parking lot, leaving a black autograph.   8. The hermit, who lived for seven years in an abandoned outhouse, established a legal claim by "Squatter's Rights."   9. Swearing to tell the whole tooth and nothing but the tooth, the nicely-dressed dentist testified in a malpractice suit.   10. The daughter of the doddering rancher spied a bull-shooting rustler hiding in the rustling bullrushes, listening to bluegrass as he smoked.

Ex. 1.1.   1-B, 2-A, 3-A, 4-A, 5-B, 6-A, 7-B, 8-A, 9 (both okay), 10 (both poor).
Ex. 1.2.   1. With this approach, there's a transfer of power from speech to writing, which increases the options of style.   2. This approach, which transfers power from speech to writing, increases style options.

Ex. 2.1.   1-A, 2-A, 3-B, 4-A, 5 (both okay), 6-B, 7-B, 8-A, 9-A, 10-A.
Ex. 2.2.   1-B. Her brother, who was tall, smiled with energy that was vibrant. 2-B. Impatiently and briskly, he rubbed his chin, which was covered with tough and unshaved stubble.   3-A. All the husky, uniformed athletes stood with restlessness; the band played the national anthem.

Ex. 3.2.   1. My writing style, like a fingerprint, is unique and personal.   2. It may be bare or modified, direct or indirect, active or passive.   3. But, unlike a

fingerprint, my writing style can be consciously altered.   4. I may decide to stress sentence openers or I may experiment with transformations that interrupt—temporarily—the flow of expression.   5. Because choices determine emphasis in sentences, they force me to think about my writing habits, which are mostly unconscious.   6. This increasing awareness may not alter my experience or training, but it should help me to make more informed decisions about style.

Ex. 3.4.   1. Error will slip through a crack, while truth will stick in a doorway. 2. Instruction ends in the classroom, but education ends only with life.   3. Being a woman is a terribly difficult task, since it consists principally in dealing with men.   4. Regret is an appalling waste of energy; you can't build on it; it's only good for wallowing in.   5. Science without religion is lame; religion without science is blind.   6. A hearty laugh gives one a dry cleaning, while a good cry is a wet wash.   7. When we read, we fancy we could be martyrs; when we come to act, we cannot bear a provoking word.   8. Fast tempos invariably raise your pulse, respiration, and blood pressure; slow music lowers them.   9. We are all sculptors and painters, and our material is our own flesh and blood and bone. 10. The splendid discontent of God with chaos made the world; and from the discontent of man the world's best progress springs.

UNIT FOUR (exercises within unit)

1. I go to work on simple, indented exercises.   2. If a kernel appears before a base sentence, the writeout has an up-front modifier.   3. If a kernel is interrupted by a slash, an internal modifier—sometimes set off by punctuation—interrupts the resulting writeout.   4. I have already learned these two patterns—one introductory, the other interrupting.

5. I study the first practice exercise for the umbrella signal, whispering the words to myself.   6. Feeling confident about my skills, I then go on to the next exercise, a slightly more difficult problem.   7. These three exercises, all using umbrella signals for embedding transformations, have not been much trouble.

Introductory pattern.   Everyone seems to understand conjunctive adverbs used as a margin signal; therefore, in this example we'll review punctuation patterns. *Embedded pattern.*   Everyone seems to understand conjunctive adverbs used as a margin signal; in this example, therefore, we'll review punctuation patterns.

8. New exercises confront me and demand my intellectual attention.   9. Staring at kernels and studying signals, I can hear writeouts taking shape.   10. I sometimes try to hold these sentences in my mind, but they quickly fade from consciousness like whispers in the night.   11. This "fading" not only occurs in combining exercises but also happens in note-taking situations.   12. Spoken language is elusive; consequently, I need to capture it quickly through careful transcription.

Ex. 4.1.   A. A large hole makes for a small doughnut.   B. The muscular people on the beach are lifting fake weights.   C. After throwing fifteen perfect interceptions in a row, our quarterback was named their Most Valuable Player.   D.

Our neighbors, a friendly couple whose house is all glass, should probably pull their shades. E. I like all types—fat ones, foxy ones, sleek ones, sexy ones. F. If you drink fresh goat's milk and eat raw onions, you might possibly live longer. G. The soldiers, bathing in a small pond that supplied their drinking water, seemed less than intelligent. H. After she had purchased fermenting oranges at a fruit auction, she decided to make wine. I. He wants to marry a person who fixes greasy motorcycles and wears chains around her neck. J. Although the restaurant had a world-famous reputation, our dinner party—a raucous class reunion—could not order pizza.

Ex. 4.2. A. The discontented cow sat on the belligerent mouse. B. Wearing the wrong hubcap can be an outrageous embarrassment. C. The subway is a swell place for a picnic at 5:00 p.m. D. Under the typewriter we found a flattened, decayed waffle. E. Your hand-rolled cigarette has an odd, sweet smell. F. Let's use her new toothbrush for scrubbing tarnished bike spokes. G. At lunch I saw him dive end over end into the wine vat. H. After class, wild nonsense makes complete sense to you and me. I. There are unique features to this business suit made of form-fitting plastic. J. To amuse her giggling friends, she sometimes flirts with her barrel-shaped shop teacher.

Ex. 4.3. A. Tony's jelly-filled tacos were awful, yet his burritos were even worse. B. You shouldn't bait your fishing hook or you may have to clean fish. C. Most teachers frown upon blackmail and extortion threats. D. One may dream about a cure for hiccups; finding it, however, is something else. E. We enjoyed backpacking in Central Park, but we didn't have a mugging permit. F. After the game they demanded chili-flavored ice cream, whereas I wanted dill pickles. G. Either Tonya should take a hot, soapy bath or she should sleep outside tonight. H. Not only did the rock group play a "heavy" number for enthusiastic senior citizens, but it also bought them cocoa. I. Grab your partner, boogie over to the Union Hall, and stomp some hand-picked grapes. J. Turning with a coy smile, she lowered her dark, thick lashes; then she told him to get lost.

Ex. 4.4. 1. Fried rice seasoned with spice is rather nice, yet I still prefer spuds with a glass of cold suds. 2. Kent's last fast—a campout in a cramped, damp tent—occurred at Lent. 3. In spite of a riot, the class was quite quiet; then people embraced, making weird words in waste space. 4. Spitting and hitting, fighting and biting, some critters turn babysitters into quitters.

UNIT FIVE (exercises within unit)

Transition Footnote Signal. (Your name) has studied the preceding examples. Not surprisingly, he/she is therefore able to use transitions in his/her writeouts. In addition, he/she has paid close attention to punctuation. Consequently, these practice writeouts are correctly punctuated.

Subordination Footnote Signal. Before me are exercises that have footnote signals. Although I am weary and do my best to ignore them, I find myself scanning the kernels. My brain, which cannot leave sentences that are uncombined alone,

clicks into action. Before I know what has happened, I have combined four write-outs that demonstrate my skills.

Footnote Signal and SOMETHING. I tell myself that I can resist temptation and ignore these exercises. But the fact that I keep doing them suggests otherwise. I sometimes wonder if I may have acquired a strange addiction to combining. Why I want to work with them, even though I don't have to, is a puzzle.

Split Footnote Signal. It seems obvious that I can kick my combining habit if I really want to. But it is not clear why I should give up a process that I find so enjoyable. Moreover, for an addict to quit "cold turkey" is sometimes traumatizing. Since it is undeniable that there are worse things to be addicted to, perhaps I should be thankful for my addiction.

Word Form Footnote Signal. After transcribing sentences tentatively, I sometimes pause. I can picture the book's author, reading silently over my shoulder. Of course, writeouts belonging to (your name) are always flawlessly perfect!

Ex. 5.1. A. In other words, they might be compared to signposts that guide the reader's attention. B. Some signposts are of course more visible and explicit than others. C. For example, the word *however* is a quite obvious transition that points to contrast. D. On the other hand, the phrase *of course* is a more subtle transition that points to added emphasis. E. Second, transitions serve to advance writing from point to point toward a conclusion. F. To put it another way, they show the physical, cumulative building of ideas. G. Thus, words like *indeed* and *in fact* signal insistence. H. Similarly, words that include *in addition* and *furthermore* signal amplification. I. In conclusion, transitions are very important in writing because they mark turns in logic and show the building of ideas. J. Not surprisingly, skilled writers therefore pay close attention to transitions.

Ex. 5.2. A. Bless the people who have a grasp on reality. B. You will hear a gasp as the floor drops away. C. When the windows are open, they are not closed. D. The college was led by men who wore ties and T-shirts. E. Because we are hurried, we'll use the mistakes that were incorrectly published. F. The sadness occurs whenever we leave the natives who worship us. G. Although avocado is delicious, I would not like it in my beard, which is always well groomed. H. Our boss, a complete perfectionist, demands loyalty, even though she is not loyal to us. I. When Winston hears the news, he turns it off because it makes him informed, which makes him uneasy. J. Journalists who interviewed the football team that had not showered wrote pungent articles.

Ex. 5.3. A. I told him that he shouldn't chase dogs with my truck. B. What Wanda had in mind soon became clear to Reggie. C. The fact that it is fun to mutilate a board is no justification for your behavior. D. She complained that watermelons made her lunch lumpy and smashed her sandwiches. E. He announced that he had swallowed a tooth, which turned out to be the truth. F. Just because she has breath that curls your mustache doesn't mean you can ignore her. G. Since it is a nice evening, I don't see why you should go skinny-dipping

alone.   H. Laboratory tests show that women will not buy Pungent Cologne even though they are moved by its fragrance.   I. Because we heard that flying saucers had landed, we sent for the Welcome Wagon, which is sponsored by the Chamber of Commerce.   J. Although Mildred wanted to marry Horace, his mother (who loved her son dearly) said that she would have to tuck him in at night.

Ex. 5.4.   A. Nurse Kathy thought it strange that her date howled at her window. B. For Throckmorton to make a fool of himself seemed inevitable.   C. It seems reasonable for you to volunteer to wash your teacher's car.   D. It was unclear what the fraternity had cooking.   E. It doesn't matter how often you boycott the school's cafeteria.   F. It comes as no surprise that scientists are investigating how kissing spreads germs.   G. It might be predicted that marriages which are born of necessity will continue to occur.   H. It is difficult to understand why today's fashions call for argyle socks that extend over the knee.   I. It would seem slightly presumptuous for Howard, who is not yet engaged, to invite wedding guests.   J. It was uncertain whether the weather, which we watched wistfully, would worsen.

Ex. 5.5.   A. By belatedly declaring itself incompetent, the Council restored public confidence.   B. Not wanting to face the dishes that were piled high in the sink, Richard stopped going back to his apartment.   C. It is still difficult to understand why Hubert's gelatin was eaten so insensitively.   D. The defense rested its case, insisting that the defendant had an honest face.   E. Attempting the impossible, she balanced precariously on the high wire, her weight supported by one toe.   F. The fact that Snodgrass was continually absent helps to explain why he was fired.   G. Instead of groveling at our feet, trying to flatter us, you should consider selective bribery.   H. Assuming that these figures are correct, our company is now broke, relieving us of worry.   I. Although it was clear that Manuel's attempt to train alligators was doomed, his friends—not wanting him to quit—cheered him on.   J. After arguing vociferously for hours, the committee finally reversed itself, deciding to give itself an enormous raise.

UNIT SIX (exercises within unit)

Grayson stood astride his motorcycle, revving the engine. The sound, a harsh, spiraling bark, filled his ears. Tense but sure of himself, he eyed the steep hill. His stomach was clenched, his heart pounding.

Bridget stood near Grayson, shouting "Go for it!" Her outfit, a checkered jumpsuit tucked into Gucci boots, caught his attention. Now aware of her presence, Grayson was unable to concentrate on the hill. His mind went blank, his senses numb. Waving to her, he unthinkingly released the motorcycle's clutch—a disastrous mistake.

Ex. 6.1.   Rick sat alone at his training table, deeply depressed about his grades. Confused by hard assignments and by big words, he was having a hard time in school. These worries—aggravated by a losing season, no pro offers, and strained pectoral muscles—were taking their toll. Even his attempts at cheating had failed,

fumbled first in the planning and further bobbled in the coverup. Heavy-hearted and humbled by circumstances, Rick worked at a huge steak, considered the situation, and decided to go look for trouble.

Wendy, late for class, jogged across campus. Breathless and disheveled, she opened the classroom door and slipped inside. So did her dog—mangy, flea-bitten, and hyperactive. Angry with her instructor's directive to put the dog outside the door, Wendy protested loudly in class. She contended that her dog had educational rights—natural and therefore irrevocable.

A sparkplug for the team, Sally sprang to her feet. The pep assembly, mostly enthusiastic boys, went wild. Noise—a wave of shouts and whistles—crashed through the gymnasium, a dome-like structure. Sally called for silence, a moment of quiet. Then the school band struck up the familiar fight song, and she did her award-winning routine, a "rally ballet."

Casey lounged on his unmade bed, his eyes glazed and dilated. One hand was outstretched, the other clenched. Stereo music—its sounds milky, swirling, and distant—burbled in his ears. His mood was relaxed, his thoughts vacant. His mantra echoing in his ears, he rocked slowly back and forth.

Ex. 6.2.   1-A. Sitting in a study hall, Gertrude thumbed slowly through *Brides* magazine.   1-B. Gertrude sat in a study hall, thumbing slowly through *Brides* magazine.   2-A. Eager to get married, she was preoccupied with finding a man. 2-B. Preoccupied with finding a man, she was eager to get married.   3-A. Her fantasies centered on Troy, the campus dreamboat.   3-B. Troy was the campus dreamboat, a center for her fantasies.   4-A. She pictured herself with him, their lives being joined.   4-B. She pictured herself with him, imagining their lives being joined.

Ex. 6.3.   1. Bridget, dressed in frilly, eye-appealing pinafore, strolled with Grayson.   2. The nearly deserted promenade was illuminated by moonlight shining through leafy trees.   3. Casey Spacey, leaning over the balcony above the boardwalk, watched the couple who paused to embrace.   4. Unaware of Casey's presence, they struggled vainly to untangle the braces on their teeth.

UNIT SEVEN (exercises within unit)

A.   2   Toothpick in his mouth,
         2   his eyelids lowered seductively,
     1   He swaggered across the room toward Bridget with a bike chain hanging around his neck.

B.   1   He swaggered across the room toward Bridget—
         2   toothpick in his mouth,
         2   his eyelids lowered seductively,
         2   a bike chain hanging around his neck.

A.   2   Pale,
         2   panicked,
     1   Bridget seemed frozen where she sat and unable to speak.

B. 1 Bridget—/—seemed frozen where she sat.
       /2/ pale,
       /2/ panicked,
       /2/ unable to speak

C. 1 Bridget was pale and panicked,
       2 unable to speak,
       2 seemingly frozen where she sat.

A.   2 A "macho" symbol,
       2 a gesture of bravado,
    1 his greasy chain was brandished before her.

B. 1 His greasy chain—/—was brandished before her.
       /2/ a "macho" symbol,
       /2/ a gesture of bravado

C. 1 His greasy chain was brandished before her as a "macho" symbol,
       2 a gesture of bravado.

A.   Meanwhile,
       2 Standing in front of another mirror—
          3 his hair fluffed,
          3 his moustache trimmed—
    1 Troy eyed his own image and wondered what his date would look like.

B. 1 Meanwhile, Troy stood in front of another mirror, / , and wondered what
       his date would look like.
       /2/ eyeing his own image—
          /3/ fluffy hair and a trimmed moustache—

C. 1 Meanwhile, Troy stood in front of another mirror,
          2 wondering what his date would look like as he eyed his own image—
             3 fluffy hair,
             3 a trimmed moustache.

D.   Meanwhile,
       2 wondering what his date would look like,
    1 Troy stood in front of another mirror,
          3 his eyes on the image of his fluffy hair and trimmed moustache.

Ex. 7.1. 1 Casey's mother—/—rapped at his door.
              /2/ apparently upset,
              /2/ somewhat bewildered

       1 Her questions were met with silence,
          2 Casey's refusal to talk.

          2 Her eyes narrowed,
          2 her face pinched,
       1 she pleaded with him to switch from astronomy to astrology.

1   The door arced opened up slowly,
    2   creaking on its hinge,
    2   revealing the murkiness of his star-filled observatory.

1   He stumbled down the stairs—/—and checked her biorhythm charts.
  /2/   unwilling to argue,
  /2/   seemingly full of despair

1   Rick—/—still felt a little queasy.
  /2/   bandaged,
  /2/   limping badly

1   His head was pounding,
    2   his muscles aching and convulsed.

1   He vaguely remembered his last goal line stand—
    2   a scene of violence,
    2   an occasion of bone-crushing contact.

    2   Primitive,
    2   violent,
    2   emotionally satisfying,
1   it had been a complete free-for-all.

1   Now he was in the cafeteria,
    2   nursing his wounds,
    2   thumbing the sports section,
    2   looking for his name in print.

Ex. 7.2.
    2   With her backpack full,
1   Wendy trudged up a hiking trail,
      3   trying to have fun.

1   She paused for a moment—
    2   sweaty and discouraged—
      3   asking herself, "Why do this?"

    2   Without warning,
1   Grayson roared up beside her,
      3   jazzing the engine on his dirt bike,
        4   a gutsy machine that gave super performance.

    2   Looking at him,
      3   a show-off who obviously needed attention from women,
1   Wendy had a terrific idea.

    2   Like the classic "damsel in distress,"
1   She collapsed at his feet—
      3   helpless,
      3   pathetic—
        4   knowing full well that she would soon be riding the motorcycle and he would be packing the yogurt and granola.

2 Flicking out the lights,

1 Troy whipped himself into grim sociability,

    3 a "grin-and-bear-it" attitude.

1 Gertrude grew suddenly agitated,

    2 her breath coming in short spurts,

        3 wheezing through her nostrils.

    2 An opportunist—

        3 desperately poor and cunningly amoral—

1 Troy considered Gertrude's wealth,

           4 wondering about the possibility of alimony.

    2 Smiling up at him,

1 Gertrude wondered about the compatibility of their astrological signs—

        3 his Scorpio,

        3 hers Taurus.

1 Troy leaned forward —/—and then kissed her jowly bulldog,

   /2/ his eyes tightly closed

        3 thinking that it was Gertrude.

Ex. 7.3. 1. Doing cartwheels down the sidelines, bouncing high into the air, Sally worked the crowd into a frenzy. 2. Slender, graceful, ready to be heard, she then grasped the microphone stand. 3. She breathed hard into the microphone, her excitement like an electric force, galvanizing the crowd, bringing people to their feet. 4. Happy with the crowd's response, Sally decided to cartwheel her "rally ballet"—a routine never before attempted.

Ex. 8.1. 6. The submersion is for as long as four minutes. 8. The stay is for less than ninety seconds. 10. The dive is successful. 11. It brings up a shellfish. 12. It brings up a rock. 13. The rock is flat. 14. An otter floats on its back. 15. An otter puts the rock on its chest. 16. An otter smashes open the shellfish. 17. The otter's chest is particularly thick. 18. The otter's chest is loose-skinned. 19. It is adapted to this operation. 20. The operation is smashing shells. 21. The otter wants to wash off food. 22. The food is spilled. 23. The otter rolls over in the water. 24. The rolling is every half-minute or so. 25. It grasps the food. 26. The food is remaining. 27. The grasp is with its front paws. 28. The paws are thick. 29. The paws are handlike. 30. This routine is well-practiced. 31. This routine is methodical. 32. An otter eats 20–25 percent of its body weight. 33. An otter is an adult. 34. The otter may weigh up to a hundred pounds. 35. The eating is every day. 36. The otter shares its distinction. 37. The distinction is using tools. 38. The distinction is shared with chimpanzees. 39. The distinction is shared with the Galapagos woodpecker finch. 40. The distinction is shared with an Egyptian vulture. 41. The distinction is shared with man.

Ex. 8.2. *Running & Being,* Dr. George Sheehan, Warner Books, 1978, p. 84.

I reached my peak in creativity when I was five. I could draw and paint and sculpt. I could sing and dance and act. I possessed my body completely. And with

it became completely absorbed in a life that was good and beautiful and joyful. I examined and tested and explored. I could not bear to watch.

Gift From The Sea, Anne Morrow Lindbergh, Pantheon Books, 1955, p. 44.

When one is a stranger to oneself, then one is estranged from others too. If one is out of touch with oneself, then one cannot touch others. How often in a large city, shaking hands with my friends, I have felt the wilderness stretching between us. Both of us were wandering in arid wastes, having lost the springs that nourished us—or having found them dry. Only when one is connected to one's own core is one connected to others, I am beginning to discover. And, for me, the core, the inner spring, can best be refound through solitude.

The Bell Jar, Sylvia Plath, Bantam Books, 1971, Harper & Row, p. 1.

New York was bad enough. By nine in the morning the fake, country-wet freshness that somehow seeped in overnight evaporated like the tail end of a sweet dream. Mirage-gray at the bottom of their granite canyons, the hot street wavered in the sun, the car tops sizzled and glittered, and the dry, cindery dust blew into my eyes and down my throat.

Desert Solitaire, Edward Abbey, Ballantine Books, 1968, p. 14.

The generator is a small four-cylinder gasoline engine mounted on a wooden block not far from the trailer. Much too close, I'd say. I open the switch, adjust the choke, engage the crank and heave it around. The engine sputters, gasps, catches fire, gains momentum, winds up into a roar, valves popping, rockers thumping, pistons hissing up and down inside their oiled jackets.

Wanda Hickey's Night of Golden Memories, Jean Shepherd, Dell Publishing Company, 1971, p. 243.

I half dozed in front of my TV set as the speaker droned on in his high, nasal voice. One night a week, as a form of masochistic self-discipline, I sentence myself to a minimum of three hours viewing educational television. Like so many other things in life, educational TV is a great idea but a miserable reality; murkey films of home life in Kurdistan, jowly English authors being interviewed by jowly English literary critics, pinched-faced ladies demonstrating Japanese brush techniques. But I watch all of it religiously—I suppose because it is there, like Mount Everest.

Ex. 8.3. *Changing,* Liv Ullman, Bantam Books, 1977, p. 200.

The woman is made to feel guilty if she wants or needs to work and let others look after her child. Because she is a woman, the child needs her at home. Because he is a man, it is normal that he gives prior attention to his profession.

When the man and woman don't marry, she is the mother with an illegitimate child.

She has the responsibility. She has to arrange eighteen years of her life in accordance with what is best for the child. She has to refuse work and contact with other people when she cannot afford or get help.

Writing Without Teachers, Peter Elbow, Oxford University Press, 1973, pp. 15–16.

Control, coherence, and knowing your mind are not what you start out with but what you end up with. Think of writing then not as a way to transmit a message but as a way to grow and cook a message. Writing is a way to end up thinking something you couldn't have started out thinking. Writing is, in fact, a transaction with words whereby you *free* yourself from what you presently think, feel, and perceive. You make available to yourself something better than what you'd be stuck with if you'd actually succeeded in making your meaning clear at the start. What looks inefficient—a rambling process with lots of writing and lots of throwing away—is really efficient since it's the best way you can work up to what you really want to say and how to say it.

A Reverence for Wood, Eric Sloane, Ballantine Books, 1965, p. 29.

In the pioneer days, doors were often symbols. Just as girls filled hope chests, young men planned doors for the houses they would someday build. A house might be built of local pine and chestnut, but the door was considered something special and the wood was often sassafras panels, apple or cherry, or even mahogany brought from the West Indies or Central America. A godly man might prefer a Christian door with stiles (vertical pieces) and rails (horizontal pieces) that formed a Christian cross. A superstitious person might put a Maltese cross in the lower section and thereby make a "witch door" to keep out evil spirits, or frame the door with ash to make the spell more potent.

Zen and the Art of Motorcycle Maintenance, Robert M. Pirsig, Bantam Books, 1974, pp. 66–67.

The romantic mode is primarily inspirational, imaginative, creative, intuitive. Feelings rather than facts predominate. "Art" when it is opposed to "Science" is often romantic. It does not proceed by reason or by laws. It proceeds by feeling, intuition and esthetic conscience. In the northern European cultures the romantic mode is usually associated with femininity, but this is certainly not a necessary association.

   The classic mode, by contrast, proceeds by reason and by laws—which are themselves underlying forms of thought and behavior. In the European cultures it is primarily a masculine mode and the fields of science, law and medicine are unattractive to women largely for this reason. Although motorcycle riding is romantic, motorcycle maintenance is purely classic. The dirt, the grease, the mastery of underlying form required all give it such a negative romantic appeal that women never go near it.

Ex. 10.1.   1. Sullen, hostile-looking students filled every desk.   2. He made a visible effort to swallow his fear, fixing his stare on the empty bulletin board.   3. His lips quivered wordlessly as sweat beaded his round, smooth forehead.   4. He now wondered why he had chosen a teaching career when he was afraid of unfamiliar people.   5. A student sneered and raised his beefy hand.   6. The instructor felt a fresh surge of raw panic.   7. Awaking from his nightmare, he

pulled back the tumbled bed covers and quieted his fierce breathing.   8. His thudding heart could not deny his fear of meeting his first class.

Ex. 10.2.   1. *Lean, direct:* We recognize that devices such as starchy openers, internal modifiers, passive voice, and inversion have their uses. *Flabby, indirect:* For us, there is a recognition that there is a use for devices which include starchy openers, internal modifiers, passive voice, and inversion.   2. *Lean, direct:* We are aware that they can provide variety and emphasis by creating special stylistic effects. *Flabby, indirect:* That special stylistic effects can be created so that variety and emphasis are provided is a part of our awareness.   3. *Lean, direct:* Our concern centers on misuse and overuse of these devices. *Flabby, indirect:* Centering on the fact that these devices are misused and overused is our concern.

Ex. 10.3.   1. An absence of starchy openers marks lean writing.   2. Flabby prose usually has many such openers.   3. Lean sentences usually have tight noun clusters.   4. Flabby writing typically expands such clusters.   5. Word economy characterizes lean writing, whereas verbosity marks its flabby opposite.   6. Similar differences exist for direct and indirect prose styles.   7. Direct sentences favor active voice, use strong verbs, and put grammatical subjects first.   8. Indirect sentences favor passive voice, use weak verbs, and emphasize grammatical objects.   9. Direct writing commonly features straightforward word order, whereas indirect prose often inverts sentences.

Ex. 10.4.   1. The sun, noon-high and glaring-hot, blistered the parched, rocky canyon.   2. Paulo had left his car at the canyon's rim and was now making his way down the narrow trail.   3. Snakes, lizards, scorpions, and spiders had long since retreated for shade; and leaves on shriveled desert shrubs were folded inward.   4. Like filmy veils or ripples on water, the heat waves shimmered in the distance.   5. A pair of black vultures glided ominously on the silent horizon.

GLOSSARY

This glossary is a handy reference for class discussion and review. Here you'll find quick definitions (and often examples) of key terms used in the text. For more detailed explanations, examples, and practice exercises, refer to appropriate units of the text.

Absolute: A type of *free modifier* usually modifying an entire *base sentence*. Example: "Absolutes are classy free modifiers, *their structure requiring care and control.*" Refer to Units 6 and 7.

Addition (sentence addition): See *free modifier*. Refer to Units 6 and 7.

Addition (the process): Joining parts of *kernel sentences* to a *base sentence* with the connecting word *and*. The resulting *writeout* has pairs of words or phrases (compounding) or a series of words and phrases. (*Addition* is analogous to *coordination*.) Example: "I read this sentence *and* first see compounding; then I push on further, study the second part of the sentence, *and* recognize a series of phrases." See *embedding*. Refer to Unit 2.

Adjective cluster: A type of *free modifier* usually describing a noun. Example: "*Eager to recognize an adjective cluster,* I stare at italicized print." Refer to Units 6 and 7.

Base sentence: The "foundation" sentence to which *modifiers* are attached; the main focus of meaning in a sentence combining *cluster* or the resulting *writeout*. Refer to Units 1–7.

Cluster: A group of *kernel sentences* to be combined into a *writeout*. Refer to Unit 1.

Connotation: The emotional "coloring" of words, ranging from positive to neutral to negative. Connotation not only depends on context but also differs from reader to reader. See *tone; usage levels*. Refer to Unit 9.

Coordination: Two or more *base sentences* grammatically joined for a balanced emphasis. There are four methods of coordination: 1) using a coordinating conjunction; 2) using a semicolon; 3) using a semicolon plus a conjunctive adverb; 4) using a correlative conjunction. Refer to Units 3 and 4.

De-combining: The process of analyzing existing prose into its constituent *kernel sentences*. Refer to Unit 8.

Embedding: Putting parts of *kernel sentences* into a *base sentence* without using connecting words. The resulting *writeout* has words that modify the main words in the *base sentence*. (*Embedding* is similar to *subordination* in its basic outcome.) An example: "I *carefully* study the *italicized embedded* modifiers *in this sentence.*" See *addition* (*the process*). Refer to Unit 2.

Flabby, indirect writing: Prose with a maximum of *starchy openers, internal wordiness, passive voice,* and *inversion.* Writing that is dull, difficult to read, and obfuscates rather than clarifies. See *lean, direct writing.* Refer to Unit 10.

Footnote signal: A subordinating conjunction, transition word or phrase, or word ending (*-ing/-ly*) at the bottom of a *cluster* of *kernel sentences.* These signals specify how kernels can be combined; however, they should be covered up with a notecard as one works through the combining process. In this way, the human *brain* supplies the connector. Refer to Unit 5.

Fragment (sentence fragment): An error in sentence structure. A piece of a sentence punctuated as a sentence. (The two preceding definitions are fragments.) Refer to Units 1 and 2.

Free modifier: Synonymous with *sentence addition.* A group of words such as *verb clusters, noun clusters, adjective clusters,* and *absolutes* that can be added to a *base sentence* to enrich its meaning. Refer to Units 6 and 7.

Internal wordiness: Needless words "cluttering up" the interior of a sentence. Example: "Internal wordiness, *which in this complex, fast-paced world of today is a problem worthy of attention by anyone who is interested—seriously interested—in communicating clearly, logically, and effectively with an audience, be it large or small, private or public, for business or for pleasure,* weakens writing." Refer to Unit 10.

Inversion: Sentences with unusual or "backward running" word orders. Example: "Disastrous, when overused, is the writing technique known as inversion." Refer to Unit 10.

Kernel (kernel sentence): A short, unmodified sentence. Three examples: "The sentence is short; the sentence is unmodified; the sentence is a kernel." Refer to Units 1 and 2.

Lean, direct writing: Prose with a *minimum* of *starchy openers, internal wordiness, passive voice,* and *inversion.* Writing that is fresh, easy to read, and to the point. See *flabby, indirect writing.* Refer to Unit 10.

Level of modification: The concept of *general* and *specific* as it pertains to *base sentence* and *free modifiers* respectively. Refer to Units 6 and 7.

Margin signal: A word to the left of a *cluster* of *kernel sentences* indicating a process of *coordination.* Refer to Unit 4.

Misplaced/dangling modifier: A *free modifier* that is either logically misplaced or inappropriate for a *base sentence.* Example: *"Knowing how sentences go together,* misplaced or dangling modifiers don't occur in my writing." Refer to Units 6 and 7.

Multi-level sentence: A *base sentence* plus a series of *free modifiers* of *different* types. See *two-level sentence.* Refer to Unit 7.

Noun cluster: A type of *free modifier* usually renaming or defining another noun. Example: "This glossary, *a set of definitions for the text's key terms,* can be a handy learning tool." Refer to Units 6 and 7.

Open combining: Use of "uncued" exercise to provide practice in choosing *write-outs* from a variety of stylistic options. See *signaled combining.* Refer to Units 1, 2 and 3.

Passive voice: A transformation that weakens writing when overused. Compare active example—"Tony received an 'A' on his paper!"—to passive example–"On his paper was an 'A' that was received by Tony!" Refer to Units 2 and 10.

Proofreading: The vital process of reading prose aloud, slowly and carefully, to catch errors in spelling, punctuation, capitalization, and other usage conventions. Refer to Unit 2.

Pre-combining: The process of first inventing *kernel sentences* by focusing on a scene, action, or object, and then combining kernels into more complex sentences. Refer to Unit 8.

Re-combining: The process of constructing writeouts from *kernel sentences* that have been *de-combined* from the prose of professional writers; then comparing these writeouts with the original version. Refer to Unit 8.

Run-on sentence: An error in punctuation—namely, two complete sentences with a comma (or no punctuation) between them. Example: "Run-on sentences can be avoided, it just requires care in proofreading." Refer to Units 1 and 2.

Signaled combining: Use of "cues" (*umbrella, margin, footnote*) to provide disciplined practice in making target transformations. See *open combining.* Refer to Units 4 and 5.

Starchy openers: Needless words "up front" in sentences. Example: *"It seems clear that there is little doubt that* starchy openers weaken writing." Refer to Unit 10.

Subordination: Two or more *base sentences* grammatically joined for a dependent emphasis. Three methods of subordination. 1) subordinating conjunctions; 2) relative connectors; 3) prepositions. Refer to Units 3 and 5.

Tone: The quality of "voice" in writing that results from attention to purpose, audience, and subject matter. *Usage level* and *connotation* are aspects of tone. Consistency in tone is one characteristic of successful writing. Refer to Unit 9.

Transformation: A mental process or processes; transformations convert the information in *kernel sentences* into more readable *writeouts*. Refer to Units 1 and 2.

Two-level sentence: A *base sentence* plus a series of the *same* type of *free modifier*. See *multi-level sentence*. Refer to Unit 7.

Umbrella signal: A black line above a word or phrase indicating that this information should be *embedded* into another *kernel sentence.* Refer to Unit 4.

Usage levels: Gradations of formality in writing, ranging from formal to standard to casual. Excessively formal writing is called *gobbedygook;* excessively casual writing is called *slang.* See *tone; connotation.* Refer to Unit 9.

Verb cluster: A type of *free modifier*. Example: "I study this definition, *trying to figure out what a verb cluster is."* Refer to Units 6 and 7.

Writeout: The product of sentence combining; the result of combining *kernel sentences* into more structurally complex, syntactically "mature" prose. Refer to Unit 1.

ABOUT THE AUTHOR

William Strong teaches courses in writing, English methods, and secondary reading at Utah State University in Logan. He has also taught high school English in Portland, Oregon, and worked as a language arts consultant in eastern Idaho. His educational background includes bachelor's and master's degrees from Portland State College and the University of Oregon respectively; he was a TTT fellow at the University of Illinois, where he received a Ph.D. in English. In addition to journal publications, he authored *Sentence Combining: A Composing Book* (Random House, 1973) and co-authored *Facing Value Decisions: Rationale-Building for Teachers* (Wadsworth, 1976). He has been a speaker and workshop leader at many state, regional, and national meetings and a consultant for several school districts. At present he directs the Utah Writing Project and edits the *Utah English Journal*.